Warfare, 1792–1918

How War became Global

Dr Robert Johnson, Oxford University

www.studymates.co.uk

D1336108

Contents

Preface

War is a persistent, recurrent and tragic part of human history. Anyone who visits the battlefields of the First World War cannot fail to be struck by the poignancy of the cemeteries there. Row after row of white headstones, set in immaculate order, stand silent amongst the peaceful hedgerows and fields of France and Flanders. Walking beside them, one can read the names and regiments, where they are known. Often it is the ages, some just 19 years old, which strike home, reminding us that wars are fought by the younger generation, and sadly they are called to make the ultimate sacrifice when their life has barely begun.

As the title suggests, this book is concerned with the changes that took place in warfare, and, as such, a certain emphasis will be placed on 'turning points' in organisation, technology, leadership, or in operations. Nevertheless, this book can never be more than a brief introduction to an enormous subject. Military history is a vast topic, and its study should be set within the context of the history of the period in question. Only by these means can a full appreciation of the military narrative be grasped. For example, the political upheavals of the French revolution set in motion the revolutionary wars, and these, in turn, assisted the career of Napoleon Bonaparte. Napoleon was as much a political animal as he was a military leader, and his strategic decision-making reflected his political aspirations to dominate Europe and suppress his rivals.

The book is designed as an introduction for anyone interested in how warfare changed Europe and the West in this period, but more specifically it is for A2 students and teachers engaged in the **Changing Nature of Warfare module for OCR**.

This book will, it is hoped, enable you to get straight to the main features of this subject. It will also help you to avoid the common pitfalls that have plagued the subject for years, particularly the assumption that warfare followed a linear trend of development or that it was driven solely by changes in technology. This book also draws on some examples of warfare outside of the West (Europe and North America), in order to show influences between different modes of warfare. These examples also help to illustrate why certain tactics survived amongst European forces fighting in the colonies long after their obsolescence in the West. However, *the colonial wars are not examined by OCR* and will merely provide some interest for the students on that course.

The book is divided into chronological sections, within which there are themes. These headings correspond with those provided by OCR but are also, in fact, useful starting points for the study of warfare.

I have many people to thank for the publication of this book, but mention must be made of Graham Lawler, Bill Antrobus and Martin Jones, without whom it would not have been possible. I would like to dedicate this book to the students of Richard Huish College whom I had the great privilege to teach and who accompanied me on a number of battlefield tours over the years. They have all taught me a great deal and I hope that this guide will be a help to them and many others.

Robert Johnson

1

Introduction: warfare

One minute overview – Compared with earlier epochs of history, the period between 1792 and 1918 was an era of rapid change in warfare. Weapons, tactics, and training were adapted to suit developments in gunpowder technology, but the professionalism of armies also reflected the modernisation of the European states. In the eighteenth century, the art of war had reached a sophisticated level. The co-ordination of infantry, cavalry and artillery on the battlefield and the adequate supply of food, ammunition and equipment had become something of a science. The preparation for war, and the maintenance of an army in the field, also required organisation of state finances for pay and administration, recruitment strategies, engineers and technicians to construct cannon and fortifications, and industries to support boot-making, saddlery, the manufacture of munitions, gun carriages and ships. In analysing warfare, one can identify certain principles, and recognise patterns of war and change. However, there are many examples where innovation and change brought military disaster. This reminds us that there are limitations in military history too.

In this chapter you will learn:

▶ there were changes and continuities in warfare between 1792 and 1918
▶ the nature of warfare at the end of the eighteenth century
▶ the principles of war
▶ the strengths and weaknesses of military history

A comparison of warfare in 1792 and 1918

War in the eighteenth century was characteristically on a small scale
The period 1792–1918 was a period of remarkable change in the history of warfare. In this period of little more than one hundred years, battles

ceased to be places where one could stand and see an entire army arrayed, where men would fight at close quarters and where events could be decided in one day. In the 1790s soldiers might march into battle on foot, or on horseback, with weapons that had changed little in two hundred years. They were supplied from huge baggage trains, or lived from goods procured from the surrounding countryside. Their commanders could often see their armies from a single point whilst in the saddle, issuing orders face to face. The thick smoke of black powder weapons obscured the battlefield and necessitated brightly coloured uniforms and visible banners around which units could rally, and the beat of drums or the sound of bugles to signal changes in direction.

War in the twentieth century
In the First World War entire regions could be engulfed in an impersonal and long-range struggle lasting several days, weeks or even months. In 1918 troops could travel to the front in trains and steamships. They were armed with machine guns and magazine rifles with greater accuracy and rates of fire. Their artillery could fire high explosive shells several kilometres, deep into enemy positions. They could release poison gas across the battlefield, or squirt liquid fire into entrenchments. Aircraft guided this artillery, but could also strafe and bomb ground positions too. Command and control was maintained by telephone, flag signals, heliograph and wireless radio. Smokeless powder and high velocity, quick-firing weapons forced soldiers to take refuge beneath the ground or in dispersed formations, and armies universally adopted camouflaged clothing. Supplies, ammunition and equipment were produced on a vast scale. The whole economy of a country could be directed towards the war effort. Wars took place over greater distances, on a greater scale and with a far greater intensity than ever imagined in 1792.

Although there were differences, there were also continuities
However, despite these changes and the corresponding historic changes in economics and society, there were continuities. The nationalist cause, which sustained the French revolutionary armies, and helped to mobilise the support of the people, was still a recognisable feature of the enthusiasm for war in 1914. The guerrilla resistance of the Spanish against the French invasion in the Napoleonic Wars was similar to the Boer guerrilla resistance to the British during the South African war in 1900–1902. Despite railways, the soldiers of 1914–18 still advanced against their enemies on foot, and occasionally 'crossed bayonets'

(fought hand to hand), just as their forebears had done. Balloon observation had been used in the American Civil War of the 1860s, but was still being used extensively sixty years later. Although great strides had been made in medicine, more men died from disease in the early twentieth century than from enemy action, just as had been the case in the 1790s. Commanders still led by personal example in 1918, often face to face with their subordinates.

Did technology determine the outcome of wars?

A controversial aspect of warfare in this period concerns 'technological determinism'. The outcomes of wars were dependent on a combination of factors. An obvious element was technology and many histories of warfare have concentrated on how technological superiority produced victory. However, battles and wars were not won by technology alone. There are countless examples of how leadership, logistics, tactics, strategy, numerical superiority and morale could affect the outcome of a conflict too.

There are dangers in only examining European warfare

There should be caution about an exclusively Eurocentric viewpoint. Much writing in the West has concentrated on changes made by Europeans, and how they succeeded in their wars against Asians and Africans. Indeed, many books still focus exclusively on Britain and European warfare at the expense of the rest of the world. This is ironic when one considers that many of the colonial campaigns of the nineteenth century were conducted by Asians and Africans under European officers. The exclusion of non-European modes of warfare means that Africans and Asians are deprived of any acknowledgement for tactical awareness, the ability to adapt, or success, even though they inflicted a number of defeats on European or mixed forces. Indeed, the Europeans spent more time in the period 1793-1918 fighting non-Europeans than each other, so a balance is essential. Nor were developments in technology solely a response to wars in the West. Anti-guerrilla tactics evolved in colonial campaigns such as the North West Frontier of India. Nevertheless, colonial wars forced European armies to retain tactics that might otherwise have disappeared. Close order formations, a reliance on the 'square', or on cavalry, were increasingly obsolete in Western warfare but essential in African campaigns.

Warfare at the end of the eighteenth century

The 'gunpowder revolution' had changed warfare
The historian Geoffrey Parker described the period between the fifteenth and seventeenth century as a 'military revolution', primarily because of the far-reaching changes in technology and the organisation of armies in Europe. Crossbows and longbows had given way to handguns, and mechanically operated catapults like the trebuchet had been replaced by cannons. In sieges, cannons had forced radical changes in fortress architecture: towers and thick stone walls were replaced by lower, earth filled bastions and smaller, outlying forts. On the battlefield, massed volleys from musketeers, or a salvo of cannon balls, could decimate the packed formations of an opponent, pierce armour and crush limbs.

Gunpowder weapons had their own drawbacks
However, this 'gunpowder revolution' in weaponry was not a smooth development, and there were some key problems. Handguns, arquebuses and later matchlock muskets were inaccurate and took time to load. This meant that they were vulnerable to attack and they had to be protected by infantrymen with pikes (a long 'lance' tipped with a spike which was effective in keeping cavalry at bay). Cannons were not easy to manoeuvre and, like all gunpowder weapons, they could be rendered useless by a sudden downpour of rain, unless the crews could keep their powder dry. Gunpowder also produced thick smoke, which, on windless days, could reduce the field of view to a few yards. It was necessary to clothe troops in bright uniforms to assist in identification, and to carry large, highly visible standards (or 'colours') as rallying points in the disorientating smoke-filled zone of battle.

There had also been radical changes in organisation
The Dutch had pioneered the greater professionalism of their officer corps and imposed a strict discipline on their troops in the 1590s. This meant that leaders studied and applied the lessons of battlefield success. Their troops rehearsed getting into formation, moving at speed and working alongside different arms (cavalry, artillery and infantry). By the seventeenth century all European states had 'standing armies' of full-time, paid and trained troops. In addition, many European states still retained irregular and mercenary forces; troops hired to fight on a temporary basis and often from peoples they dominated. For example, Cossacks had been recruited by the Russian Tsars in the seventeenth

century, whilst Swiss soldiers had traditionally served in a voluntary manner in a number of armies across Europe from the 1400s.

Linear formations emerged in the seventeenth century to maximise firepower
The introduction of prefabricated cartridges by the Swedes greatly increased the rate of fire of musketeers in the Thirty Years War (1618–1648). This meant that the numbers of supporting pikemen could be reduced and musketeers deployed in lines three deep (rather than in deep blocks). In addition, Gustavus Adolphus (the King of Sweden as well as the field commander) trained the cavalry to charge knee to knee in three ranks and fight hand to hand, abandoning the traditional *caracole* (of troopers advancing to discharge pistols and retiring). Moreover the cavalry were given specific roles to attack flanks, the rear areas, to carry out a pursuit, or ride down enemy skirmishers. The Swedish artillery was standardised in calibre and charges. Guns were subdivided into categories and the lightest guns were deployed alongside the infantry. Twenty years of battlefield experience had wrought these changes which culminated in the victory at Breitenfeld (17 September 1631). After the Thirty Years War wheel lock muskets and bayonets were introduced, and gradually pikemen were phased out. By the beginning of the eighteenth century, flintlock muskets were in use by the British army. In 1702 the Duke of Marlborough won a significant victory against the French (who had persisted with matchlocks) at Blenheim. Despite the success of linear formations, the Russians under Peter the Great relied on sheer weight of numbers to defeat the Swedes in the Great Northern War (1700–1721).

Frederick the Great: manoeuvre or firepower?
Frederick of Prussia, initially, on the advice of the leading military philosopher Maurice de Saxe, decided to downplay the importance of infantry firepower in favour of manoeuvre in his armies in the mid-eighteenth century. Frederick's use of the 'oblique order' (extending the flank from the line of march under the cover of hills or woods to avoid being outflanked and to envelop the enemy line) was legendary but not a system Frederick relied upon every time. The emphasis instead was on flexibility: he adapted his tactics to suit the situation. Napoleon Bonaparte later appreciated this point and avoided 'formulas' himself.

The citizen army of America and the revolution influenced Europe
In 1775 American colonists engaged regular British forces at Lexington at the outbreak of the American Revolution. Unable to stand against

the British redcoats, the Americans conducted a withdrawal giving harassing fire when any opportunity presented itself. At Bunkers' Hill (17 June 1775), by contrast, the colonists were able to repulse two British attacks by sheer weight of fire from behind entrenchments. When they ran out of ammunition, a third assault carried the position. Throughout the war that followed, the British and the Americans fought each other to a standstill. The British troops were highly disciplined and well trained. The British had already adopted skirmishers of hand-picked marksmen from their experience of fighting Indians in the wooded countryside of the Seven Years' War, but 'light infantry companies' began to make their appearance across the army. The Americans were most effective in guerrilla fighting and hit and run raids, but their command centres were local and able to respond more quickly than the British (whose headquarters were in London). However, as mercenary forces from Europe joined the Americans against the British, the American army adopted more formal tactics and training. When the French expeditionary force and the French irregulars returned to France, they took with them the revolutionary ideas they had seen in action in America.

How gunpowder weapons worked

The devastating effect of close range musketry, fired in controlled volleys, was frequently demonstrated in the eighteenth century. Although still slow to load and fire (three aimed shots a minute would be exceptional), the use of these simple weapons in large numbers was effective. The musket consisted of a barrel lying on a 'furniture' of wood, a pan (a bowl for gunpowder) and a trigger-operated arm with a flint attached. The musket was fired by tapping a measure of gunpowder into the pan, before pouring the rest down the barrel followed by a lead musket ball. When this was rammed home, the musket could be put into the aim position. Pulling the trigger made the flint swing forward on its arm into the pan. Sparks from the flint ignited the powder, and, by means of a touch hole, the flames passed from the pan into the barrel, setting off the main charge. This propelled the ball out of the barrel. Artillery inflicted considerable losses too. At longer range, artillery fired metal 'shot', or cannon balls, aiming to pitch them just in front of enemy infantry and cavalry formations. The balls would bounce, jump and ricochet through ranks and files, often killing several men at once. At close range, artillery would fire chain shot (two balls connected by a chain that scythed through ranks) or canister (a cylinder filled with small balls that burst on leaving the muzzle of the cannon, spraying out like a shotgun).

The use of firepower was a hallmark of modern warfare
Infantry fought in linear formations to maximise the effect of their muskets, but there was an option of charging forward to close with the enemy in hand to hand fighting with a bayonet. Cavalry made use of this shock effect, combining their speed and mobility with the advantage of height to cut down with sabre or thrust with sword point. Given that muskets and cannons still took time to load, and that formations moved slowly (a speed of 110 paces to the minute was not uncommon), the decision to use 'cold steel' could be practical as well as psychological.

The principles of war

Certain principles of warfare can be identified
No reliable analysis of warfare can be based solely on one battle, and the outcomes of wars, like their causes, are the result of manifold factors. However, there are certain themes which help identify success, and which, to a lesser or greater extent, played their part in all wars: surprise, concentration of effort (known as the *Schwerpunkt*), co-operation of all arms, control, simplicity, speed of action and the initiative. Added to these principles were the factors of training, discipline, unit cohesion, technology, leadership, the use of reserves at the critical moment and sound logistics.

Terms require definition
In warfare, certain terms are helpful in defining the processes involved. War itself is a prolonged conflict between rival political groups by force of arms, thereby including insurrection and civil war, but excluding riots, or individual acts of terrorism or violence. Grand strategy is the co-ordination of all the resources of a nation, or group of nations, towards a common political objective. Strategy is the art of deploying military means (troops and supplies) to fulfil a particular policy. Tactics are the dispositions, techniques and control of military forces in actual combat. Campaigns are the periods of military activity, perhaps a series of manoeuvres and battles that take place as each side tries to fulfil its strategy.

The causes of war require separate study
This book is not so much about the causes of war and the impact of war on society as the changes in warfare itself. However, no account of

warfare can completely ignore the causes of war since they influence strategy. David Chandler, in reference to the deadlock of the First World War, pointed not to the devastating technology of artillery and machine guns, but the willingness of the participants to engage in total war. More recently, Jeremy Black has argued that the willingness to resort to war, the inherent 'bellicosity' of states to fulfil objectives by force of arms, is the main cause of war. Von Clausewitz (1780–1831), the military theorist, famously remarked that 'war is nothing but a conti- nuation of politics with the admixture of other means' whilst a pacifist slogan in 1936 ran simply 'war will cease when men refuse to fight'. Detailed histories are required, however, if the outbreak of particular wars are to be understood. Wars, like other events in history, are not the result of some overarching theory or doctrine, but the product of unique historical forces. Nevertheless, some truths are irrefutable. War is a persistent human activity. Failure to prepare for conflict invites defeat and subjugation. This reminds us of the warning, in an adapted form, given by Vegetius (c. 4th century AD): '*Si vis pacem, para bellum*' ('if you want peace, prepare for war').

The strengths and weaknesses of military history

Military history is an important facet of human history
In military history there are certain problems which confronted the commander of every age. Whilst weapons, communications and trans- port changed, the basic building block of any army was the individual soldier. What mattered to the commanders was the way he was led, fed, and clothed, and the way that he endured, dug in, marched, and above all, fought for the cause. Military history is of immediate use to any soldier trying to understand the need for professionalism, organisation and certain skills or qualities. Military history is also of immense value to any historian trying to understand the condition of war which has prevailed over European history for so long. Military technology acted as a spur to industrialisation. New firing mechanisms for muskets, the rifling of barrels, and the demand for weapons of standard dimensions in large numbers catalysed specialist foundries, machine tools and factories. War is a human condition and it would be difficult to under- stand any period of human history without reference to its conflicts. Certain political leaders made their reputations on wars, and others were crushed by war. Entire civilisations were built on the success of their armies, and the rise of European empires in the nineteenth century was to some extent dependent on war. By studying military

history, one is aware that the fate of nations, communities and even individuals could rest on a single campaign or battle. The outcomes of battles themselves could be the result of a range of factors, but even the preparation for them could have a profound influence on a region or an entire state. The presence of garrisons often affected a local economy, changed social relations, or altered the political balance of power.

The study of military history produces problems of bias

The danger of military history is that it is often exposed to the engineering of hindsight to make sense of a confusing encounter, or worst still, to fulfil a political agenda. Unit histories in particular armies might be selective in their recording of events in order to create an *esprit de corps* based on the courage and success of their forebears. Official histories, too, tend to fall victim to portraying what they felt should be believed rather than what actually happened. These histories tend to ignore or play down mutinies, desertion, murder and cowardice. Barbara Tuchman once remarked that, in British military history, there had never been a retreat or a defeat that was not redeemed by utmost gallantry in the face of adversity. Less unkindly, the military historians had focused on the efforts of the individual when the general situation was bad. David Chandler offered a four-part solution. One, that it was a subject that required a study in depth in order to see the various factors that influenced a particular outcome. Two, it should be studied from the perspective of every level of command, from the general to the private soldier, in order to obtain a grasp of 'the hidden factors that shaped strategic decisions [down] to the experience of the battlefield'. Three, it is a subject that must be studied across the ages in order to appreciate the changes and continuities that would be obscured by too narrow a view. Four, an awareness of the historical context is vital, such as the limits imposed by international relations and resources, or the general political, social and economic background to a particular conflict.

Conclusions

Professor Jeremy Black, in *War and the World*, reminds us that too often there is a narrow focus in the study of warfare. Usually this takes the form of analyses of European modes of warfare and decisive battles, leaving out the civil conflicts such as the 1848 revolutions. Moreover, since Geoffrey Parker argued that there had been a 'gunpowder revolution' in the early modern period (a point, incidentally, which Black disputes, arguing that the 'revolution came as late as the eighteenth century), many historians have focused on the technological changes at the expense of the continuities. Military history often suffers from a 'whig view' of the past (where human society makes continual improvement and progress), when it is evident from spectacular setbacks, or colonial wars, that tactics and doctrine did not always 'advance', especially outside of Europe. A section on Chinese and African modes of warfare is included in this book to illustrate this. However, whilst military history is subject to various limitations, it is no more a victim than other aspects of history. Frequently the study of history raises more questions than answers. Moreover, historians often disagree about the reasons for change in warfare, or the outcomes of some historical events, but this debate exposes an aspect of history to deeper scrutiny, fresh perspectives, and, through dialogue, a more accurate understanding of the past. Military history is important and relevant. It does not necessarily 'teach lessons' (the trick, even if it does, is to know which ones it is teaching) or help in the construction of some over-arching universal theory. It does not make men more clever, but it does perhaps make them wise forever.

Summary

To make the comparative study of different periods easier, certain themes can be identified under the headings below. Throughout the book these headings will be used to help you keep track of the changes and continuities in warfare, and to assess which factors were paramount in producing the outcomes of certain wars. They are **leadership, quality of troops, technology, planning and preparation, strategy, tactics, alliances and domestic factors** (organisation of the state for war – such as mobilisation plans – media and public opinion, civil–military relations and industrial development). In addition, the key developments of the period and their primary outcomes can be tabulated as shown opposite.

Tutorial

Progress questions

1. How did gunpowder affect the development of weapons technology up to 1792?
2. Why did many battles take place at close quarters in the eighteenth century?
3. Why should historians approach military history with caution?

Debatable turning points	Main developments	Outcomes
1792-1815 Revolutionary and Napoleonic Wars (Chapters 1–3)	Ideological warfare State resources mobilised for war Napoleon as a leader Napoleonic offensive warfare Corps system Meritocracy	Wars of peoples/nations Mass conscription Conquest and new states Short, decisive campaigns Military reforms Limited social reforms outside France
1815-1854 Peace and Reaction (Chapter 4)	Vienna Settlement and Holy Alliance Long service professional armies Jominian interpretation of warfare Start of industrialisation Railways	Rejection of the French Revolution Reaction against mass armies Short, decisive campaigns based on concentration preferred Mass production of rifled weapons Potential for rapid mobilisation and supply
1854-1871 Mid-Century Wars (Chapters 5–7)	Crimean War: rifles and minié bullets Wars of Unification: railways Moltke and von Roon General Staff The needle gun and Krupps artillery The American Civil War	Logistical shortcomings revealed Potential and use Strategy and reforms Efficacy and mobilisation Effects on defence and mobility Mass casualties, attrition and mobilisation of resources
1871-1914 Minor Wars, Technology, Industry, Democracy, Nation States (Chapters 9-10)	Technological developments: breech-loading, high explosives, machine guns, aircraft, field defences, naval design Industrialisation Democratisation and militarism Conscription Nationalism and social Darwinism	Destructiveness and lethality of weapons, advantages to defence Mass production Public opinion and popularity of military Mass armies War more acceptable
1914-1918 The First World War (Chapters 11-13)	Failure of war plans Trench warfare Technological developments Home fronts	Mobilisation of mass armies Heavy casualties and stalemate New weapons Total war, domestic morale, revolutions

Seminar discussion

1. What are the advantages and disadvantages of studying one battle to understand change in warfare?
2. Which was the most important development of warfare in the eighteenth century: linear tactics or technology?

Practical assignment

Investigate further warfare in *one* of the following campaigns in order to understand the nature of war in the eighteenth century:

1. The Seven Years' War in North America
2. The British struggle with the Indian states and the French in south Asia
3. The American War of Independence

In particular, you should try to find out what weapons were used and what tactics were employed. Moreover, try to understand how the organisation of the states involved played a part in determining their outcome.

Study tips

1. Note that to understand war also requires an understanding of the period, the nature of society, the level of industry, the availability of resources and political organisation. War cannot be understood in isolation from its historical context.
2. Notice that changes in warfare were often developed as responses to experiences on the battlefield. Technology was developed to fit a purpose or need, it rarely emerged on its own. However, some technologies developed for entirely different purposes were adapted for war.
3. Organise your notes under clear headings. Remember that the aim of this book is to identify change, and cannot cover the history of all the wars between 1792 and 1918. It may be necessary to conduct your own research in more detail, and a uniform pattern of headings will make comparison easier. For example: campaign, significant battles, commanders involved (thumb nail sketch), quality, size and type of forces, tactics used, and other changes under the headings at the end of this chapter.
4. Be aware of the limits of military history. Determine the agenda of the author and the period in which the text was written.

2

The Revolutionary and Napoleonic Wars, 1792–1807

One minute overview – French history dramatically changed direction after the French revolution of 1789, but the revolution was harnessed by the inspirational military leadership of Napoleon Bonaparte. Napoleon dominates the period. He sought to impose his personal will not only on France, but also on the whole of Europe. He possessed a visionary grasp of military science to complement his grandiose plans of a French Empire on the continent, and he inflicted a series of defeats on the European powers. He introduced a number of changes in the French army, or built upon innovations from the revolutionary period. Unlike the warfare of the eighteenth century, he aimed to bring his opponent to battle, marching his men at high speed to inflict a decisive defeat. Short campaigns ended with the imposition of some new settlement in Napoleon's favour. However, the British remained defiant and retained naval superiority, preventing an invasion of the British Isles.

In this section you will learn:

▶ the fortunes of the French Revolutionary Army
▶ the reason for Napoleon's success

Quality of troops: The French Revolutionary Army

The French Revolution began because of 'taxation without representation'
Revolution broke out in France because of several factors. The emerging middle classes were excluded from politics, but subject to taxation which they resented. The incompetent financial management of the state meant that taxes were unfair, subject to corruption, and badly audited. The lower classes resented the *taille* tax (which the clergy and nobles did not pay) and feudal dues. The nobles were angry with government attempts to create new exemptions. Intellectuals influenced by the American slogan 'no taxation without representation', and by

ideas of liberty from England, added a spirit of disobedience to the anger of the classes. On 5 May 1789, the King called the 'Estates-General' representing the nobility, clergy and 'Third Estate' (dominated by the middle classes and lesser nobles) to amend the financial system. However, the Third Estate, under the leadership of the Abbé Sieyès, declared itself to be a National Assembly, and on 20 June pledged itself, in the Tennis Court Oath, to give France a Constitution.

Fear of the French army led to revolutionary violence
Concern that the King might deploy troops to crush the National Assembly (which were unfounded) led to the storming of the Bastille prison in search of arms. Parisians adopted the tricolour and cockade as their symbol, and formed a citizens' army called the National Guard. The National Assembly passed reforms to abolish the remnants of feudalism and privilege. The King favoured constitutional change but was a hostage of the National Assembly. His attempt to escape in June 1791 failed, further reducing his power. The French army was divided. Many officers fled (as *émigrés*) to join an army in exile of the Rhine (led by the Comte de Artois, the King's younger brother). However, the National Guard had its own difficulties: it was forced to fire on a mob in the 'massacre of the Champ de Mars' (17 July 1791) to maintain order. The now elected National Assembly, which met in October, was dominated by the progressive Girondins and Jacobins. They forced the King to abandon his selected, right-wing ministry, and a Girondin Government was formed.

Ideological war: the outbreak of the Revolutionary War
Initially relieved that the French monarchy faced internal difficulties, the ideological pronouncements of the National Assembly soon persuaded the conservative rulers of Europe to act against France. The Austrians and Prussians settled their differences and concluded the Declaration of Pillnitz in August 1791. This document stated that, should other European partners join them, they would intervene to assist the French monarchy. However, the British, although rivals of France, saw no reason to go to war. They had already successfully contained French expansion during the Seven Years' War. Nevertheless, the Legislative Assembly Girondin party decided to pre-empt foreign intervention. It was already concerned by the existence of an *émigré* army in the Rhine which Austria refused to disperse. On 20 April 1792 the Legislative Assembly declared war on Austria. It was supported by the monarchists in France too, hoping for a restoration of confidence in

Louis XVI if victory was secured. The Girondins also needed a distraction from the famine and disorder in the countryside. Marat observed that a war was 'necessary' to rid France of 300,000 brigands.

Quality of troops: the Revolutionary Army in 1792

The enthusiasm of the men was not matched by the quality of the officers
Despite the absence of many of its professionals and officers, the rump of the old French army was leavened with enthusiastic but inexperienced volunteers and National Guardsmen. However, the 'army of the north' was brushed aside by the Austrians in September and its commander, Marshal Rochanbeau, resigned. He was replaced by the veteran of the American War of Independence, the Marquis de Lafayette. However, when the King was stripped of his powers in that autumn, Lafayette defected to the Austrians, and was replaced by General Dumouriez. Dumouriez marched his forces to support General Kellerman's 'army of the centre' against the 80,000-strong Austro-Prussian army.

The early French victories made an extension of the war more likely
At Valmy on 20 September 1792, 36,000 French faced 34,000 Prussians. The French had pushed forward an infantry screen to cover its withdrawal from a weak position, but the appearance of the Prussians convinced Kellerman to fight using artillery to cut down Prussian infantry as it emerged through the morning fog. However, both sides engaged in an inconclusive artillery duel and the Prussian advance was recalled soon after it began. The main cause was the respect for the French artillery, which was the only branch of the army that could be regarded as professional. However, the Prussian withdrawal demoralised its soldiers and they retreated as if defeated. The French, by contrast, believed that their army had saved France. In October the French annexed Savoy and Nice, then overran the Austrian Netherlands after the battle of Jemappes (6 November 1792). This expansion made a general European war more likely, but political announcements gave the French army an ideological role. The events of 1792 indicate that enthusiastic, untrained men could hold off high-quality professional troops.

The Revolutionary War in 1793

The ideology of revolution gave the war a new intensity
The development of the war was the result of French ambition. The Jacobin Party replaced the Girondins as the political leaders of France. The Republic was established on 21 September 1792, when, by a majority

of one, the Jacobins succeeded in condemning the King to death as a trai-
tor. He was executed on 21 January 1793. Added to their regicide, the
revolutionaries declared an Edict of Fraternity (November 1792) promising to aid all foreign peoples in their overthrow of their own kings. The
generals were told to implement a new order in captured territories by
abolishing feudalism, confiscating the property of the clergy and aristocracy, and declaring the sovereignty of the people (democratic government). In addition, the 'doctrine of natural frontiers' (January 1793)
claimed the right to extend the French borders to the Rhine, the Pyrenees
and the Alps. Most flagrantly of all, the French sent warships down the
Scheldt to Antwerp, despite its official status of neutrality. France then
declared war on Britain, Holland and Spain.

The invasion of France was a disaster for the Revolution
A massed invasion of France was launched from the German states and
the Netherlands by six powers: Austria, Prussia, Sardinia, Holland,
Britain and Spain. On 18 March 1793 Dumouriez was defeated at Neer-
winden and he defected to the allies. His successor was killed in action,
and General Custine was guillotined after a defeat at Valenciennes (21
to 23 May). There were rebellions against the Jacobins in Toulon (which
asked for British support) and in the north in the Vendée. Fearful of
royalist intrigues, the Jacobins began a wave of executions known as
'the Terror'. The value of the assignat currency fell by 22 per cent and
prices rose encouraging hoarding and financial speculation. General
Houchard was guillotined for failing to drive the Austrians out of northern France, and Girondins were also executed *en masse* by Robespierre
and his Jacobin clique. Racked by internal fear and dissension, and
faced by the onslaught of external enemies, France seemed doomed. In
particular, it had no effective leaders to command the army.

The organisation of the state for war: the recovery of the French Army

Two factors saved France: military reforms
Lazare Nicholas Carnot (war minister of the Committee of Public
Safety) reorganised the French army. He implemented training, which
complemented the enthusiasm of the troops. He created corps of all
arms that could operate independently as miniature armies. The infantry were taught to attack in tightly packed columns, giving each man
the psychological support of his friends and a shock effect on the enemy.
The columns, bearing down on their opponents, were preceded by

sharpshooters (a lesson picked up from America). The advantage of this training was that it could be completed in just two months. Moreover, as General Hackett observed, the aim was the crushing of their opponent, 'The age of limited war (of the eighteenth century) was over'. The soldiers were told they were fighting the privileged elites of Europe, but, above all, they were defending France. The stirring *Marseillaise* became the national anthem.

The second factor: the mobilisation of French troops
The second factor was the mobilisation of the nation's resources, particularly the manpower of France. In the 'Levée en Masse' all unmarried men between 18 and 25 were conscripted into the army, whilst many married men were drafted into factories. The death of the generals focused the commanders solely on victory; by contrast, Austrian and Prussian troops were unwilling conscripts or mercenaries, often led by indifferent commanders. The Austrian Duke of Brunswick disagreed with the Prussian king on the best strategy to defeat France. Moreover, both Austria and Prussia were eager to complete the dismemberment of Poland in 1792 and 1795. The British expedition to Flanders in 1795 was indifferently executed, primarily because Austrian troops were transferred to the border with Prussia, but also because they had been defeated by General Jourdan at Fleurus (26 June 1794).

The French army drove off its enemies
Toulon was recaptured using the plan of the Corsican artillery officer, Napoleon Bonaparte, in December 1793. Napoleon believed the siege depended on two forts and he sited guns personally to reduce their walls. On 17 December he led an attack and was wounded but the city was taken and he was promoted to Brigadier General. An *émigré* French army was routed at Quiberon Bay in 1793 by General Hoche. Holland and Spain withdrew from the war. Prussia, by the treaty of Basle (April 1795), gave France a free hand on the Rhine, providing France did not intervene in north German affairs. Carnot also implemented a new system of logistics. Although control depots still provided munitions, its supplies were requisitioned from the countryside (which compelled armies to stay outside of France). The mobilisation of the state's resources was therefore effective.

Leadership: the rise of Napoleon Bonaparte

Robespierre's reign of terror generated enemies, especially when it was clear political opponents were being eliminated to preserve his power, such as Hébert and Danton. In 1794 he aimed to replace Christianity with the 'Cult of the Supreme Being' and establish a utopian 'Republic of Virtue'. In 1795 the Jacobins were replaced by the moderate 'Thermidorians' who established a new convention and an executive, or Directory of five. Napoleon was placed in command of troops in Paris and crushed an uprising, the 'Coup d'état of 13 Vendémaire', thus saving the new regime. Given the wartime conditions, the convention handed power over to the Directory. Carnot decided, now that Spain, Holland and Prussia were out of the war, to defeat Austria by a pincer movement. One thrust, through the German states, would be led by Generals Jordan and Moreau. The other, through northern Italy, would be led by 27-year-old Napoleon, who replaced the ineffective Schérer and had got the political backing of Barras in the Directory (because he had crushed the Paris uprising).

Planning: Napoleon prepared his campaign in Italy carefully
The initial operations in Italy and Germany in 1795 had made little progress, so Napoleon began his campaign by stiffening discipline in the army, introducing reinforcements and better administration. He won respect by delivering the supplies that were needed, giving firm orders and constantly visiting the troops. Napoleon also prepared his strategy in advance. Whilst in Paris, he noted that the 60,000 defenders were concentrated in four pockets on the western border of Italy, with a mobile reserve 60 miles (96.5 kilometres) in the rear. Napoleon could command 46,000 ragged soldiers but he planned to outflank, or take in the rear, each of the enemy detachments and use surprise. The concentration of artillery fire and greater numbers, along with his personal leadership in the critical attacks, improved the morale of his own men after each success. Baron Colli's 25,000 Piedmontese and General Johann Beaulieu's Austrians failed to combine, and Napoleon drove a wedge between them, attacking each in turn. This was called 'Central Position'. He maintained battlefield flexibility by dividing his cavalry into two divisions and keeping an artillery reserve for use at the critical point.

Napoleon inspired his men by personal example
Having driven the Piedmontese from Dego and Mondori (21 April), he

faced 'cordon defence' by the Austrians along the river Po. Giving the impression of attacking elsewhere by a series of 'feints', Napoleon struck across the river at Piacenta, and, by threatening the Austrian lines of communication with Mantua, he compelled the Austrians to withdraw. However, a rearguard at Lodi denied the French a viable line of communication of their own. A long causeway across the river was dominated by a strong Austrian position. Siting the guns himself, Napoleon urged his infantrymen to attack. Initially they were thrown back, but a second assault carried the position. The bridge at Lodi was immensely significant. Napoleon's reputation as a brave and bold commander was established. He had won over his troops (they affectionately called him 'the little corporal' because of his visits and his siting of the guns), and his success encouraged a popular following. Moreover Napoleon himself began to conceive greater ambitions.

Case examples: the battles of Castiglione and Arcola

The Austrians counter-attacked in northern Italy with two armies under General Quasdanovich and General Würmser. Unable to sustain the siege of the Austrian fortress city Mantua, Napoleon's subordinate Sérurier lost 179 cannon, and Massena was forced to abandon Verona. Napoleon kept his 'central position' between the two wings of the Austrian pincer, dispatching Augereau to hold up Würmser, whilst he defeated Quasdanovich. Augereau's success, just 5 miles away, was rewarded when Napoleon turned and prepared to take on Würmser's force at Castiglione on 5 August 1796. A frontal assault would be supported, at the critical moment, by the arrival of Sérurier's division in the Austrian rear and reinforcements under Despinois on the left. However, in the event, Sérurier was ill and replaced by an impetuous General Fiorella. Delays in the advance of the French infantry were overcome by Napoleon's personal intervention and by the timely arrival of 18 guns under Auguste Marmont that pounded the Austrian line. French grenadiers broke the Austrian left, Despinois' men arrived and the Austrians broke off.

A combination of factors gave Napoleon victory in Italy

The Austrians quickly recovered. Würmser despatched (in August) two further columns to relieve the renewed siege of Mantua. Each was destroyed in turn, again, by local superiority in numbers. There was a third Austrian assault in September, trying to sandwich Napoleon between two armies under Alvintzi and Davidowich, and Mantua itself. Napoleon despatched holding forces under Massena, Vaubois and

Guieu. Napoleon's main force tried to push across the river Alpone at Arcola on 15 November but he was almost drowned when pushed into the river and, when it appeared Vaubois had been defeated, Napoleon withdrew. The arrival of Austrian reinforcements meant Napoleon was unable to effect a crossing on the 16th and so decided to outflank the Austrians to the west. Massena was ordered to pin the Austrians at Arcola, and carried out a spectacular ambush on advancing Austrian troops by concealing his men in ditches and marshes.

Napoleon demonstrated his desire to act independently
In 1797 the Austrians again tried to relieve Mantua, making diversionary attacks on Verona and Legnano. Napoleon decided to stand at Rivoli on 14 January 1797. Alvintzi planned to attack in five columns (with two on each flank for an envelopment) but Napoleon's reinforcements kept arriving all day, doubling his force by mid-afternoon. The centre fell back, but a counter-attack drove the Austrians from the field. Mantua capitulated on 2 February 1797, having sustained 18,000 casualties (mostly through disease). Napoleon marched on to a point just 95 miles from Vienna dictating peace terms without consulting Paris (confirmed as the Treaty of Campo Formio, 18 April 1797). Belgium was ceded to France and Austria recognised the French satellite, the Cisalpine Republic, in Northern Italy.

The limits of Napoleonic military ambition
The French could not defeat the Royal Navy
Napoleon had been successful in Italy because he had moved his troops rapidly, made use of the corps system and often led by personal example. Despite Napoleon's success in Italy, the next French plan to invade Ireland and Britain (and thus defeat the only power still opposed to them) was dependent on naval supremacy. Britain had captured the islands of Martinique, St Lucia and Tobago from the French in 1794. On the 'Glorious 1 June 1794' Lord Howe defeated the French fleet off Ushant. When Spain declared war on Britain in 1796, Britain took the island of Trinidad the following year. These events indicated that Britain was the dominant power at sea.

Great Britain remained defiant of France despite some internal problems
The Spanish fleet was defeated by Jervis off Cape St Vincent, whilst the Dutch, who had already surrendered Ceylon and the Cape of Good Hope to the British, were defeated by Duncan at Camperdown (October 1797). Proposed French landings in 1796 to support the Irish led to a

rebellion there in 1798. General Humbert's French and Irish were forced to surrender to Cornwallis, whilst a landing at Fishguard in Wales was soon contained. Nevertheless, the Royal Navy was not immune from French revolutionary ideas. At Spithead, sailors mutinied in protest at bad pay, poor quality food, the unfair division of prize money, excessive harshness by their officers and flogging. Lord Howe, 'Black Dick', persuaded the men to return to duty, but at the Nore, sailors expressed anger at the articles of war and demanded some say in the selection of officers. The Thames was blockaded and two Royal frigates were fired upon by the mutineers, but eventually they surrendered. The ringleaders were hanged and the rest pardoned. Duncan's successful deception of the Dutch during the mutiny, and his victory at Camperdown with the fleet, proved that both conciliation and firmness had been vital.

Case example: the campaign in Egypt

As they could not defeat the Royal Navy, the French planned to cut Britain off from its Indian possessions and thereby weaken its Empire. Eventually, Napoleon envisaged the restoration of French colonies in South Asia. He captured Malta and invaded Egypt with 40,000, successfully evading the Royal Navy. He defeated the Mamloukes in the Battle of the Pyramids (July 1798) and the Turks at Mount Tabor (April 1799) and Aboukir (July 1799). However, Nelson destroyed the French fleet at Aboukir Bay in August 1798 and captured the French siege guns.

Despite setbacks in Egypt, Napoleon rose to power in France
Campaigning into the Holy Lands, Napoleon secured the citadel of Jaffa, but executed 3,000 unarmed prisoners, probably through frustration at the delays the garrison had caused. Sickness followed the army, including plague (which killed 2,000) and morale collapsed. Unable to retreat along the North African coast, Napoleon left for Paris and, by means of a *coup d'état*, became one of the three members of the Consulate, a body which replaced the unpopular Directory (of five). The French army in Egypt was defeated at Heliopolis (1800) and Aboukir (1801), then capitulated. Nevertheless, Napoleon's reputation was untarnished. He was regarded as First Consul and, in his person, combined the civil, diplomatic and military leadership of France. Napoleon was able to achieve power because he was decisive, he had earned a reputation for success at a time when France faced defeat, and he symbolised order and discipline in a period of chaos. He was ruthless

with opponents (because he believed he was guided by destiny), but he had been fortunate in his political allies.

Alliances: the allied counter-offensive (the Second Coalition)

The British Prime Minister, William Pitt, persuaded Tsar Paul I of Russia to join a coalition against France. Austria, Portugal, Naples and Turkey also joined and mounted a counter-offensive. An Anglo-Russian army was to advance from the Netherlands. Archduke Charles of Austria defeated the French at Lake Constance (March 1799), whilst a combined Austro-Russian-Neopolitan army of 9,000, under Marshal Alexander Suvorov, defeated 40,000 French at Cassano (27 April 1799), but not before the Neapolitan army had mutinied and the French had established the Parthenopean Republic. Suvorov divided the French and defeated each force in detail, recovering Milan and Turin lost in 1796. By June 1799, Suvorov's force was reduced to 40,000 and he faced 50,000 in southern France, but he took a portion of the army and defeated the French at Trebbia, and then concentrated all his men in August to inflict another defeat at Novi, pursuing them through the Appenines. Marshal Mélas completed the rout of the French at Genoa.

Despite allied successes, there were also setbacks
The Duke of York was unable to invade northern France through Flanders, whilst Massena checked the Austrians in Switzerland and almost trapped the Russians there. When Napoleon returned from Egypt, and had secured political authority by his *coup d'état* of 18 Brumaire, he created a new 'Army of the Reserve' at Dijon. This was largely because the army of Italy was in disarray. Desertions, increasing failure to report if conscripted, the draft of unwilling conscripts, the string of defeats, low morale and attempts to murder the officers illustrated the collapse of the force which had been Napoleon's instrument of conquest in 1796-7. This indicates that Napoleon had been the main factor in improving the quality of troops in Italy. However, it was in Italy he decided to take the offensive.

Strategy: Napoleon's second campaign in Italy 1799-1800

On 8 March 1800 Napoleon moved his army of 37,000 across the snowy St Bernard Pass, arriving in May on the North Italian plain. Twenty thousand more passed through the Simplon, St Gotthard and Mont Cenis passes. It was a major gamble. The troops were dispersed and the risk of delay due to bad weather was great. Cannon barrels were laid on sledges and 20 men hauled each one. Ammunition supplies had to be halved. However, surprise was achieved. On 25 May the fort at Ivrea was taken when guns (with wheels covered with straw) were hauled by gangs of 50 men in silence up to the walls. On 2nd June Napoleon took Milan and therefore cut the lines of communication. Nevertheless, Genoa's French garrison capitulated on 4 June.

Marengo was a 'meeting engagement' that Napoleon won by luck
Napoleon dispersed his small army to forage for food. The roads were guarded with a small reserve to maintain a barrier against the Austrians. General Lannes was in advance of Napoleon's main position. General Melas of the Austrian army initially remained inactive against the French whilst he concentrated his forces around Alessandria. Meanwhile General Ott (with 18,000 Austrians) left Genoa to effect a junction with Melas. Lannes attacked Ott with just 8,000 men at Montebello on 9 June. He reported his success to Napoleon who believed that it was evidence that the Austrians were retreating to Genoa. However, they were in fact advancing. On 13 June the two advanced guards clashed (Napoleon thinking he had made contact with Melas' rearguard). The following day at Marengo 31,000 Austrians drove the French back and Napoleon pleaded for his distant detachments to come to his aid. Just as Napoleon faced defeat, Kellerman's cavalry and Desaix's infantry arrived on the Austrian right flank, causing them to fall back. Napoleon was outnumbered and outgunned, but it was the Austrians (who felt unable to restore their lines of communication) who negotiated a withdrawal to Lombardy. Later Napoleon would downplay his 'rescue' by Desaix and Kellerman, even though his 'victory' had depended on their initiative.

Peace was restored in Europe in 1802
Napoleon's success in Italy coincided with the collapse of the second coalition. Russia withdrew from the war, quarrelling with Austria and concerned that Britain had acquired Malta. The Tsar was also angered by the British 'right to search' all vessels of neutral powers. In 1799, the Duke of York's expeditionary force evacuated Holland, and the Russians and Swedes concluded an alliance against Britain. In 1800 they were joined by Prussia and Denmark in the Armed Neutrality of the North but, with the prospect of these powers' fleets joining Napoleon against Britain, Lord Nelson 'copenhagened' the Danish fleet in 1801 (that is, he launched a preventative attack and destroyed it). The Austrians were defeated by General Moreau at Hohenlinden in Germany, as well as by Napoleon in Italy. By the Treaty of Lunéville in

1801 Austria recognised the French control of Holland, Switzerland and Italy and the loss of all territory on the left bank of the Rhine. Unable to come to grips with Britain, France concluded the Treaty of Amiens in March 1802. Britain agreed to restore Malta and her colonial conquests except Ceylon and Trinidad. France returned Egypt to Turkey, evacuated Rome and relinquished Southern Italy.

Changes in the technology of warfare

Napoleon's strategy had been concentration of force at the precise moment, both in terms of manpower (hence the need to drive a wedge between opponents' forces) and in artillery fire. The devastating power of artillery, with its ability to lob cannonballs effectively up to 1,300 yards (1,183m) made it a weapon that would dominate the battlefield right through to 1918. However, there were already other developments in technology that transformed warfare. At the battle of Fleurus in 1794 Captain Coutelle of the French army had used a hot-air balloon to observe enemy positions and ultimately direct artillery fire. Howitzers and mortars used plunging fire to toss bombs (explosive with a fuse) over obstacles, and in 1784 Henry Shrapnel invented a shell that would explode in mid-air, spraying the ground with a lethal cone of balls, a particularly effective weapon against troops in the open.

Industrialisation and experimentation affected warfare in this period
To speed up production, the English firm Boulton and Watt laid down the first flow-line engineering works in 1796 called the Soho factory. Each specialist workshop (drilling, turning, pattern making) supplied the next one, a practice soon adopted by armaments works. Similarly, in 1800, Henry Maudsley (formerly of the Woolwich arsenal) invented the precision screw cutting lathe. In 1798 Eli Whitney of New England set up mass production of muskets, setting a pattern that would enable armies to arm vast numbers of conscripts. In 1792 Claude Chappé introduced semaphore signalling which soon meant that messages could be transmitted 150 miles in 15 minutes through chains of relay stations, or shorter distances on the battlefield or at sea. The British army adopted rockets as weapons, having been subjected to rocket attacks by HyderAli of Mysore in 1780. In 1806 William Congreve's rockets were used in a bombardment of Boulogne but their battlefield use was limited because of their inaccuracy. A testament to the greater professionalism in warfare was the opening of the first military academies for officers at Sandhurst (1802) which complemented the training

of British artillery officers at Woolwich (following the establishment of a Staff College at High Wycombe in 1799). The American West Point (1802), the French College of St Cyr (1808) and the Russian War Academy (1810) followed suit.

Summary
Weapon effectiveness

▶ Artillery British 6- & 9-pounders could fire roundshot 1,000 yards, grapeshot 300 yards. Rate of fire: 6 r.p.m. (rounds per minute).

▶ Muskets British 'Brown Bess' had an effective range of 200 yards at best but battle range was shorter (hence 'wait until you see the whites of their eyes'. 3 r.p.m. Best used *en masse.*

▶ Rifles British Baker rifle could fire out to 300–500 yards, but fired only 1 r.p.m. In the Peninsular war it was calculated that one bullet in 459 was effective, but many engagements were at close quarters so the hit rate improved. Used by sharpshooters.

Tactics

Most armies fought in a series of lines so as to maximise the number of muskets that could be brought to bear on an opponent. However, the French used columns that would offer soldiers the psychological comfort of numbers, and bear down on their opponents whilst singing, chanting or shouting and firing ragged shots from the front. This mass of men would intimidate and unsettle troops in lines and then crash into them in a hand-to-hand fight. Once the enemy lines were pierced, cavalry would charge in dense formation into the broken enemy formation, causing confusion and panic. Artillery was used to blast great holes through the enemy lines. However, columns were vulnerable to the fire of cannons. In addition, if determined men in lines were prepared to stand and continue firing in a disciplined and effective way, they could demoralise the leading men in a column and cause the attack to falter. Moreover, if infantry formed a square formation and kept their nerve, they could repel cavalry. Time and again, disciplined British troops were able to use these techniques to defeat French attacks.

Strategy and tactics: Napoleon's campaign of 1805

Preparations began for the resumption of war with Britain
With the peace of Amiens (27 March 1802), Napoleon concentrated on domestic reforms, and was created 'First Consul for Life' (2 August 1802). However, Napoleon was determined to defeat Britain and the fragile peace was shattered on 16 May 1803. Napoleon had supported rebellious Maratha princes against the British in India, had attempted to establish a colony in Australia (1800–1803), tried to capture San Domingo in the Caribbean (1802), had refused to evacuate Southern Italy (claiming that he would not do so until Britain gave up Malta), had placed French troops in Dutch fortresses, seized Parma, annexed Piedmont and gained extensive control of the Swiss army. In 1804 Napoleon concentrated an army at Boulogne in preparation for an invasion of Britain. He assembled a Franco-Spanish fleet ready to win supremacy of the English Channel, and on 2 December, at the height of his powers, he was crowned (placing the crown on his own head) 'Emperor of the French' on 2 December 1804.

The Third Coalition and the strategic victory of Ulm
To survive, Britain needed the support of continental allies. In April 1805 Britain obtained the support of Russia to drive the French from Switzerland and Holland. Encouraged by the concentration in the west and the presence of only 50,000 men under Massena in Italy, Austria joined the coalition in August, and Sweden also joined. Faced by this new landward threat, Napoleon abandoned the invasion project. Any hopes of gaining naval supremacy and resurrecting it were crushed by Nelson's victory at Trafalgar on 31 October 1805 (Nelson broke with the tradition of naval warfare, by crossing the battle line of enemy warships and closing with them in close quarter fighting, a feat that required good seamanship and courage). The Austrians focused on Italy, but General Mack commanded a force of 50,000 men in Bavaria, which had paused at Ulm waiting for the 100,000-strong Russian army. Napoleon swung his 210,000-strong force in a wide concentric arc, in six columns around the Austrian right and rear, whilst Joachim Murat's French cavalry demonstrated in front of Ulm to pin the Austrians down. Eventually two Austrian attempts to break out, at Haslach (11 October 1805) and Elchingen (14 October 1805), failed but Archduke Ferdinand managed to escape with just 2,000 cavalry. Mack capitulated, which meant that Napoleon had defeated an Austrian army by manoeuvre alone. Moreover, as the Austrians tried to withdraw from Italy, Massena prevented them from crossing the Alps and they played

no part in the campaign. Napoleon pressed eastwards, despatching two corps (Ney and Marmont) to cover the alpine routes and 50,000 to protect his extended lines of communication. Vienna was captured and garrisoned with 20,000 men, but, faced by the approach of the Russians, Napoleon was compelled to concentrate 70 miles to the north and take up a defensive position. He had with him 73,000 men of the 'Grande Armée'.

Strategy and tactics: Napoleon's defensive battle at Austerlitz

The battle of Austerlitz was the pinnacle of Napoleon's career. His own skill, and the quality of his army, contrasted with the weaknesses of his opponents. The Austro-Russian plan was to outflank Napoleon by smashing his right wing, thus severing him from Vienna to the south. A feint would occupy and pin the French left. However, Napoleon had chosen his ground carefully. When the allied attack began at 4 a.m., Lannes held off the attack on the left. As the Russians crossed the Prat-zen heights on their way to attack his right, Napoleon unleashed Soult in the centre which cut the allies in half. The Russian Imperial Guard, held in reserve, tried to destroy Soult, but Napoleon's Guard Cavalry hurled them back. At this critical moment of allied confusion, Napoleon then committed the Imperial Guard. The allied troops, who had been cut off, tried to escape across frozen lakes, but were cut down. It was a total victory for Napoleon, but the cost was appalling. One eighth of the Grande Armée were casualties, and one third of the allies, with 16,000 killed or wounded and 11,000 prisoners. The Austrians sued for peace (they were forced to pay 40 million francs as a war indemnity), the Russians withdrew and Britain was again alone against France. Under the terms of the Treaty of Preisburg (26 December 1805) the Bavarian and Wurtemberg rulers were promoted to kings and agreed to provide Napoleon with troops.

Napoleonic offensive warfare

Napoleon commanded a European army in 1806

At the end of 1805 Napoleon promised Hanover to Prussia, partly to reward her neutrality during the war, but also in return for the ceding of Ansbach to its new ally Bavaria. In Britain the death of William Pitt (23 January 1806) ushered in a new ministry under Fox who immedi-ately began peace negotiations. Napoleon, having already embittered the Austrians, now incensed the Prussians by promising to restore Hanover to the British. The Prussians demanded the withdrawal of the

French, invaded Saxony to control its armed forces and joined a fourth coalition (Britain, Russia, Prussia and Portugal). The Grande Armée, stationed in Southern Germany was a multinational force. Amongst its ranks were Dutch, Italians, Swiss and Germans, as well as French men. However, to win, Napoleon realised he had to move quickly and defeat the Prussians before the Russians arrived in force.

The battle of Jena did not follow Napoleon's plan
Starting on 8 October the French army marched at top speed in three vast columns shielded by light cavalry on a front of 30 miles, covering 15 miles a day. Each corps was a self-contained army, and Lannes was able to inflict a minor defeat on the Prussians as soon as he made contact at Saalfeld (10 October 1806). Nevertheless, thinking Lannes had made contact with the Prussian main body, Napoleon concentrated his army before Jena. In fact, General Friedrich von Hohenlohe was covering the withdrawal of the main force under the Duke of Brunswick with 51,000 men. On the morning of 14 October 1806, 90,000 French troops had assembled. Napoleon's plan to envelop the Prussians on the right, with two corps, was jeopardised by an unauthorised and impetuous attack in the centre by Marshal Ney of VI corps. Ney was attacked and almost surrounded by Prussian cavalry until relieved by Lannes. The situation stabilised and Napoleon used his artillery to batter the Prussian infantry for two hours, inflicting appalling casualties. At 3pm the French advanced again and defeated them. To the north, Davout's corps had encountered 50,000 Prussians, but parrying a series of uncoordinated attacks, the 27,000 Frenchmen had been able to defeat the Prussians at a cost of 40 per cent casualties. The Prussians lost 25,000, and thousands more were captured. Berlin fell on 24 October. Napoleon then issued the Berlin and Milan decrees, banning the European states from trading with the 'nation of shopkeepers', the British. In response the Royal Navy blockaded France and the north German coast. Thus a trade war extended the military–naval conflict between Britain and France.

Napoleon turned to the defeat of Russia
Having defeated the Prussians, Napoleon marched east to engage the Russians. He advanced to the Vistula and occupied Warsaw whereupon two French corps independently engaged the Russians under General Bennigsen in December, but they withdrew having suffered 12,000 casualties. With poor roads, supply in winter was almost impossible and Napoleon decided to follow the usual practice of billeting his men

in winter quarters. Even so, mud, snow and freezing temperatures meant the supply system almost collapsed. However, Bennigsen attacked French outposts in January and Napoleon's plans to trap him failed when bad weather delayed couriers to Bernadotte, and a complete set of plans fell into Russian hands.

Tactics: the battle of Eylau was fought in terrible conditions
Napoleon took up a defensive position at Eylau on 7 February 1807. Temperatures fell to −30°C, but blizzards at dawn on the 8th made visibility poor. Napoleon decided to stay on the defensive until Ney and Davout's corps arrived from the north and south respectively, then he launched them into the Russian flanks. However, Davout was unable to make progress. Soult, in the centre, was under pressure from massed Russian batteries of sixty guns. To buy time for Ney to arrive, Napoleon sent in the corps of the ailing Augereau, but blinded by the snowstorm, his force lost direction and was cut to pieces as it emerged in front of the Russian battery. They fell back, the loyal 14th Line Infantry sacrificing itself on a small mound to cover the retreat. The Russians pressed on to Eylau itself. Desperate now, Napoleon launched the massed cavalry of Murat, 10,700 strong, into the Russian infantry. They broke through, reformed in the Russian rear and then cut down the Russian gunners as they withdrew to the French lines. Davout made progress but the arrival of 9,000 Prussians under General Lestocq tilted the battle back in the Russians' favour. At that point, Ney arrived and the French regained their positions by nightfall. However, despite Napoleon's claim that it was a victory, it was, at best, a draw. There was no pursuit, but the Russians were checked in their offensive.

The battle of Friedland was also hard fought
In the spring Napoleon renewed his offensive by besieging Danzig, and parried Bennigsen's attempt to crush Ney's corps. On 10 June Napoleon attacked the Russians indecisively at Heilsberg, and was compelled to march around the flank to turn a defensive position. Bennigsen withdrew on Friedland although Napoleon initially mistook the move as a Russian withdrawal to Königsberg. Both sides reinforced their armies on 14 June: Napoleon to 80,000 with 118 guns, Bennigsen to 60,000 with 120 guns. However, the Russian position was weak. Almost the entire army was on the west bank of the river Alle, so that, if attacked, they would be forced to squeeze back over a single bridge into Friedland itself. At 5 pm Napoleon sent Ney in to attack the Russian right but, despite success at first, a Russian massed battery on the far bank

checked the French attack. Bennigsen then switched cavalry from his right and centre to the threatened point.

Artillery had a devastating role at Friedland
Napoleon realised Ney might now fail, so he sent forward Victor's corps and the Imperial Guard from his right-centre. The Russians gave ground and, at this point, a remarkable event occurred. General Senarmont, the commander of Victor's corps artillery, sent forward his guns, battery by battery, each covering the movement of the next. They reduced the range to 450 yards, then 250 yards and finally to within 60 paces of the Russians. Unsupported, artillery would never ordinarily have been used this way, but it demoralised the Russian troops and they began to pull back. The Russian Imperial Guard made one last attempt to turn the tide, but failed. Only the lack of a determined pursuit saved the Russians from further losses. The Russians appealed for an armistice, and Tsar Alexander met Napoleon on a raft in the middle of the river Nieman. There they concluded the Treaty of Tilsit: German territories were partitioned, Poland became a satellite state and a trade embargo was enforced against Britain.

Conclusion: the Napoleonic Wars marked a change in the nature of war
Napoleon's position was one of great significance. He was master of Western and Central Europe. He had compelled Russia to be his ally and he controlled Italy. Once again, only Britain remained defiant. Under French occupation Napoleon had imposed reforms, and changes to frontiers, even renaming several states, such as the Cisalpine Republic of Northern Italy. Napoleon's campaigns had been short and decisive. His aim had been to defeat enemy armies in battle in order to impose a peace settlement on his own terms. However, he was less successful in protracted operations. The Napoleonic Wars were therefore different from the wars of the eighteenth century: the French gave warfare an ideological dimension.

Tutorial

Progress questions
1. How did the quality of troops affect the outcome of the Revolutionary Wars?
2. What were the *Levée en Masse* and the Corps system?

3.   What qualities and techniques made Napoleon successful in warfare?

Seminar discussion
1.   Is Napoleon's success and innovation more myth than reality?
2.   Which was the most important factor in determining the outcome of the wars between 1792 and 1807: leadership, quality of troops, technology, tactics or logistics?

Practical assignment
Create a sketch map of Europe in 1792–1807. Plot each of the campaigns and major engagements on it. Identify changes in national borders. Annotate a brief summary of each campaign around the edge of the map.

Study tips
1.   The period is dominated by the ideology of revolution and the rise of Napoleon, so it is worth being familiar with these aspects.
2.   Note the changes that took place in warfare: you will not be examined on the details of each battle or campaign. However, it is worth knowing a few case examples to use as evidence in support of your arguments.

3

The Napoleonic Wars, 1807–1815

One minute overview – Despite Napoleon's occupation of central Europe and his ability to redraw the map of the Continent, France faced continued resistance from Great Britain. The occupation of Spain led to a long drawn out conflict and desultory guerrilla fighting against the Spanish people, which only served to drain and demoralise the French army. Yet Napoleon's reputation as a leader was such that his presence on the battlefield, it was said, was worth an additional 10,000 men. Nevertheless, Napoleon was unable to defeat Russia in 1812, and the combined strength of the European powers in the years 1813–1815. In particular he was unable to defeat Great Britain, which wrested Spain from his grasp in 1814. After a brief period out of power in France, Napoleon returned to challenge Europe a second time. Ultimately, at Waterloo in 1815, Napoleon's bold strategy proved ineffective against the determined resistance of an allied army. Nevertheless, the European powers continued to regard the containment of France as a common policy for the next 40 years.

In this chapter you will learn:

▶ how the Napoleonic offensive faltered in Spain and Central Europe
▶ the role of the British Army in 1812
▶ the consequences of Napoleon's invasion of Russia
▶ how Napoleon was defeated

Ideological war: the conflict in Spain and the Peninsula War, 1808–1811

The Spanish guerrilla war was a bitter irony for the French, who had themselves championed the idea of a people's army, made up of enthusiastic rather than trained mercenaries. Just as the advocates of revolution had been consumed by their own monster, so now France, the advocate of patriotism, faced a patriotic war in Spain against them.

Napoleon planned to secure his southern flank in Spain
Napoleon imposed the 'Continental System', a blockade against Britain in 1807, but he was eager to occupy Portugal, Britain's ally, and perhaps replace the Spanish monarchy with a Bonaparte, just as he had done in Italy. This would also secure his southern flank. When Napoleon sent General Junot through Spain, there was no resistance (the Spanish army, on loan to Napoleon, was in Denmark). In December 1807 Junot occupied Lisbon and the Portugese royal family fled to Brazil. Napoleon then sent Murat with 100,000 men to occupy the entire Iberian peninsula in March 1808. The monarchy was replaced, prompting an uprising in Madrid on 2 May. The brutal suppression of this rebellion initiated a guerrilla war by the Spanish under local juntas against the French army of occupation.

Spanish guerrillas used different tactics to British and French forces in the region
The guerrillas benefited from the remote, mountainous terrain, poor roads and summer heat. The regular Spanish troops were less successful. In the siege of Saragossa citizens assisted in the defence of the city, but field armies under General Cuesta were defeated at Cabezan and Medina del Rio Seco. At Baylen, a French force of 17,500 men was isolated and forced to surrender, but Spanish irregulars massacred the French troops or sent them to prison hulks. With Junot cut off in Portugal, the British despatched an expeditionary force under Sir Arthur Wellesley. Junot was defeated at Roleia and Vimiero. However, the more senior British commanders, Burrard and Dalrymple, arranged, under the convention of Cintra, the evacuation of the French without further fighting. Command of the British forces then passed to Sir John Moore, an advocate of light infantry tactics and marksmanship. In the Peninsular War that followed, the fine discipline and musketry training, or 'skill at arms' of the British army that he promoted was highly successful. This contrasted with the French emphasis on mass and shock, caused by columns of enthusiastic but less well-trained soldiers. The British put their faith in firepower, the French favoured the psychological effect of advancing blocks of men. At the risk of exaggeration, the French tactics reflected the momentum of the revolutionary crowd, the British the iron discipline of the industrial revolution.

Leadership: British troops were well led by Arthur Wellesley and Sir John Moore
In September 1808 Moore was ordered to move into Spain, to coordinate with the juntas. When the Spanish leaders proved unwilling he advanced on Salamanca, hoping to draw Napoleon, who had recently

arrived with 100,000 men, into action. Nevertheless Moore, with only 35,000, was forced to fall back on Corunna in mid-winter where he inflicted, at the cost of his own life, a defeat on Soult (16 January 1809). The British army was evacuated but Napoleon, leaving an army of occupation, also left Spain, believing the campaign to be over. Saragossa fell on 20 February 1809, but the British established a base in Lisbon and helped retrain the Portuguese army. Wellesley launched an offensive and drove Soult from Oporto. Soult was surprised by Wellesley's audacious plan: The Buffs (the East Kent Regiment) were ferried across the River Douro and captured a small seminary. There they held off counter-attacks and were soon assisted by reinforcements (and a popular uprising in the town of Oporto itself). The French were broken and chased from the town. In less than three weeks, Wellesley had liberated Portugal and morale in Britain was restored. However, despite promises, the Spanish regular army failed to assist the British, leaving Wellesley to fight off repeated French attacks at Talavera (28 July 1809).

Wellesley adapted his strategy to suit the strengths of his troops
Wellesley knew that the Spanish troops were unreliable, so he drew them up behind the walls of Talavera and a mile deep just to its east. His British and German troops were extended eastwards, making use of reverse slopes to protect his men from artillery, but also to conceal his outnumbered force. He controlled the battle, and the deployment of reserves, from a small hill. As French columns came up, the British leapt up and fired steady volleys. As the French faltered, bayonet charges were made, thus adding to the psychological impact of the musketry.

Wellington proved a skilful commander in defence
Outnumbered, Wellesley (now known as the Duke of Wellington) withdrew to Portugal. In 1810 Soult resumed the offensive by besieging Cadiz (which lasted until 1812) which became a symbol of 'free Spain'. In May Massena invaded Portugal and Wellington took up a defensive stance at Busaco, aiming to delay any French thrust towards Lisbon. Massena's reconnaissance failed to provide the information he needed because, once again, Wellington concealed his men on reverse slopes. Intending to roll up Wellington's flank, the French were cut down by steady and disciplined British musketry. The morale of the Portuguese troops, fed, clothed, equipped, trained and, in senior command, led by the British, was greatly increased.

The French were unable to pierce the British defences in Portugal
Defensive works were drawn up to protect Lisbon known as the Torres
Vedras lines. These were a triple line of 108 redoubts with 447 guns,
held by the Portuguese militia. Under Wellington's instruction the front
of this formidable earthwork was a 'scorched earth' to deny food and
forage to the French army. Massena, unable to tempt Wellington out,
withdrew without attempting an assault. The following spring his
wretched army was harried out of Portugal by guerrillas.

Quality of troops in Spain

Spanish guerrillas demoralised the French army
The guerrillas cost the French 100 men per day during their occupation.
They continually severed communications, attacked convoys and
isolated detachments. However, the morale of the French army was
severely affected by the massacre and mutilation of captured troops,
the wounded and camp followers (including women and children). In
one incident every man in a hospital of 400 patients was murdered and
a further 53 were buried alive. The French response was counter-terror,
a policy which fuelled yet more atrocities.

Despite successes, the British suffered heavily too
In 1811 General Graham was sent to break the French siege of Cadiz,
but the Spanish regulars again failed to support the British, yet claimed
the victory at Barossa (5 March 1811) as their own. Wellington
blockaded Almeida, and as Massena marched to relieve it, Wellington
fought another defensive battle at Fuentes d'Oñoro (3 and 4 May 1811).
In southern Spain General Beresford encountered Soult at Albuhera
(16 May 1811), but was strongly attacked on his right flank. Three things
went wrong: the Spanish troops refused to deploy, the piecemeal arrival
of reinforcements meant that a counter-attack was costly and ineffective, and the sudden appearance of French cavalry after a hailstorm
caused heavy casualties. An infantry charge by the British fusilier
brigade finally tipped the battle against the French. The English regiments suffered very heavy losses but remained cohesive, a testament to
their courage and endurance. The 29th (Worcesters) lost 336 out of 476
men, the 57th (Middlesex) 428 out of 616, the 48th (Northamptons)
280 out of 646, the 31st (Huntingdons) 155 out of 398. Under heavy
French fire Colonel Inglis gave his regiment its distinctive nickname by
calling out 'Fifty-Seventh, *die hard!*' as he lay dying.

Rebellion in central Europe

The French setbacks in Spain encouraged the Austrians to establish their own people's militia or Landwehr (despite fears of its revolutionary potential) in June 1808 to support the regular army. In December the war with France was renewed. As Napoleon left Spain, the Austrians invaded Bavaria (9 April 1809), central Germany and Italy. However, the anticipated Prussian support failed to materialise and only Brunswick troops joined the Austrians. An Austrian resistance group in Tyrol under the patriot Andreas Hofer also tried to liberate his province from Bavaria (a French ally). On 6 April the Austrians won a victory against French forces in Italy at Sacile, but Napoleon gathered his forces in southern Germany and, once again, took up a 'central position' to split the Austrian forces. He defeated one wing, under General Hiller at Landshut, then despatched Lannes' corps to assist Davout who had pinned the second Austrian wing under Archduke Charles. However, as the bulk of the Archduke's men withdrew to the walls of Ratisbon, Napoleon wanted to avoid a siege and ordered an immediate assault. Lannes' men were twice repulsed, but Lannes himself grabbed a storming ladder and inspired a third assault. The city fell and Napoleon occupied Vienna on 13 May. Napoleon said he did not aim to capture the capital, he wished to 'exterminate' his opponent's army.

Meritocracy

Lannes was typical of the inspirational leadership of the Napoleonic Army. Favouring promotion on merit, rather than on class or seniority (as in Britain), young officers strove to excel in the hope of promotion and reward. Michel Ney was made Duke of Elchingen in 1805 after distinguished service in battle. However, it was not universal. Marshal Soult and Marshal Grouchy were both aristocrats. In Britain, it was possible to purchase a commission in the army and the practice, although long discredited, continued until its abolition in 1870. The officer corps of the central European states was drawn exclusively from the privileged élites and landed nobility. The French revolutionary army, with its system of meritocracy, represented a threat to the established order of classes in the rest of Europe. This helped to foster an alliance between the European powers' leaders and a determination to defeat Napoleon.

Napoleon was defeated at Aspern and Essling
Because he crossed the Danube on a single pontoon bridge and had

made insufficient reconnaissance, Napoleon was exposing himself to counter-attack from the Austrians in 1809. The French troops failed to fortify the villages of Aspern and Essling on the perimeter of the bridge-head (which gave their name to the battle) and an Austrian attack achieved surprise. A French counter-attack on 22 May was repulsed and Napoleon evacuated the *tête du pont* (bridgehead) using the Young Guard to 'break clean' (cause a pursuer to pause), no doubt aware of the folly of fighting on a narrow front with a river at his back. Napoleon thus suffered his first defeat. He lost 21,500 men, including his talented friend and subordinate, Lannes.

The battle of Wagram was costly but restored Napoleon's power in Europe
In six weeks, Napoleon built up his army to 188,000 men and he took Archduke Charles by surprise by a renewed crossing of the Danube on 4–5 July 1809. He established a 15-mile bridgehead. As he built up his forces, the Archduke counter-attacked at Wagram just as Napoleon himself launched his own attack. The most significant aspect of the battle was the damage done by the 112-gun massed French battery. Indeed, the battle witnessed the greatest ever concentration of artillery to that date: 554 guns against 480 Austrian guns. The casualties were appalling: approximately 40,000 each. It is interesting to note that in the Seven Years' War the average size of the armies was 47,000, but 84,000 in the Napoleonic Wars. Whilst in the eighteenth century there had been an average of three guns to every 33,000 men, there were three guns to every 5,000 men in the *Grande Armée*. Between 1756 and 1763 there was an average of 1.4 battles a year, in the period 1792–1815 there were seven.

Domestic factors: the effects of economic war
The Berlin and Milan decrees, setting up the Continental system, alien-ated the merchants and rulers of Europe and badly affected the French economy. Smuggling increased, especially after the British capture of Heligoland island off the north German coast in 1807. Although the Royal Navy contained France, the people of Britain suffered high prices for food. Nevertheless, the French army wore overcoats manufac-tured in Leeds and shoes from Northampton, showing how ineffective the French blockade really was. The alienation of the powers was evident in Portugal's alignment with Britain, the Austrian war in 1809 and later, the defiance of Russia.

Napoleon defeated his central European enemies and was at the height of his powers
By the Treaty of Schönbrunn (14 October 1809), Austria lost territory and access to the Adriatic Sea, her army was reduced to 15,000 men and she was made to pay another war indemnity. This time, however, Napoleon forged a Franco-Austrian alliance and married Marie-Louise (the Emperor's daughter) which linked the Bonapartes with the Habsburg dynasty. This tie brought together the military domination of Napoleon and the prestige of the Austrian royal house and was designed to make rebellion less likely in the future. To underline the point, Hofer and his Tyrolean guerrillas were crushed and Hofer was executed (February 1810). Nice, Savoy and the left bank of the Rhine were annexed. Poland was brought under the control of his ally, the King of Saxony (titled the Grand Duchy of Warsaw). The German states were reorganised as the Confederation of the Rhine and Jerome Bonaparte ruled the new state of Westphalia in 1807. Louis Bonaparte ruled Holland, Sweden was ruled by Marshal Bernadotte (a relation through marriage). Italy was still officially Napoleon's own kingdom from 1805.

Quality of troops: the strengths and weaknesses of the British forces

The French were unable to defeat the Royal Navy which dominated the coast of Europe. Trafalgar (1805) was a turning point in that Napoleon was unable to challenge British naval supremacy and abandoned the idea of invading the British Isles. The British order in Council (which permitted the seizure of European shipping) had turned the Russians against Britain in 1807, but Napoleon's insistence on the Continental system (a blockade of Britain) now turned the Tsar against France. The Royal Navy again destroyed the Danish fleet and bombarded Copenhagen on 2 September 1807, an 'act of great injustice', in order to prevent their use by France. In the Peninsular War the British had often put their faith in unreliable Spanish commanders and exposed themselves to attacks by greater numbers of French troops, but their musketry was superior and Portugal's Torres Vedras lines were impregnable, providing the British with a continental base. However, the Walcheren Expedition (July–December 1809) exposed the weaknesses of the British army. Forty thousand British troops descended on Antwerp, but delays meant that the city was fortified, and a French fleet protected it. Poor administration led to a shortage in drinking water and proper accommodation. By September 11,000 men were incapacitated by disease, and, after a temporary occupation of Walcheren Island, the expedition withdrew.

Discipline had been poor, commanders had argued about objectives and the transport and supply system, the Commissariat, was a disaster.

The Peninsular War in 1812 demonstrated Britain's determination to resist Napoleon

As Napoleon drew troops away from Spain to central Europe, Wellington seized the initiative and stormed the fortresses on the Spanish–Portugese frontier: Cuidad Rodrigo (19 January) and Badajoz (6 April). Having sustained heavy casualties in the assault, British troops exacted a terrible revenge on the inhabitants for two days. The threat of hangings was the only way to restore order but, with discipline enforced, the British Army did not engage in the atrocities against the Spanish that the French did. Later, in France, Wellington's men actually won over the local French population whilst their own army, under Soult, continued its brutality and alienated the population. Wellington advanced to cut lines of communication between the main two French armies in Spain, Soult in the South and Marmont (who replaced Massena) in the centre. Marmont tried to cover all Wellington's axes of approach by deploying in a 4-mile line outside Salamanca, but Wellington's cavalry pierced the line and Marmont was routed on 22 July 1812. However, the convergence of Soult and reinforcements under Marmont compelled Wellington to withdraw from Madrid. Southern Spain was, nevertheless, free and Portugal safe. The only setback was the campaign by Sir John Murray, who, despite victory at Castalla, couldn't exploit his success. Although the Anglo-Portugese army was still outnumbered by 200,000 French troops, Soult, Marmont and Suchet were harassed by guerrillas and deprived of the best troops, most of whom Napoleon had employed in Eastern Europe.

War of nations

Napoleon's invasion of Russia, 1812, was his greatest error

The invasion of Russia was conceived in 1811, probably in an attempt to reduce the power of his eastern neighbour to that of Austria and the German states. Alexander I was concerned about French designs in Poland and angry with the demands of the Continental system. In the Spring of 1812 Napoleon mustered the 'army of 20 nations', a gigantic force of 614,000 men (with a further 61,000 support services). As he would be unable to sustain this *Grande Armée* by traditional foraging, a vast supply chain was devised but, even so, it was inadequate for the task. Napoleon envisaged another swift campaign, crushing the

Russian field army and concluding with harsh terms. However, he underestimated the protracted nature of operations over huge distances, the determination of Russian resistance and the enormous supply needs. Three great columns advanced slowly eastwards, failing to exploit disagreements between the two Russian commanders Barclay de Tolly (Minister of War) and General Begration. However, the Russians adopted a 'scorched earth' policy as they withdrew deep into Russia. Napoleon was forced to deploy garrisons along his extended lines of communication against Cossack hordes. Disease, desertion and skirmishes also depleted and demoralised the French.

Napoleon's strategy was to draw the Russians into a decisive battle
Napoleon tried to draw the Russians into battle by a frontal assault on Smolensk (16–17 August 1812) but the Russians continued to edge away. Napoleon faced the dilemma of halting for the winter (with stretched supply lines), withdrawing (to improve the supply situation) or pressing on in the hope of bringing the Russians to a decisive engagement, but at the risk of enduring the fierce winter (as he would be unable to return westwards in time).

The battle of Borodino did not give Napoleon decisive victory
With the appointment of General Kutuzov as commander, the Russian withdrawal, which had never been a considered 'policy' to lead Napoleon on, was halted. Fieldworks were thrown up at Borodino to protect the artillery (a tactic used frequently in the eighteenth century) in a series of fortified positions. Kutuzov commanded 120,000 men against Napoleon's 133,000 but the French launched expensive frontal assaults. Davout's suggestion of a flank assault was rejected and Napoleon seemed lethargic. By 5pm both sides were exhausted and 44,000 Russians and 30,000 French had been killed or wounded.

Napoleon's army was destroyed in the famous retreat from Moscow
Kutuzov withdrew, but as Napoleon entered the deserted Moscow the Russians set fire to the city to deprive the French of winter quarters. On 19 October 1812 the 100,000 men of the *Grande Armée* began their catastrophic and harrowing 'retreat from Moscow'. At once, Russian irregulars attacked the French supply routes. Supplies at Maloyaroslavets were attacked. Discipline in the French army began to crack up. At Vyazma Davouts' Corps was cut off, then rescued on 13 November, but it disintegrated as a fighting unit. At Krasnyi on 16–17 November, the French were temporarily cut in half and, at the river Berezina, on 26

November Napoleon had to fight for two days whilst engineers repaired the bridges. Napoleon abandoned his men to restore order in Paris, but the army descended into a group of fugitives. Only the rearguard, under the personal command of Ney, held off Russian attacks. Starvation, cold and incessant assaults reduced the remnant to 20,000 ragged troops and a mob of survivors.

Britain was unable to capitalise on the French defeat in Russia
Napoleon's defeat in Russia, and his inability to subdue the British, Spanish and Portuguese in Iberia, were turning points in his fortunes. Nevertheless, he was still able to conduct successful operations in 1813 and 1814. Moreover, the British had become embroiled in an unnecessary war with the United States over three issues: an escalating trade war, a dispute over the nationality of deserters from the Royal Navy and a breakdown in diplomatic relations. American attempts to invade Canada were repulsed (although York was burned), but so too were British landings (again after the successful destruction of Washington) in 1813 and at New Orleans in 1814. The 'War of 1812' distracted the British when a full effort against Napoleon was required.

Alliances: the emergence of a new coalition pushed Napoleon back onto the offensive
When the Prussian contingent of the *Grande Armée* negotiated a separate treaty with Russia, King Frederick William III began to set up a new army in Silesia (based in part on the secretly organised 'Black Reichswehr') and then declared war on Napoleon in March 1813. Meanwhile, Napoleon had used the winter months to build up an army, and 200,000 of a projected strength of 700,000 were to be despatched to Germany. However, many of the new soldiers were inexperienced conscripts or 15- and 16-year-olds. The best troops were those extracted from Spain whilst, in France itself, the National Guard was mobilised, coastal artillery units were transferred to infantry regiments and pensioners and invalids were recalled. To defeat the new Sixth Coalition (Britain, Russia, Spain, Portugal and Prussia), Napoleon decided to take the offensive and deal with each opponent separately.

Despite victory in the field, Napoleon failed to end the war
As he advanced on Leipzig, his inexperienced cavalry failed to reveal a 75,000-strong allied army under General Wittgenstein to the south. At Lützen on 2 May Wittgenstein attacked, but Ney held the position and Napoleon arrived, gradually building up his force to 110,000. He bombarded the allied centre, then committed the Imperial Guard at

7pm, breaking the allies completely. Without cavalry and nearing darkness he couldn't pursue but, when Wittgenstein tried to stand at Bautzen, Napoleon pinned the centre and sent Ney's corps on a flank attack. The battle lasted two days but Ney failed to completely cut the allies' line of retreat so, although victorious, 80,000 allied troops escaped. Napoleon hoped to negotiate, but an armistice merely encouraged Sweden and Austria into the war on the allies' side. Thus, as hostilities resumed, Napoleon faced 230,000 Austrians in the 'Army of Bohemia' (Schwarzenburg), 195,000 Prussians in the 'Army of Silesia' (Blücher) and 110,000 (Swedish, under Bernadotte) in the 'Army of the North'.

Napoleon was encircled in Germany

The allied plan was to defeat Napoleon's outlying corps and converge on Napoleon himself. At Dresden (26–27 August 1813) Napoleon managed to build up his forces when St Cyr's Corps successfully held the city. As Schwarzenburg's Austrians tried to stove in Napoleon's centre, the French enveloped their flanks and compelled the Austrians to withdraw. However, as Vandamme's corps set off in pursuit it was cut off and forced to surrender at Kulm (29 August 1813). In addition, as Napoleon planned to use Leipzig as a base for operations east of the Elbe river, he learned that Ney had been defeated at Dennewitz by the Swedes and a combined Prussian and Swedish army was bearing down on him. Meanwhile, the Austrians pressed up from the south. Bavaria declared war on France, the Confederation of the Rhine began to crack up and Napoleon's weary troops were short of equipment and ammunition. Napoleon was being defeated by massed armies, as the European powers conscripted ever larger forces.

Napoleon escaped defeat at the Battle of the Nations

Napoleon decided to make a stand at Leipzig and it was to be the largest of the Napoleonic battles: the French mustered 195,000 and 700 guns, the allies 365,000 and 1,500 guns. On 16 October Napoleon parried the attacks from the north and the south and General Betrand of IV Corps pushed back Austrian attempts to encircle the French in the west. However, to maintain his defensive perimeter, Napoleon could not manoeuvre to defeat any of the three armies against him. On the 17th a further 100,000 allied troops arrived. Worse, the French army was perilously short of ammunition. On 18 October the final phase of 'the battle of the nations' was played out. The Saxon corps in French service defected, and, in nine hours of fighting, Napoleon cut his way out to the west. However, a French engineer corporal prematurely blew the only bridge out of the city, leaving the 20,000 strong French rearguard stranded. Despite the successful extraction of the bulk of his forces, Napoleon had lost 73,000 men (compared with allied losses of 54,000) and most of his equipment. Leipzig marked the beginning of the end of his European empire. As he was pursued, he defeated a Bavarian army at Hanau on 30–31 October, but 16,000 stragglers dropped out and were captured in the retreat. Back in France, he could muster only 70,000 men.

Allied victory in the peninsula 1813–1814

Wellington was made the supreme commander of all allied forces in Spain and, although still outnumbered by the French, he outman-oeuvred them and retook Madrid. The French under Joseph Bonaparte and Marshal Jordan made a stand at Vittoria. On 21 June 1813 Wellington attacked both flanks and the French line split and collapsed. One hundred and forty-three out of 150 guns were captured and the French occupation forces were withdrawn to defend France along the Pyrenees under the command of Marshal Soult. Wellington laid siege to San Sebastian and Pamplona, the fortresses astride the invasion route, then turned to defeat Soult's attempts to relieve them in 'the battle of the Pyrenees'. The fortresses fell at the end of August and October and Wellington pushed on into France. He defeated Soult at Nivelle (10 November), Nive (9–12 December) and Orthez (27 February 1814). Hoping to be joined by Suchet, Soult tried to hold Toulouse, but Wellington assaulted the city (19 April 1814) leaving southern France totally in allied hands. These battles established Wellington's reputation as an excellent leader.

Offensive warfare: the campaign of 1814

Napoleon reorganised the state for the defence of France
The situation for Napoleon in the winter of 1813–14 seemed hopeless. One hundred thousand of his men were scattered or besieged in Germany and he had assembled barely 80,000 men to cover a frontier of 300 miles against allied forces numbering over 300,000. Moreover, the French economy was nearing exhaustion, Wellington had already invaded southern France. However, Napoleon resurrected the old revolutionary cry of '*La patrie en danger!*', reinvigorating himself and his people. He and his staff scoured France for manpower, calling up 936,000 conscripts (including 150,000 younger men not yet due for military service), and uniformed services such as forestry, customs officials and gendarmerie were enrolled as combatants. The Young Guard

of the Imperial Guard was expanded by taking the most experienced men from the line regiments. Propaganda urged greater civilian as well as military efforts. However, many conscripts failed to report, Murat defected (taking the control of Italy with him) and Denmark, the last ally, capitulated. To gain time, Napoleon offered to restore the Spanish monarchy and thus sow division among the allied leaders.

The allies advanced on Paris
Austria, Britain and Sweden all hoped for a negotiated settlement. When Napoleon was asked to restore the pre-1792 borders (thus losing the Netherlands), he refused and the allies began a three-pronged offensive. Napoleon tried to defeat the Prussians first by attacking at Brienne, but the Prussians, under Field Marshal Blücher, counter-attacked and forced Napoleon into a costly battle. However, in a celebrated 'Five Days' of fighting, Napoleon tackled each corps in turn and inflicted a series of defeats. He made one final thrust at Blücher at Vauchamps, but the withdrawal had to continue as Napoleon turned his attention to the Austrians. Napoleon force-marched to engage the Austrians at Montereau on 18 February 1814 using a massed battery to inflict heavy casualties. The Austrians withdrew but, when the Prussians regrouped, Napoleon had once again to turn against Blücher. With Napoleon distracted, the Austrians resumed their advance on Paris. Against overwhelming numbers, the French corps failed to stem the tide. Ney was repulsed at Craonne and Marmont at Laon (7 March). Still undefeated, Napoleon marched to Reims, interspersing himself between the Russians and Austrians and routing an isolated Russian corps there under General St Priest. Napoleon was unable to deflect their relentless advance on Paris. On 26 March he attacked Schwarzenburg at Arcis sur Aulse, but the Austrians were reinforced to 80,000 and the 28,000 French troops withdrew. The dwindling detachments of Frenchmen were defeated, Paris occupied and Napoleon was compelled to abdicate. Although the *Levée en Masse* had failed, Napoleon refused to begin a guerrilla war 'having delivered France from the revolutionaries'. He attempted suicide by poison but failed and was confined to the island of Elba.

The 100 days' campaign and Waterloo, 1815

As the allied powers began the restoration of Europe's former frontiers, after only a few months Napoleon escaped from the island of Elba,

Figure 1. Napoleonic Europe

quickly winning over the garrison of Grenoble. Although many of his former marshals refused to join him, old soldiers flocked to rejoin the Eagles and he assembled a force of 188,000 men. However, despite the extensive use of propaganda (in stark contrast to the restored Bourbon regime), Napoleon knew he did not have time to enlist more men, or compel the more reluctant to come forward, for the allies were eager to concentrate and destroy Napoleon's forces. In the Netherlands an Anglo-Dutch army of 95,000 and a Prussian army of 100,000 lay closest to France. Schwarzenburg had 210,000 Austrians on the Rhine, whilst a further 75,000 occupied northern Italy. Barclay de Tolly was moving slowly westwards with 167,000 Russian troops. Murat, who had defected in 1814, now realigned with Napoleon but was defeated at Tolentino (2 May). Napoleon decided to attack the allies before they could concentrate, but he made his best two field commanders, Davout and Soult, Minister of War and Chief of Staff, appointing the impetuous Ney and lethargic Grouchy as his principal subordinates in the field.

Napoleon's strategy of 'central position' worked initially

Napoleon quickly advanced on Charleroi hoping to establish his 'central position' between the Anglo-Dutch and Prussians. As the allies concentrated their forces, Napoleon sent Ney to hold the Anglo-Dutch off at Quatre Bras whilst he attacked Blücher at Ligny on 16 June 1815. The attack was little more than a frontal assault with Vandamme's corps attacking on the right. However, Napoleon had planned for D'Erlon's corps, half-way between himself and Ney, to march around the Prussian right-rear and envelop them. Ney, though, issued his own orders to D'Erlon, insisting he join him at Quatre Bras; consequently, D'Erlon played no part in the battles. Napoleon considered using the Imperial Guard to smash the Prussian centre, and renewed the assault, but Blücher avoided a rout with a cavalry charge (in which he participated and was almost killed).

The Prussians withdrew but continued to support the Anglo-Dutch army

The Prussians withdrew in good order. Gneisenau, the chief of staff, urged a withdrawal to Namur and Germany, but Blücher was determined to maintain contact with Wellington and the Anglo-Dutch. Napoleon, thinking Blücher's Prussians defeated, despatched Grouchy to pursue them 'with a sword at their back', but he failed to appreciate the Prussians' endurance. Using muddy and rutted tracks, and in appalling wet weather, the troops of 'alte Marschal Vorwärts' (Old Marshal Forwards) toiled towards Waterloo.

Wellington took up a strong defensive stance at Waterloo

Meanwhile Wellington, having contested the Quatre Bras crossroads, had fallen back behind a screen of cavalry to a low ridge at Mont St Jean, near Waterloo, placing his troops on reverse slopes. He extended a screen to his right to prevent any outflanking manoeuvre, and placed troops in the walled chateau of Hougoumont, the farm of La Haie Sainte and the hamlets of Papellotte, La Haie and Frischermont. He commanded 68,000 troops with 156 guns (against Napoleon's 72,000 and 246 guns), but only one third were British. Other than German contingents (such as the Hanoverians and King's German Legion), Wellington was unsure of the reliability of the Dutch-Belgians who, until recently, had been in French service. With many Peninsular veterans still returning from the United States following the conclusion of the War of 1812, many of his British troops were untested in battle. Heavy rain made the battlefield muddy and Napoleon was forced to delay the attack until 11.30. Napoleon sent the corps of Reille and Jerome against Hougoumont to draw Wellington from his centre, but the British footguards fought on all day without assistance, even when the buildings burnt down around them.

The French attacks at Waterloo failed to break Wellington
Unable to wait any longer, Napoleon sent forward D'Erlon against the allied centre, hoping that his massed batteries had had their effect. In fact, Napoleon's commanders warned him about the disciplined firepower of Wellington's British infantry: Napoleon dismissed their fears. As Wellington later noted, the French came on 'in the old style' and were driven off 'in the old style'. Picton's men stood up and fired volleys into the French columns, artillery discharged 'canister', and, at the critical moment, Lord Uxbridge sent forward the British heavy cavalry which routed all but one French division of D'Erlon's corps. However, pursuing too far, they were attacked in turn by French cavalry. By now Napoleon was aware that the leading elements of the Prussian army had arrived on his right flank so he despatched the Young Guard to hold them off. While he dealt with this Prussian threat, Ney ordered the French cavalry to attack Wellington's centre (thinking, wrongly, that the Anglo-Dutch were withdrawing). For two hours the French horsemen surged around the British formed in 'square', a formation that presented four walls of bayonets. Decimated by artillery and musket volleys, Napoleon countermanded Ney and withdrew them. Had this cavalry attack been coordinated more efficiently with D'Erlon's earlier assault, Wellington's position may have been very different. As it was, Wellington was able to cling on to the ridge. At 4.30pm the Prussians were in action, but Wellington had already suffered heavy casualties, some of the allied troops had fled and the King's German Legion, holding La Haie Sainte, were overwhelmed, leaving a gap.

Napoleon was defeated but it was a 'near run thing'
French artillery was wheeled up and began to destroy the allied units behind the ridge: the 27th Foot suffered so heavily they lay dead in a square. Pleading for reserves to exploit the attack in the centre, Ney's request for more men could not be fulfilled because they were being absorbed by the Prussian attack. The only reserve troops left were the Imperial Guard, but such was the desperate nature of Napoleon's position, they were committed in two columns against (mistakenly) the

strongest part of the line held by the British Guards. Commanding in person, Wellington gave the crucial order. His men leapt up and fired at 40 yards whilst the 52nd Light Infantry enfiladed the Imperial Guard. Blasted by their volleys, the French gave ground and were repulsed. The defeat of the Imperial Guard was the signal for the collapse of Napoleon's army and, with the Prussians arriving in greater numbers, the battle was effectively over. Wellington remarked that it had been close: a 'near run thing'.

The results of Waterloo
The battle had cost the allies 22,000 and the French ca. 40,000 dead and wounded. The French armies, and support for Napoleon, evaporated. He was exiled to St Helena but, even after his death, his legend grew. The balance of power shifted towards Britain, Austria, Russia and Prussia, and never again would the Revolutionary or Napoleonic armies dominate Europe.

Conclusion
Despite resistance across Europe, Napoleon's rapid movement and decisive victories continued to hold his empire together. However, even before he embarked on his ambitious and ultimately doomed march into Russia, he was already complaining that the guerrilla war in Spain, the 'Spanish Ulcer', was draining his army. Moreover, the British were able to reinforce and supply an army in Portugal and Spain by sea. Ably led by the Duke of Wellington, the British and their Spanish allies eventually drove the French from the Iberian Peninsula. In the Russian campaign, Napoleon had compelled the other European states to supply him with troops, so it was an international force that set out in 1812. However, the defeat of Napoleon's *Grande Armée* signalled the outbreak of rebellion across Europe which, after a further two years of fighting, led to the collapse of France.

Napoleon's leadership
Napoleon was an exceptional leader who personalised his command. He was able to encourage his men to believe they were an élite and he rewarded the courageous, regardless of background. Soldiers sought glory so as to achieve fame in the Parisian 'bulletins'. However, his highly effective system of *corps d'armée* was invented by Lazare Carnot. The concept of living off the countryside, rather than relying only on depots and slow-moving baggage, meant his armies were highly manoeuvrable. Napoleon's success often lay in this flexibility and speed.

He was only able to achieve a 'central position' to defeat larger enemy forces in detail because of his speed. Speed also enabled him to concentrate forces to achieve local superiority. He claimed to have worked out his movements long in advance, but the evidence for this is inconclusive. He was certainly able to conceal the point of his attack by using screens of light cavalry, swarms of skirmishers, and the famous *ordre mixte* (a mixture of columns and lines). Massed artillery became a feature of Napoleonic battles which made dense formations vulnerable. Cavalry continued to be used to pursue broken opponents. Correlli Barnett argued that Napoleon did not deserve the reputation as a tactician and innovator he has enjoyed since. Barnett pointed out how poor discipline and an inadequate supply system weakened the army, and how many errors Napoleon actually made in his battles. There was little development in weaponry, his men were often pitched into battle poorly fed, led and trained. Napoleon never achieved naval supremacy against the British and he failed to appreciate the determination of the Spanish resistance, or the effectiveness of the British army. However, Napoleon understood the diplomatic dimension of war and exploited divisions amongst his enemies. His success in dominating Europe was remarkable.

Some of Napoleon's legacies survived

Napoleon's successes in battle were carefully studied decades after his final defeat in 1815. Some elements of his strategy proved difficult to replicate, particularly the concept of 'central position'. Changes in weapons technology also made the use of dense infantry columns in attack an anachronism. However the independent corps organisation survived, giving generals considerable flexibility over the formerly unwieldy massed formations of troops. The idea of large conscript armies, whilst abandoned in mid-century, was later revived in the First World War. Above all, military theorists wanted to know how Napoleon had been so successful for so long. Was it a unique genius, or could it be scientifically analysed and reproduced?

Tutorial

Progress questions
1. Why did the Spanish fight so bitterly against the French from 1808?
2. What factors made the British army in the Peninsular War so successful?
3. What role did alliances play in the defeat of Napoleon between 1812 and 1815?

Seminar discussion
1. Which factor was the most important as a turning point in Napoleon's fortunes?
2. Why did the allies win at the battle of Waterloo: was it their successes or Napoleon's errors?

Practical assignment
Calculate the distance from Warsaw to Moscow and back, and the time taken to travel this distance. On a sketch map plot the route and losses of the *Grande Armée*, and the campaigns of 1813 and 1814. Locate the key towns mentioned during the Peninsular War. Now write an essay of approximately six to eight paragraphs on the following: 'Napoleon's concept of offensive warfare reached its limits in the campaigns in Spain and Russia in 1812, and in the central Europe theatre in 1813–14'. Do you agree?

Study tips
1. Having an atlas to hand and locating the main events helps you to 'picture' the narrative in your mind and therefore remember the events more clearly. Remember, you are asked to focus on change.
2. Continue to make your own notes under the headings listed at the end of Chapter 1. A paragraph explaining the main changes and then a case example on each will be sufficient. This will give you an excellent set of notes with which to construct arguments and just enough evidence to support each point. You do not need to become an expert on all the campaigns, instead look for the themes. Try to connect these themes to identify the changes from the earlier period.

4

Peace and reaction, 1815-1854

One minute overview – The period after the Napoleonic years was characterised by a desire to restore Europe to its pre-revolutionary war status. However, the conservative powers of Europe were not always successful in suppressing liberal movements across the continent and many states were temporarily overthrown by revolutionaries in 1848. There were changes to the armies of Europe too. Rifled firearms were gradually improved and adopted as standard weapons for all infantrymen from the 1840s. Artillery was also rifled, giving it greater range and accuracy. Armies contracted in size and became more professional. Conscription continued to be used by the European powers, although Great Britain's all-volunteer force was the exception, with the result that most Europeans had to perform several years' service in the army followed by a reserve liability. Analyses of Napoleonic warfare also emerged, the most influential being that by Baron de Jomini.

In this chapter you will learn:

▶ how the European powers reacted against the ideas of the revolutionary period
▶ how Napoleonic warfare was interpreted by Baron de Jomini
▶ changes in technology

The Vienna Settlement

The Vienna Settlement rejected the Napoleonic redrawing of Europe
Napoleon redrew the map of Europe, creating new states in Italy and in Eastern Europe (the Grand Duchy of Warsaw and the Confederation of the Rhine). The Low Countries (Belgium and Holland) had been annexed by France, whilst Austria and Prussia had been occupied. The conservative statesmen of 1815 wanted to reverse the Napoleonic arrangements, restore the original rulers and expunge the ideas of

liberty, equality and fraternity amongst the lower classes. They began by reducing France in size, and created a fully independent Netherlands and a Switzerland free of French influence. They restored the rulers of the German and Italian states and abolished the Grand Duchy of Warsaw. Northern Italy came under Austrian control. In addition, there was a determination to prevent the outbreak of revolutions in Europe. The 'Concert of Europe' was a body made up of representatives from the European powers who would aim to co-operate to maintain the status quo of 1815. France was to be contained by the strengthening of Piedmont (Northern Italy) and Prussia (North Germany), but not so much that they posed a challenge to Austria.

The Holy Alliance was a force opposed to revolution anywhere in Europe
The three conservative, autocratic powers of Austria, Prussia and Russia formed a Holy Alliance. They aimed not only to uphold the Vienna Settlement, but also to oppose any revolutionary outbreak in Europe and, by definition, any liberal movements in the continent. This was unacceptable to Britain, a country with a limited constitutional monarchy and a liberal parliamentary democracy (albeit with a narrow franchise). There were diplomatic disagreements in 1820 when the Troppau Protocol became the first point of division. Arguing that the Europeans should adopt a non-interventionist stance, Britain's relations with Austria were soured when Austrian troops crushed a liberal uprising in Piedmont in 1821.

The split between Britain and the Holy Alliance powers
The split widened in 1822 when French troops reoccupied Spain to support the absolutist and brutal monarch Ferdinand. Britain was firmly opposed to intervention in the Iberian Peninsular, and initially refused to participate in the suppression of disorder in Portugal. Britain also refused to intervene against the independence struggles in South America. However, British troops were sent to protect national interests in Argentina and British liberals supported the cause of Greek independence in 1827. Britain's policy favoured liberal movements which aimed to create constitutional monarchies. When Turkish troops massacred 25,000 islanders at Chios, intervention was more likely. The Royal Navy's fleet under Admiral Codrington destroyed the Turkish fleet at Navarino Bay in 1827. However, this action made a negotiated settlement, which the government sought, less likely. Indeed, encouraged by the Turkish setback, the Russians invaded the Ottoman Empire and engaged in a long and exhausting campaign in the Balkans. In 1829 the

Russians reached their own separate settlement with the Turks by the Treaty of Adrianople. However, the consequences of the Turkish defeat were that all the European powers began to speculate that Turkey was now the 'sick man of Europe' and would eventually collapse. Suspicious of Russian designs on the region, the British developed a considerable fear and loathing of Russian imperialism called 'Russophobia'.

Revolts in Europe and their suppression

Rebellion in Belgium in 1830 against Dutch rule heightened the possibility of French intervention in the strategic 'cockpit of Europe', so Britain persuaded other powers to accept Belgian independence swiftly. Britain undertook to guarantee Belgian territorial integrity by the Treaty of London in 1839. However, a similar revolt in Poland in 1830 failed to attract any external support. Initially successful, the Poles were defeated by large Russian forces. The Holy Alliance partners reacted in the same way to disturbances in Italy in 1831, the Austrians retaining an army of occupation there. Britain and France co-operated to support the liberal constitutional monarchists against absolutism in Spain and Portugal in 1834. Despite this success, Britain's anxieties about French ambitions in the region meant that joint action had broken down by 1836. Britain did not endure chaos that faced other Europeans in the 'year of revolutions' in 1848 because it already had a liberal constitution. Massive uprisings in Paris once again overthrew the monarchy, whilst revolutionaries piled up barricades in the Italian states, the German Confederation and in Austria. All the uprisings were eventually suppressed by military action. Russia even assisted the Austrians in putting down the Magyar (Hungarian) revolution.

The rejection of mass armies
The French Revolution and the revolts in the decades that followed demonstrated the risks in arming vast numbers of citizens. The use of small, professional and therefore loyal and élite regiments was preferable to unwieldy numbers of conscripts of uncertain allegiance. Moreover, it became common for troops to be housed in permanent barracks instead of being billeted on the local population. This separation would ensure the troops did not infuriate the local population and that the soldiers did not fraternise with politicised citizens who opposed the government. Armies and regiments developed 'clan' loyalties – forged by shared hardship and identity – from which civilians were excluded.

The separation of soldiers and citizens reinforced that sense of difference. The sheer cost of sustaining a mass army was also prohibitive. Smaller professional forces were cheaper. However the problem remained of how to mobilise larger numbers of men at short notice against a foreign invasion. The revolutionary armies had used a system of *amalgame*. Recruits received a week's basic training and then joined a unit. Veterans and inexperienced soldiers were mixed together, thus 'stiffening' morale in the newcomers. But the system had still relied on a call-up of all available men within a certain age range. In the 1850s, the Prussians brought in a system of reserves. After a short period of military service, soldiers would return to civilian life. This gave the state the chance to cut the costs of a large standing army, but have a ready made and highly trained reserve that it could call up. Despite this system, soldiers continued to enlist for long periods. Twelve-year engagements were common in the British Army and troops in the colonial stations rarely, if ever, returned to Britain on leave. In the Russian army recruits' families would hold the equivalent of a funeral for the departing men, since they never expected to see them again.

Baron de Jomini's interpretation of Napoleonic warfare

Jomini believed there were essential principles in war
Born in Switzerland, Jomini (1779–1869) served in both the French and Russian armies. He wrote about war and advocated a scientific footing for its study. The most influential of his writings was the *Summary of the Art of War* (1837–8). Jomini argued that there were two principles which guided everything else. First, all operations should seek to destroy or disrupt the enemies lines of communication whilst protecting one's own. Secondly, the key to victory was concentration of all forces at the 'decisive point' (which could be both a time and a place). In German this is called a *Schwerpunkt*.

Jomini analysed Napoleon
Jomini greatly admired Napoleon: he felt that Napoleon had rightly taken the offensive in order to seize the initiative and dominate the enemy. This praise of the offensive was to be very influential in Europe and America for decades. Yet the need to protect lines of communication made him feel that operations should be on 'interior lines' (and therefore he should have really been advocating a defensive stance),

even though Napoleon had often fought wars by using 'exterior lines' and envelopment (such as the campaign of 1800 which ended with Marengo). Jomini appreciated the value of surprise but emphasised the need for planning and commented that surprise was difficult to achieve at the strategic level. Following Napoleon's thinking, Jomini thought the destruction of an enemy army was a condition of victory, but he still measured success in terms of territory gained. He felt that maps and terrain were vital, often dictating where the 'decisive point' would lie.

There were shortcomings in Jomini's interpretation

According to Daniel Moran, Jomini failed to grasp Napoleon's ability to improvise, adapt and seize opportunities. If anything, Jomini represented the thinking of the *Ancien Régime* with its stress on order, planning and structure. Yet this approach appealed to the conservativism of the post-Napoleonic period (with their small professional armies). Jomini's praise for the attack and quick, decisive victories was certainly appealing. During the wars of the later nineteenth century, and particularly colonial wars, the speed with which operations were concluded seemed to confirm the idea of the superiority of the attack. However, these views tended to linger even though technological changes made weapons far more lethal over greater ranges. Jomini failed to appreciate that, in the future, firepower could also provide a *Schwerpunkt*. Jomini's views were the mainstay of military thinking in the USA before the Civil War (1861–65), but the advent of mass, citizen armies and the experience of attrition warfare in the last two years of the war discredited his views there. However, these lessons were not learned by the European powers as they regarded the American Civil War as exceptional. The use of exterior lines by Moltke in the Seven Weeks' War also seemed to prove another of Jomini's theories wrong.

Jomini was eventually overshadowed by von Clausewitz

Clausewitz argued that war was not scientific but a clash of wills, a release of social energy and 'the extension of politics by other means'. It was subject to the 'friction of war', such as error, chance and genius. Jomini's influence nevertheless continued to exert itself in a continuing faith in the attack and in emulation of the Napoleonic offensive. However, most military analysts agree that there are certain 'principles of war' which, if applied, will produce victory. This, in fact, is Jomini's real legacy.

Technological change

Changes in weapons technology was slow

Weapons technology evolved slowly in the forty years after Waterloo. Many of the world's armies continued to arm their men with smooth-bore muskets because of their simplicity and cheap manufacture. Rifled barrels did, however, become the standard feature of small arms in European armies. The greater accuracy that could be achieved by the spin of a bullet, and a flatter trajectory, were appreciated as necessary for modern armies despite the increased cost and complexity of manufacture. The Royal Navy's vast fleet was a feature of its strength, but warship design did not change rapidly even when steam ships appeared in the 1820s. Although screw propellers were introduced in the 1850s, captains could still manoeuvre using sails and skilled seamanship.

The psychology of warfare retained its attraction despite changes in weapons

The psychological features of Napoleonic warfare were harder to jettison. The mass attack in close order, accompanied by drums, shouts and songs, was thought to have been the secret of the French army's success in the Napoleonic years. The French army continued to clothe its soldiers in bright uniforms and stressed that its *élan* (style/morale) depended on headlong infantry assaults with the bayonet. However, weapons technology was not entirely neglected and the French army adopted rifles and, by the 1860s, machine guns at the same pace as other European armies. Yet, the significance of the Napoleonic era had been an increase in firepower, from Napoleon's massed batteries to the fire discipline of the British infantry. To overcome the weight of fire, increasingly large numbers of troops were required. The firepower–manpower ratio continued to tilt in favour of the former in Europe throughout the nineteenth century. Not all battles were determined by this fact, but operational success depended on a careful balance of firepower and mobility.

The effects of industrialisation

The mid-nineteenth century was a period of economic transformation in Europe. Industrialisation enabled states to reproduce weapons to a uniform design in vast numbers. Developments in rifle firing mechanisms made them more attractive as the standard weapon of the infantryman. Internally housed parts and a waterproof percussion cap (with an all-metal hammer to operate it) replaced the flintlock and open pan, and therefore gave greater battlefield reliability in poor weather conditions. Artillery barrels could also be cast and cut on the same pattern far more quickly than before. The era of mass production meant that it would be far easier to equip large numbers of citizens with weapons should the need arise. Industrial processes also enabled weapons to be more finely engineered and this precision led to further refinements in weapon design.

Conclusion

The Vienna Settlement had attempted to restore Europe to its status before 1792, but its provisions did not last and international co-operation soon broke down. In the decades after the Napoleonic Wars, the ideas that had been promoted by the French Revolution did not disappear as the autocratic powers had hoped. The outbreak of revolutions in 1848 seemed to herald a new liberal era in Europe, but the defeat of the liberal movements confirmed the supremacy of conservatism. Yet one concept from the French Revolution fused their peoples more closely together, and that was nationalism. This concept enabled conservative statesmen to accept the broadening of their small professional armies and the introduction of reserves. The introduction of railways during the industrial revolution seemed to offer great potential for the rapid mobilisation of troops and the fulfilment of the Jominian idea of a quick victory. Weapons technology advanced slowly at first, but gradually industrialisation began to have an effect on the ease of manufacture and in the sophistication of design.

Tutorial

Progress questions

1. What were the aims of the Vienna statesmen and how successful were they?
2. Why was there a preference for smaller armies after 1815?
3. What lessons did Jomini derive from his study of Napoleon?

Seminar discussion

1. Did Jomini learn the wrong lessons from his study of what was successful in warfare?

2. How successful were the statesmen of Europe in preventing another Napoleon or another Napoleonic War?

Practical assignment

Construct a mind map or diagram of all the changes in warfare and its study from 1792 and 1854. Try to memorise the key developments then take a break for 15 minutes. Now take a fresh piece of paper and try to map out all the headings again. Which ones did you miss out? Check to see which ones you couldn't remember and add those to the new diagram. Repeat this exercise in two weeks' time to see if you can remember more.

Study tips

1. It is a good idea to try to remember what the Vienna statesmen tried to achieve and why. Without the benefit of hindsight, like Jomini, they tried to learn lessons from the wars.
2. Practise answering questions under timed conditions. Even writing a paragraph on each heading will help you build up a set of useful revision notes and retain the information in your memory.

5

The Crimean War, 1854–1856, and Italian Wars of Unification, 1859–1861

One minute overview – Several developments took place in the nature of warfare in the decades after the Napoleonic Wars that were certainly manifest by the mid-nineteenth century. The most significant European conflict, from a military point of view, was the Crimean War. Although there had been a rebellion against Ottoman rule in Greece between 1821 and 1829, and a series of revolts across Europe in 1848 which required that armies be deployed in counter-revolutionary operations (such as the bombardment of Prague, 1848), the Crimean campaign demonstrated a number of changes in warfare between European powers. These included the continued importance of artillery, the impact of the Minié bullet and rifled small arms, press coverage of war, and the need for improvements in medical services. These developments were also manifest in the Italian Wars of Unification.

In this chapter you will learn:

▶ the causes of the Crimean War
▶ the problems encountered in the opening phases of the Crimean War
▶ the key battles and turning points of the Crimean War
▶ the Italian Wars
▶ changes in warfare

The causes of the Crimean War

There was rivalry between the Great Powers
In the 1848 revolutions across Europe, the Austrians had relied on Russian support to restore order, a fact they resented. In addition, a revolution in France had opened the way for Louis Napoleon, the nephew of Napoleon Bonaparte, to come to power in a *coup d'état*. The temporary paralysis of the German states and Austria had highlighted

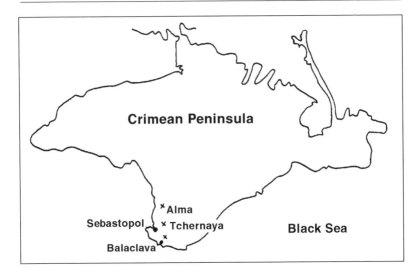

Figure 2. The Crimean War, 1854–56

that central European powers were weak, and so France and Russia emerged as rivals for influence as the dominant power over Europe. Nicholas I of Russia saw his country as the gendarme of Europe against revolutionaries and he was full of disdain for 'the adventurer' Louis Napoleon who had been crowned Emperor Napoleon III and who shared the name of the man who had invaded Russia in 1812. In addition, Nicholas believed, as many others did, that the Ottoman Empire was on the verge of collapse. He was determined that Russia would exert its influence over the decaying Ottoman provinces, and 'protect' the holy places of the Orthodox Christian Church in the near East. However, Napoleon III was eager to legitimise his rule by championing the Roman Catholic Church which claimed exclusive right of control over the same holy places. The British interpreted the Russian demand for 'protection' of all Christians living in the Ottoman Empire as a prelude to annexation of the Balkans, and possibly the establishment of naval bases on the Aegean (which might threaten the trade route to British India). The British regarded the Ottoman Empire as a bulwark to Russian expansion.

The Sinope massacre prompted Anglo-French action against Russia
When the Turks rejected the Russian demands for supervision of all Christians, the Tsar ordered the occupation of the Turkish provinces at

the mouth of the river Danube. Negotiations failed and the Turks declared war on 5 October 1853. Shortly after the Turkish declaration of war, the Russian fleet from Sebastopol (the naval base on the Crimean peninsula) engaged the Turkish navy at Sinope. In a matter of hours they had sunk and damaged the Turkish flotilla with rifled guns and exploding shells. The Turkish ships were all wooden sailing ships and the battle marked the end of the 'wooden walls' of the Napoleonic era. In future, warships would adopt ironclad hulls, or be of an all-metal construction. Sinope was also significant in that it convinced the British public of the need for military action. The Russian attack was described as a 'massacre' inflicted on the Turks, and there were calls for revenge. Public pressure for war was also an unexpected dimension for the diplomats and politicians. Newspaper interest would be a salient feature of the campaign that followed.

Strategy: the problems encountered in the opening phases of the war

The war in the Baltic and the Balkans failed to produce any lasting results
The allies' greatest strength lay in their naval forces, but an Anglo-French fleet failed to make any real impression on the Russian defences in the Baltic Sea. Later, the strength of Russian coastal defences at Sebastopol would also preclude an effective naval bombardment. Whilst Ottoman troops prepared to defend the Danubian fortress of Silistria, a joint British and French expeditionary force landed at Varna on the Bulgarian coast. Faced by this threat, and in control of the economically important mouth of the Danube river, the Russians saw no need for any further advance and lifted the siege of Silistria. Moreover, Austrian and Prussian pressure compelled the Russians to withdraw from the occupied principalities. Meanwhile, the allies' troops remained inactive for weeks, but an outbreak of cholera devastated the ranks of these armies: eight per cent of the British force was suffering from cholera in August 1854.

A new plan emerged to destroy the Russians' naval strength
A withdrawal at this point would have merely played into the patient Russians' hands. The Tsarist troops would advance as soon as the allies had left. It was necessary to find a way of inflicting a defeat on the Russians, and thus create a better bargaining position for peace. As the Russian capital of St Petersburg was so heavily defended (by Kronstadt)

and the Russian Baltic coast equally well held, an attack here would be a waste of lives. With memories of Sinope still fresh in their minds, the most obvious target was therefore Sebastopol in the Crimea. Supplied from the sea, the allies could make an amphibious landing and destroy the Russian port. Such a strategy utilised their greatest strengths, their navies, and stretched Russian lines of communication whilst avoiding a campaign deep in the interior of Russia. Russian troops in the Crimea were estimated to be somewhere between 45,000 to 120,000. The British and French were able to land 63,000 men and 128 guns in four days at Calamita Bay, but they were initially short of cavalry, the British Light Brigade being the only mounted force. The British had had some difficulty in preparing an expeditionary force because its all-volunteer army numbered only 120,000 in total and it was widely dispersed across the British Empire.

Technology: innovations in warfare

The British and French had superiority in weapons systems
British Enfield rifles (introduced 1853) were superior to the Russian smooth bore muskets, although formations were unchanged both in attack and defence. British infantrymen advanced in two-deep lines, thus maximising the firepower they could deliver to their front. The bullets they fired took a flatter trajectory, greatly aiding accuracy. Rifling, the spiral grooves inside the barrel, gave their Minié bullets (replacing the old musket ball) a spin and also improved accuracy. Minié bullets expanded when fired, fitting the barrel more snugly, increasing power and therefore range. British riflemen were therefore more likely to hit their target. By contrast, Russian infantry relied on the cohesion and mass of dense columns that might advance and overwhelm their opponents by weight of numbers and momentum. Russian officers found that British riflemen could engage them at greater ranges and therefore shoot down the leading ranks, thus demoralising the rest, before they could close with the enemy. Moreover, the greater muzzle velocity meant that bullets might hit, pass through and kill more than one man. The dense formations also made them vulnerable to artillery fire.

Logistics and co-ordination were weak
The chief weakness of the allied forces was its lack of supply transport and logistical support. In Bulgaria the allies had been unable to trans-

port all their supplies just a few miles inland, and medical services were overwhelmed by the numbers of cholera cases. Co-ordination within the British army was also problematic. The Ordnance (artillery) was independent of the other fighting arms, the former under the Master-General of Ordnance and the latter under Commander in Chief at Horse Guards in London. The civilian Ordnance Department supplied military equipment, but the Commissariat (under the Treasury) supplied food and transport. In addition, the navy was controlled by the Admiralty and the British field commander, Lord Raglan, had no local authority over the naval officers. Co-ordination difficulties also existed between the allies. Unlike the Duke of Wellington's supreme command of the allied forces in Spain, Raglan had to rely on the voluntary co-operation of the French (under Marshal St Arnaud) and the Turks (under Osman Pasha). The campaign began late in the summer, but when hopes of an early victory faded the troops faced a Russian winter with inadequate accommodation (using lightweight tents), food supplies (over several hundred miles), fuel and warm clothing. This caused much suffering amongst the men. The commissariat broke down causing further misery. In order to supply the troops besieging Sebastopol, a light railway was later constructed from the port of Balaclava.

Steam shipping began to feature in the Royal Navy
The Royal Navy made use of steam ships as early as 1828 (HMS *Lightning* was laid down in 1823), but the vulnerability of paddle wheels, the restrictions of space and fields of fire, and the continued versatility and expertise in sailing meant that steam-powered vessels served alongside the traditional fleets for many years. It was not until the completion of the first French steam-powered ship of the line, the *Napoleon*, in 1850 that a race in naval design truly began. In 1852 the first British steam-powered warship, HMS *Agamemnon*, was commissioned and this was followed in 1860 by the Navy's first ironclad, HMS *Warrior* (a response to the French *La Gloire* of the same design). By the 1890s, the naval race with France had resulted in torpedo boats and, in 1882, the first operational submarine, *Nordenfeldt I*, although no Royal Navy submersible was commissioned until 1901. In 1875 241 ships were in commission, of which 20 were ships of the line, and Royal Navy personnel totalled 34,000. Fifty-two of these vessels were in home waters, 18 in the Mediterranean, 22 in Chinese waters, 13 in South East Asia and 15 in North America and the West Indies, with the rest divided between the Cape, South America, Australasia and a collection of naval stations. Their

duties included combating piracy in the Red Sea, protecting mission-
aries and traders, anti-slave trade patrols, debt collection in South
America as well as support for army operations in Egypt, China or on
the Nile. In 1898 the number of commissioned vessels was 287, but 52
of them were battleships. Personnel had increased to 97,000 but, other
than the Mediterranean and Home fleet, the distribution of strength
was not vastly altered. Thirty-eight vessels patrolled the Mediterranean, but the home defence contingent had been reduced to 15, albeit
with a greater number of battleships.

The Royal Navy's key role remained the protection of British trade routes
The Navy's role, other than the defence of British waters, remained the
protection of the vast merchant marine which brought in some £200
million every year, and which was regarded as the lifeline of Britain's
future prosperity. There was even a significant shift in the source of Britain's foodstuffs – whilst in the 1830s 90 per cent of Britain's food was
grown at home, by the turn of the century a third was imported.
Between 1857 and 1875 annual corn imports rose from £19.4 million to
£51.7 million and meat rose from £3.5 million to £13.8 million. Britain's merchant fleet was the largest in the world, and operated across
the globe, and demanded from the Royal Navy an ability to respond
whatever the circumstances, with greater strength. Added to this
demand was a desire to continue to be the largest navy in the world as a
symbol of Britain's power and prestige. It is significant that the aim of
the Crimean campaign was the neutralisation of the Russian naval
threat.

Strategy: the course of the war

The Battle of the Alma, 20 September 1854, did not provide a swift conclusion
The commander of the western Crimea, Prince A.S. Menshikov,
decided to engage the allies before they could reach Sebastopol. He
drew up his 33,000 infantry and 116 guns along the heights above the
river Alma, spread along a front of five miles with a concentration at
the mid-point of the line, on two hills called Telegraph Hill and Kourgane Hill. His left flank, closest to the sea, was only lightly guarded,
but he held a large number of troops in reserve under his direct
command. The allies' plan was for the French to assault the Russian
left, and, once they had secured the flank, the British would advance to
take the Kourgane Hill. However, the French attack was much slower

than expected and the British troops were subjected to heavy fire from two redoubts (earthworks) on the Kourgane Hill. As a result, the British were compelled to make a frontal attack before the French had secured their objectives. The British 2nd and Light Divisions advanced directly up the hill, but were recalled when it was thought the Russians were going to envelop them. A second assault, by the Guards and Highland Brigades of the 1st Division carried the two Russian redoubts. British small arms and artillery had inflicted heavy casualties on the Russians and Menshikov had failed to deploy his reserves at the right moment. The Russian centre collapsed, pursued for a short distance by the cavalry of the Light Brigade. However, the fact that 3,000 Russian cavalry remained uncommitted (and the Russian infantry were rallied two miles to the south) deterred a full pursuit.

Sebastopol was not captured in 1854 as expected

The French delayed the allied advance after the Alma, giving the Russians three days to organise their defences. When the allies did eventually continue, the defences of Sebastopol were already formidable, and it was decided to outflank the defences to the south. Establishing a logistics base in the narrow harbour of Balaclava, the allies began a siege of the Russian port. As the open ground in front of the Russian defences would make an assault suicidal, trenches were dug some 1,200 yards from the walls and redoubts constructed to protect the artillery. The Russian garrison was 30,850 strong, but the British force, reduced by sickness, numbered 16,000. Moreover, the Russians sank ships across their harbour entrance and lined their walls with 220 guns, whilst the combined British and French arsenal was 126 guns. Consequently, when the first bombardment began, the allies were ineffective. To make matters worse, the French magazines were blown up and only 41 British guns remained in action. However, the British 68-pounders (the weight of the projectile) caused significant damage to the Russian defences. It was not enough to be sure of success for an infantry assault, so the attack that had been planned was called off.

The Russian counter-attack at Balaclava, 25 October 1854, failed

As the allies focused on the bombardment of Sebastopol, Menshikov assembled 20,000 infantry, 2,300 cavalry and 78 guns to sweep down on the port and supply route at Balaclava. Defending the port were 1,500 Turkish troops with nine guns in a line of redoubts, and, closer to Balaclava, the 93rd Highlanders, Turkish infantry and 26 guns. At dawn, the Russians seized the Turkish redoubts and, at 08.30, began to advance on the harbour defences. Before the French and British reinforcements arrived, the 93rd, although deployed in only a 'thin red line', had managed to defeat a Russian cavalry attack. In addition, the British Heavy Brigade, despite being heavily outnumbered, charged into a Russian force of 2,000 horsemen and routed them. The harbour was saved. The action of the 93rd was particularly significant: it demonstrated that infantrymen were now so well armed that a head-on attack by cavalry was unlikely to succeed.

The charge of the Light Brigade was a heroic failure
An order to prevent the Russians withdrawing with the Turkish guns captured earlier in the day was misunderstood. As a result, the British Light Brigade charged the front of the Russian army, straight into their artillery. The charge was immortalised by Alfred Lord Tennyson in poetry, but the 673 men were reduced to 197 effectives in a matter of a few minutes over a distance of 1.25 miles (2 km). The cost of the charge showed that, despite undoubted courage, cavalry could no longer dominate the battlefield as they had once done.

The battle of Inkerman, 5 November 1854, was a 'soldier's battle'
The Russian garrison had sortied from Sebastopol on 26 October, but they tried again in force on 5 November with 16,000 men and 96 guns, whilst a further 22,000 men and 88 guns would cross the Tchernaya river and assist from outside the city. Meanwhile a diversion on the northern side of Sebastopol would divert allied reserves from the battle. However, the Russian efforts were not co-ordinated. Heavy rain and a thick morning mist obscured visibility, but the allies fed troops or guns in to the firing line as dangers emerged. The battle degenerated into a fierce struggle for two battery positions, The Barrier and Sandbag Battery. Casualties were very heavy on both sides, since they still fought in dense, Napoleonic formations with weapons of greater accuracy. In total 10,729 Russians were killed, wounded or taken prisoner. British casualties totalled 2,357 and French 1,743. Personal leadership was clearly important to the British: no less than three generals were killed in the fighting in the Inkerman battle.

Military shortcomings were revealed

The latter stages of the campaign: the siege operations produced little result
The allies did not have enough men to storm the defences of Sebastopol, and, as winter drew on, it was a constant struggle to maintain adequate

levels of supplies to the troops. Without road making parties, or materials, the line of communication to Balaclava became a quagmire. The fuel ration was reduced at the coldest point in the year. The lack of land transport, which had been evident in Bulgaria, had still not been solved, so that fresh food supplies could not be moved up to the troops around Sebastopol. Raglan, the British commander, is usually blamed for this, but in fact he had no direct control of the Commissariat, even when it was transferred from the Treasury to the Secretary of State for War in the winter of 1854. A new government in Britain intensified the demands for positive results in February 1855, but it was not until April that a renewed bombardment of the city began. However, supply difficulties and consideration of new plans that ruled out an infantry assault reduced the intensity of the shelling. In May amphibious attacks in the sea of Azov disrupted Russian supplies. In June British and French troops captured Sebastopol's outworks at a cost of 6,000 men. However, a second assault was badly co-ordinated and the allies were repulsed with a further 5,000 killed and wounded. The strain of this is thought to have led to Raglan's early death on the 28th of that same month.

The battle of Tchernaya was a turning point in the war
In August the Russian commander in the Crimea, Prince M.D. Gorchakov, was pressured to attack the allies before reinforcements could arrive. Having crossed the Tchernaya river on 14 August, his troops advanced under cover of a mist the following day, only to be repulsed by the French and enfiladed by the Sardinians (the Sardinians had recently joined the war). Gorchakov failed in a number of respects: he had attacked hastily and lost two divisions, he failed to commit his remaining two divisions at the critical moments, and his plan (to secure the Fedioukine Hills before thrusting towards the allies on the Sapoune Ridge) was unlikely to succeed because of the strong allied positions. It was a turning point in the war, since it reduced the last field army in the region to a force that was only capable of defensive operations. This meant that Sebastopol could not be relieved. Attempts to reinforce and resupply the Russian armies had proved difficult due to the distances and poor infrastructure from the population centres of western Russia.

The allies successfully stormed Sebastopol
Concentrating 775 guns against the defences for four days, and with trenches just 30 yards from the key Russian bastions, the allies assaulted the defences of Sebastopol. General MacMahon's division of French

troops swept into the Malakov Redoubt and spiked its guns. General Pelissier took the Little Redan, but was compelled to withdraw. At the Malakov, the Russians counter-attacked five times, but MacMahon's force held the position. The British attack by the 2nd and Light Divisions was directed against the Great Redan. However, rocky terrain had prevented their trenches from getting any closer than 400 yards to the objective. When they rose from their trenches they had to cross this open and rising ground in the face of fire from the Great Redan and three, mutually supporting, redoubts called the Gervais, Garden and Barrack batteries. Thousands fell, but the regiments pressed forward and some members of the Naval Brigade (sailors serving guns or acting as infantrymen on land) actually got inside the defences. The attack failed. Nevertheless, as John Sweetman points out, the British had distracted fire that otherwise would have been directed against the French in the Malakov and he concludes the 'capture of Sebastopol ... was truly an allied effort'.

The end of the war was the result of Russian exhaustion
The fall of the Malakov Redoubt unlocked the defences of Sebastopol, and the port soon capitulated (although the northern suburb remained in Russian hands). The allies were released to conduct operations elsewhere on the Black Sea coast. However, cholera and typhus devastated the troops in the winter of 1855 (the French had 50,000 cases and one fifth died). Unable to continue the war, Tsar Alexander II made peace in January 1856. The Black Sea and mouth of the Danube were neutralised, and claims to protect all Christians in the Ottoman Empire were dropped. At the front, former enemies visited each other and the British invited Russian officers to a race meeting.

There were several changes in the British army
The logistical difficulties of the war prompted army reform in Great Britain. The first, and most important, was the rationalisation of the chain of command for organisation in the field (from seven to one). One civilian minister (the Secretary of State for War) and one military officer (the Commander in Chief) now controlled all aspects of personnel, supply and ordnance. A Staff College was set up in 1862 at Camberley to improve staff work within the army. The support services in the field were also rationalised. A Mounted Staff Corps became the army's police service, whilst the Land Transport Corps became the Military Train and later, in 1870, the Army Service Corps. An Army Works Corps (for construction tasks) was not continued after the war because

of indiscipline and drunkenness amongst its ranks (they were all civilians). Florence Nightingale's efforts to improve standards of health and hygiene in the military hospital at Scutari had been a landmark in the care of the wounded or sick. In 1857 a permanent Army Hospital Corps was established, and it was joined with the Medical Staff Corps of Doctors to form the Royal Army Medical Corps in 1898.

Media and public opinion

There was a new role for the media
In addition, the British army had been subject to intense scrutiny from the press, eager to meet the appetite for war news at home. Reporters, unused to war or military organisation, found much to criticise and the reputation of Raglan was severely damaged. The most celebrated journalist was W. H. Russell, the first of a new generation of war correspondents. The war also produced the first photographs of life on campaign, the most well known of which were produced by Roger Fenton.

There were changes in the Russian army
Alexander II was concerned that the Crimean defeat might cause revolution in Russia so he began a process of reform, not least of which was the Emancipation of the Serfs (1861). Dimitri Milyutin, the War Minister, supervised the reform of the Russian army. He reduced military service from 25 years to six. He brought in conscription (1874) for all males over 20, closing the loopholes that had previously enabled noblemen to escape military duty. Brutal punishments were abolished. Military service as a substitute for imprisonment was also ended. 'Military colonies', training establishments for the sons of soldiers, were closed.

There were changes in naval warfare
The Treaty of Paris regulated naval warfare, preventing strategies Britain had employed in previous decades. Privateering was abolished, enemy goods on neutral ships could not be seized unless they were 'contrabrand of war' and blockades had to be 'effective' or not imposed at all. The punitive blockades employed by Napoleon in the early 1800s were therefore condemned.

A summary of changes in warfare in the Crimean War
The British and French had demonstrated the superiority of their rifled small arms over Russian smooth bore muskets. In siege warfare, massed heavy calibre artillery was essential to overcome the Russian

defences. The Russian defences were brilliantly organised by Lieute-nant-Colonel F. E. I. Todleben: earthworks were used to absorb the kinetic energy of the enemy shot, bastions with artillery were mutually supporting and swept the glacis (approach slope) of adjacent defences, and troops were employed as reserves for immediate counter-attack or as labourers to repair the defences at night. The allies fired 1,350,000 rounds to reduce the fortifications. The allies used amphibious opera-tions to good effect, the navies often supporting land-based units with gunfire (and with sailors as land units). The vulnerability of cavalry to artillery fire was demonstrated by the charge of the Light Brigade. The time taken to cross 1,000 yards (915m) was seven minutes. At a range of 600–1,000 yards (550–915m), the Russian guns each fired nine rounds of solid shot. Four hundred yards before reaching the guns, the Light Brigade were subjected to a further three rounds of shot or canister. Finally, the last 200 yards, covered at a gallop, exposed them to two rounds of canister.

Successes in the war are often overlooked
The war initiated many advances. Medical services, staff work, the chain of command and transport units in the British army were improved. However, the success of the allies in the war itself should not be overshadowed. They succeeded in maintaining a large army hundreds of miles from their homelands, just about equipped and supplied, to bring about victory. Where Napoleon Bonaparte had failed in an invasion deep inside Russia, the allied armies succeeded in the destruction of a military base on the periphery.

The Wars of Unification

In Italy, the state of Piedmont-Sardinia struggled with Austrian occu-pation and the revolutionary patriot Garibaldi united the southern states before handing them over to the Piedmontese government. Later, in Germany, Prussia defeated the Danes, incorporated other north German states and then defeated Austria in a seven-week war in 1866 (see Chapter 7). In 1870 Prussia led the German states against France in a war that forged the German nation.

The Franco-Austrian War of 1859

There were several early attempts to 'liberate' Italy
Initially after the Napoleonic era, conservative and reactionary regimes were reinstated in the separate Italian states. In the 1820s Neapolitan troops had tried to impose a constitution on their monarch, but Austrian troops had crushed the mutiny and remained in occupation until 1828. In Piedmont a similar mutiny was crushed at Novara when Austrian forces were invited to assist the new king, Charles Felix. In the Papal States rebellions were put down with Austrian assistance in 1830-31. However, there was a growing desire for more liberal institutions which coincided with a resentment of Austria and therefore developed into a spirit of nationalism. In 1848 there were a number of rebellions across Italy, and Austrian troops were ejected from Milan and faced barricades in Lombardy. Charles Albert, the King of Piedmont, declared war on Austria to liberate Lombardy and Venetia, two states that were populated by Italians but which lay within the Austrian border. The Pope, Pius IX, condemned the cause of Italian patriotism, and his troops joined Neapolitans in the defeat of the liberal uprisings of the south. Charles Albert nevertheless managed to capture the Austrian fortress city of Peschiera and defeated an Austrian army at the battle of Goito. Reinforced, the Austrians counter-attacked and won at Custozza (25 July 1848) and Novara (23 March 1849). An indemnity of 75 million lire was imposed.

Foreign intervention denied the patriots success
Louis Napoleon of France offered assistance to the Pope when a republic was declared in February 1849. French troops under General Oudinot landed in April, but they were initially repulsed outside Rome by the revolutionary leader Garibaldi. With reinforcements and Neapolitan assistance, Rome was captured on 30 June 1849. Italian patriots had been defeated by a strong parochial loyalty and by the strength of foreign powers. Austria was strongly entrenched in Lombardy and Venetia because it controlled four fortress cities known as the Quadri-lateral (Verona, Peschiera, Legnago and Mantua). Austrian troops were well led by General Radetzky, and they enjoyed numerical super-iority. In the final siege of Venice, an Austrian artillery officer, Franz Uchatius, floated paper balloons with timers to release 30lb bombs over the city. This first aerial bombardment failed to produce any results and the city fell because of a cholera epidemic and starvation on 24 August 1849. Camillo di Cavour, who became Prime Minister of Pied-

mont in 1852, realised that Piedmont needed allies if it was to unify Italy under its own leadership. In 1855 he joined the Crimean War, hoping to secure French backing. Napoleon III hoped to reassert French influence in northern Italy and win over Catholics at home, but it took an assassination attempt by Felice Orsini in January 1858 to provoke Napoleon into action.

In the war of 1859 both sides utilised railways and massed armies
France and Piedmont concluded a military alliance in January 1859, but attempts to make Austria appear the aggressor initially failed. Cavour gave secret instructions to Italian revolutionary societies in Austrian territory, but a European congress appeared to go in Austria's favour until the Austrians delivered an ultimatum. The Emperor, Francis Joseph, appointed General Gyulai to command the troops in Italy, and relied on the advice of Count Grunne who had no combat experience. He overlooked the more efficient General Benedek and the strategist General Hess. The Austrians delayed their offensive for ten days, long enough for the French to arrive in force in northern Italy using recently constructed railways. The Austrian supply system was inadequate for their army and there was insufficient reconnaissance. Moreover, troops had to be retained in Hungary to prevent revolts there, and a second army had to be retained in southern Germany to counter a potential thrust north of the Alps. Consequently there were 90,000 men available in Italy, but Italians, Croats and Hungarians in the Austrian army deserted throughout the campaign. Approximately 80,000 Franco-Piedmontese troops clashed with the Austrians in a frontal attack at Magenta (4 June 1859) and again at Solferino (24 June). The soldiers of both sides stubbornly held their ground or made costly but ineffectual attacks. At Solferino the French claimed victory because they remained in possession of the field.

The results of the war were costly but inspired improvements to medical services
The French and Piedmontese lost 17,000 men and the Austrians 22,000 in just one day of fighting at Solferino. As in previous battles of the nineteenth century, the care of the wounded was inadequate, but European opinion was universally shocked by the scale of the losses and the reports of the suffering in the newspapers. Henri Dunant, a Swiss observer at the battle, wrote *Un Souvenir de Solferino*, an influential account of the battle and its cost. In 1864, 16 nations' representatives met at Geneva to found the Red Cross, an international society dedicated to the relief of suffering. The war of 1859 ended when Napoleon III

became anxious about Piedmontese ambitions, and the Austrians were faced with Prussian mobilisation on their northern frontiers. Austria remained in possession of northern Italy, but the French withdrew without any gains at all. However, the price for their support of Piedmontese claims to Lombardy (secured in 1859) and the duchies of Modena, Parma and Romagna was the annexation of Savoy and Nice to France.

Leadership: how Garibaldi contributed to the Italian Risorgimento in 1860

Giuseppe Garibaldi was an Italian patriot who had fled Italy in 1834 to become a successful commander of the Montevideo garrison against the Argentinians. In 1848-49 he defended the Roman republic against the French, sustaining a two-month siege before withdrawing across the peninsula. In 1859 he returned from exile to conduct guerrilla operations against the Austrians near Lake Como. With unrest growing in southern Italy (and a revolt in Sicily on 4 April 1860), Garibaldi gathered a 'Thousand Redshirts' at Genoa and prepared to make an attack on the Neapolitan government. Denied supplies, manpower or arms by the Piedmontese, Garibaldi's makeshift revolutionary army steamed south and was unofficially protected by the Royal Navy. Gaibaldi's Thousand landed at Marsala on 11 May and defeated a stronger Neapolitan force at Calatfini, a feat which caused thousands to flock to his banner and initiated a collapse of Neapolitan morale. Having captured all of Sicily by July, Garibaldi crossed the Straits of Messina on 18 August, again with British support. He continued up through the Kingdom of Naples, fighting a series of engagements on the Volturno. From the north, Cavour sent the Piedmontese army to 'restore order' in the Papal States, defeating the Papal army at Castelfidardo. Garibaldi handed over his southern conquests to the King of Piedmont, but he was to make two unsuccessful attempts to capture Rome for Italy in 1862 (halted by Piedmont at Aspromnate) and 1867 (defeated by the French at Mentana).

Garibaldi was a successful irregular leader
Garibaldi certainly contributed to Italian unification and forced Piedmont to co-operate. However, Garibaldi also understood the need for popular support in a revolutionary cause. His 'Redshirts' uniform and patriotic zeal appealed to romantic sentiments, even though many Italians remained loyal to their region or state. He was politically

aware, knowing that Piedmont would not tolerate the declaration of a republic in the south. Throughout his military campaign he had always made his cause of 'Italy and Victor Emmanuel' (the King of Piedmont) to retain Piedmontese support. However, his attempts to secure Rome brought him into conflict with Cavour and with France. He was difficult to work with, but he had inspired others when he was successful, and was a skilful tactician. In the Franco-Prussian War Garibaldi returned to mercenary warfare when he fought to defend republican France against the Germans.

Conclusion

The wars of the mid-nineteenth century were marked by improvements to small arms technology. The greater lethality of weapons certainly affected the outcomes of a number of battles. The Crimean War had revealed many shortcomings in logistics and organisation in all the armies, but the media were particularly critical in Britain. In the war, leadership was a crucial factor and many have found fault with the leaders of all the armies, believing that many of the casualties were unnecessary. In Italy, by contrast, Garibaldi's inspirational leadership enabled a small, high-quality force to overcome the Neapolitan army in 1860. Nevertheless, the lessons of the Crimean war and the 1859 War were soon applied.

Tutorial

Progress questions

1. Why was the supply system during the Crimean war unable to cope with the demands of the armies on both sides?
2. What effect did disease, and subsequent manpower shortages, have on the siege of Sebastopol?
3. In what ways did media interest affect the Crimean War or its consequences?
4. Why was Tchernaya (15 August 1855) a turning point in the Crimean War?

Seminar discussion

1. What lessons were learned from the Crimean War and the War of 1859?

2.   How important was leadership in the outcome of the Crimean War
     and the Italian Wars?

Practical assignment

Examine media reports of any recent wars. Try to determine what similarities and differences there are between the first war correspondents'
dispatches and today. What interests do military leaders have in what is
reported and the way it is reported?

Study tips

1.   The Crimean War is memorable for its mistakes and errors, but it is
     significant because of innovations and reforms that arose from it.
2.   Notice that many changes were brought about as a result of the war,
     not during it.
3.   The most significant change off the battlefield was the improvement
     of medical services. Be prepared to comment on these.

6

The American Civil War, 1861-65

One minute overview – In the mid-nineteenth century national or regional identity, and the hegemony of certain states, dominated issues on either side on the Atlantic. Whilst nations were forged in Europe, in America the Confederacy attempted to secede from the Union, but was crushed in that continent's bloodiest conflict. In this struggle there was great experimentation in warfare. Citizen armies were mobilised on a massive scale, and railways were used to transport them to the front and to supply them there with unprecedented rapidity. Telegraphic communication increased the speed of decision-making, as well as political interference. On the battlefield machine guns, rifled artillery and trench warfare forced armies to adopt more extended formations, to manoeuvre on ever expanding fronts, or to adopt a defensive posture – often using fieldworks or trenches. Field obstacles gave the sieges an appearance similar to the First World War. Formations of men standing shoulder to shoulder, advancing with the bayonet, were now more likely than ever to end in carnage. By 1864–5 battles had become conflicts of attrition, and Sherman's 'scorched earth' policy devastated part of the Confederacy's economy as well as making a deep psychological impact on the South.

In this chapter you will learn:

▶ the innovations in warfare in the American Civil War, 1861–62
▶ the key battles of 1862-3
▶ the importance of the war in the western theatre
▶ changes in warfare that were highlighted in the Civil War

The innovations in warfare in the American Civil War, 1861-62

The causes of the war and the strategies of North and South
The American states had always enjoyed a degree of autonomy, but

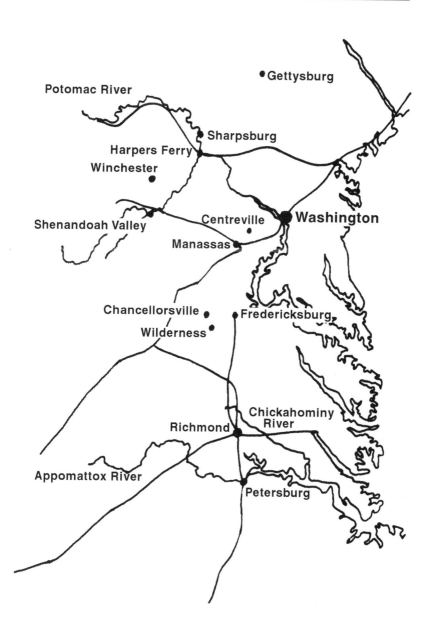

Figure 3. The American Civil War: eastern theatre

rivalry had developed between the slave owning and largely agrarian south, and the industrialised north. Objections by South Carolina and six other southern states to the election of an apparently anti-slavery President resulted in their declaration of secession from the Union. Lincoln, as President, refused to withdraw troops from Fort Sumter in South Carolina, prompting a bombardment by troops loyal to the new Confederacy of the South. When Lincoln called for 75,000 volunteers to suppress the rebellion, four more states seceded from the North. However, the South, which was populated by only seven million whites, faced the North's 20 million. The North also possessed the bulk of America's industrial capacity and the navy (which could deny the import of munitions to the South). The Southern leader, Jefferson Davis, adopted a defensive strategy, hoping to wear down the resolve of the North, whereas Lincoln anticipated a quick victory, utilising superiority of numbers and industrial material. Lincoln knew that, to suppress rebellion, total victory and occupation were necessities.

Quality of troops: the forces in 1861 were inexperienced
One of the key features of both armies was their inexperience, for the regular army at the outbreak of war had numbered only 16,000. With troops deployed in the west to contain Native American Indians, the regulars had little impact on the war, except in the provision of commanders. In April 1861 the South attracted 314 regulars, mainly officers, whilst the North could count on 3,000 men. In June the Confederacy had enlisted 112,000 men on a one-year engagement, whilst the Federals (North), expecting a quick victory, enrolled 152,000 volunteers on a three-month term. However, men from the countryside were often familiar with firearms (favouring the rural South), and some of the best leaders had joined the Southern cause. Both sides hoped to conduct mobile operations, utilising methods of warfare learnt in the wide frontier expanses of the west, but coloured by readings of European military history.

The opening months of the war went badly for the Union
The Federal invasion of the South was supposed to end in the capture of the rebel capital Richmond, but at Bull Run on 21 July 1861 the Federal attack faltered and was repulsed. Communication failure, indiscipline by troops unused to the terrors and scenes of combat, and the resolve of the Confederate leaders, were the hallmarks of the battle. Brigadier-General Thomas Jackson rallied other units when it was said he and his Virginians held their ground 'like a stonewall' against Federal attacks.

Crucially, 1,900 Confederates arrived by rail at Manassas junction from the Shenandoah Valley and turned a Federal withdrawal into a rout. Panic spread through the Northern army and was carried back to the capital Washington. The battle at Bull Run had exposed the deficiencies of the two armies but was the first tactical deployment of troops by rail. The Southerners quickly established a reputation for success, increasing their morale.

The campaign of 1862 was bloody and indecisive
The most important theatre of operations was the area between the two capitals, Washington and Richmond, where, in 1862, 22 battles were fought between General Robert E. Lee for the South and General George McClellan for the North. The region was highly populated, dissected by wooded river valleys and well served by railways. The South faced threats from four directions: the bulk of the North's Army of the Potomac in the Peninsula south-east of Richmond, 30,000 more under Brigadier General Irwin McDowell near Fredericksburg, 15,000 under General Nathaniel Banks in the Shenandoah Valley and 10,000 under General John Frémont in the Allegheny mountains (west of the Shenandoah mountains). The Confederate response was to concentrate on the defence of Richmond, but to despatch Thomas 'Stonewall' Jackson and Brigadier General Richard Ewell with 17,500 men to attack the Federals in the Shenandoah. The key result of this strategy was a successful blocking of the Union's invasion, but at a heavy cost. In the Seven Days Battle (26 June to 1 July), the longest battle to that date, the South sustained losses of 20,000, the North 16,000. By the autumn of 1862, the armies had swollen in size. At Antietam, Lee (50,000 strong) stopped McClellan's 70,000 men but the combined casualty toll was 26,000 and it ranked as the bloodiest battle of the entire war. In December, the Federals tried to storm Confederates dug in above Fredericksburg no less than 14 times, but they failed with losses of 13,000. Clearly battles were already being dominated by firepower.

Case studies: the key battles of 1862–3

Jackson's Shenandoah campaign raised Confederate morale
Jackson's Shenandoah campaign was a remarkable success. He was an aggressive leader who drove his men hard, earning them the reputation of 'foot cavalry' because of their speed. On 8 May 1862 Jackson drove off Frémont's force and marched north with Ewell paralleling in the

Luray valley to the east. Combining with Ewell, Jackson captured the Federal garrison at Front Royal and defeated General N. P. Banks at the battle of Winchester on 25 May. At Winchester the Confederates captured vast quantities of arms and stores. However, three Federal armies tried to converge on Jackson as he approached the Potomac river. Jackson's men marched rapidly out of the trap and then turned on their pursuers, defeating Frémont at Cross Keys (8 June) and James Shields' division at Port Republic (9 June). Jackson had marched 350 miles (560 km), won a series of battles, cleared the Shenandoah Valley, tied down 60,000 Federal troops and inflicted twice as many casualties as he himself had suffered.

The Peninsula Campaign failed to provide the Union with victory

McClellan had advanced very cautiously up the Peninsula towards Richmond, and General Joseph E. Johnston, the Confederate commander opposing McClellan, had retreated slowly towards the Southern capital. McClellan was hampered by heavy rains, floods, and poor maps, but he was also reluctant to commit to battle, much to Lincoln's frustration. However, Johnston fared little better. His attempt to capitalise on a temporary division of McClellan's army at the battle of Seven Pines failed as units got lost, attacked on their own initiative, or got congested on narrow roads. Johnston himself was wounded and was replaced by Robert E. Lee.

Leadership: Robert E. Lee was one of the South's best leaders

Lee ordered his men to dig in, whilst he toured each unit, inspiring them with confidence. He ordered supplies to be brought up, and the artillery was reorganised to make it more mobile. Nevertheless, at Mechanicsville (26 June 1862), Confederate divisions were unable to cross the Chickahominy Creek because reserves (Jackson's men from the Shenandoah) had not arrived and Union troops had dug in with formidable artillery support. Poor co-ordination, navigation and insufficient fire support meant that Confederate forces again faced defeat. Even so, Mechanicsville persuaded McClellan to pull back. At Gaines Mill, 27-28th June 1862, the main forces clashed. Confederate infantry advanced in parade-ground style as separate corps towards and, in places, across Boatswain's swamp. Union artillery and infantry-fire inflicted 8,300 casualties for a loss of 6,837, but they quit the field and left behind 22 guns. Moreover, after further clashes at Savage's Station (29 June), Glendale (30 June) and Malvern Hill (1 July), the so-called Seven Days Battle, Lincoln pulled McClellan out of the Peninsula altogether.

Lincoln pressured Major General John Pope to attack the South
As McClellan withdrew from the Peninsula, the Confederates formed
the Army of Northern Virginia into two wings, under Major General
James Longstreet and 'Stonewall' Jackson. After clashing with Pope's
55,000 strong army (confusingly known as the Army of Virginia) at the
Battle of Cedar Mountain on 9 August 1862, Jackson was despatched
by Lee on a rapid march to Manassas Junction, a Union supply base.
Pope turned to attack Jackson, who stood and checked the assault on 29
August. However, Lee had brought Longstreet up on a forced march.
Consequently, on 30 August at the Second Battle of Bull Run, Federal
troops launched their second attack against Jackson only to find Longstreet's corps on their left flank. The leading Union troops were cut to
pieces but the army withdrew in relatively good order to Washington.
Pope's advance had been premature. Had he waited for the rest of
McClellan's Army of the Potomac, the result may have been different,
but a combination of his own over-confidence and political pressure to
act (because of McClellan's inactivity) caused this debacle.

Strategy: Lee's first invasion of the north gave his army a formidable reputation
Having defeated Pope, Lee believed that an invasion of the North might
produce certain results: Virginians would be able to gather in the
autumn harvest without a Federal invasion, Richmond would be safe if
the North was busy defending its own territory, and a decisive victory
on Northern soil might persuade foreign powers to intervene and make
peace. Moreover, Federal elections, scheduled for the autumn, might
return a more peaceful party to government. Lee once again divided
his army and sent Jackson to capture Harpers Ferry (a Union base).
McClellan, who fortuitously obtained a set of Lee's plans, set off with
80,000 men to crush Lee, but Harpers Ferry capitulated and Jackson
hurried to join Lee at Sharpsburg.

Mass casualties: the Battle of Antietam was a bloody engagement
The resulting Battle of Antietam (17 September 1862) occurred in three
phases. The first was a Union cannonade and attack on the Confederate
left (Jackson). Eight thousand Federal soldiers fell in the attack. A
whole division was cut to ribbons around the Dunker Church when it
was caught in crossfire. The second phase of the Federal attack concentrated on Lee's centre. Initially repulsed by Confederates in a sunken
road, the Union troops outflanked the position and cut down the defenders, giving it the epithet 'the bloody lane'. The Confederates were without reserves nearby and Major General Israel Richardson, the Union

divisional commander on the spot, urged McClellan to commit his reserves immediately. McClellan refused, heeding his corps commanders' warnings that he controlled 'the last reserve of the army of the Republic'. The final phase was a Federal attempt to cut Lee off from the south. Just as Major General Ambrose Burnside's corps prepared to attack, the Confederate A. P. Hill and his Light Division (some of them wearing captured blue uniforms and flying Union flags as a ruse of war) opened fire on their left flank. Burnside conducted a fighting withdrawal. The Federals lost 12,500 men, the Confederates 10,300, making this the costliest single day of battle in the Civil War.

The battle of Antietam confirmed the confidence of Confederate troops
The two sides had fought each other to a standstill, but McClellan did not pursue Lee vigorously when the Confederates withdrew across the Potomac. Whilst McClellan had stopped the Southern invasion, there were criticisms of his lack of aggressiveness, his failure to commit reserves and his lethargic conduct in the Peninsula. He was replaced by Burnside. Lee, whilst ejected from the North, earned considerable acclaim at home. His troops, frequently outnumbered, displayed a fighting spirit that alarmed Northern commanders and troops alike. In battle, a shrieking call known as the 'rebel yell' unnerved their enemy.

The battle of Fredericksburg proved the value of defensive tactics
Burnside took the offensive, crossing the Rappahannock River at Fredericksburg on pontoon bridges. Hoping to pin down Lee's force in front of the town and outflank the Confederates' right, Burnside's men were unable to dislodge Jackson's regiments from Prospect Hill, despite initial success by Brigadier General George Meade. Lee's force was partially entrenched. Commenting on the open ground in front, one of their artillerymen assured Longstreet that 'a chicken could not live on that field'. Six successive waves of Union troops attempted to storm out of Fredericksburg, but they were each repulsed with heavy losses. Burnside was replaced by Major General Joseph Hooker. Hooker improved the morale of the Union army by developing better supply chains, better sanitation, fostering a corps identity and re-equipping his troops. By July 1863, the Army of the Potomac numbered 134,000 well drilled and confident soldiers.

Strategy: Chancellorsville, 1–4 May 1863, demonstrated Lee's skill
Hooker's plan was to hold Lee at Fredericksburg with 40,000 men under Major General John Sedgewick, send cavalry to cut railway lines

towards Richmond and march the bulk of the army around Lee's left flank, through an area called the Wilderness of Spotsylvania, and then turn towards Fredericksburg. The Union troops marched to Chancellorsville between 27 and 30 April 1863, but Lee was not inactive. Leaving 10,000 to watch Sedgwick at Fredericksburg, Lee took 50,000 to engage Hooker. Clashing just 3 miles east of Chancellorsville, Hooker lost his offensive spirit and decided to dig in around the town. Lee knew the Union left was strongly held against the Rappahannock River, and the centre now entrenched. He therefore despatched Jackson on a flanking march to the Union right. They emerged from the woods, opposite Major General Oliver Howard's XI corps with complete surprise. Half of Howard's men fell, and the commander (who had lost an arm the previous year) was unable to stem the retreat of the survivors. Jackson, riding forward in the gloom, was hit by a volley from his own men and later died. It had been a brilliant manoeuvre, conducted through tracks and woods for 5.5 miles (9 km) without detection. Nevertheless, 12,674 Confederates and 17,287 Federals had been killed or wounded. The Northerners began to doubt victory and passed a National Conscription Act.

Developments in warfare

There were several reasons for the heavy losses in the battles of 1862–3
There were a number of reasons for the high casualties of the war between 1861 and 1863. Civil war commanders adopted the close order formations of the day, partly to overcome the difficulties of controlling large bodies of partly trained men. Cohesion and morale could be sustained by close proximity between men, whereas dispersed formations made control more difficult. Numerous attempts were made to manoeuvre, but poor maps made navigation difficult, enemy reinforcements could be switched quickly using rail transport, and the close country of the east coast tended to funnel units onto the same roads and therefore costly frontal assaults. Both armies retained smooth bore cannons because of their effectiveness against troops in close quarter battle. However, by the end of 1862 the formations were changing: units adopted open order far more frequently. In addition, trench systems were dug to defend Richmond, but regiments used field fortifications, or natural cover, much more often to protect themselves against devastating firepower. Machine guns made their appearance in a defensive or siege role, but massed rifle fire could stop an infantry assault dead in its tracks.

There was a changing role for cavalry on the battlefield

As infantry and artillery firepower increased, so the mobility of units was reduced. This was particularly evident for cavalry, where charges with the *arme blanche* (swords and sabres) gave way to dismounted firing with carbines or pistol fire from the saddle. Cavalry were unlikely to succeed in the pursuit but still had a valuable role to play in reconnaissance. General J. E. B. Stuart demonstrated the value of cavalry in this function, but also its strength as a raiding force. In a famous ride between 12 and 15 June 1862, Stuart's troopers crossed the rear of McClellan's army, capturing or destroying stores and equipment, gathering information on the strength and dispositions of the Federals and causing confusion wherever it went. At Brandy Station on 9 June 1863, Stuart was screening the front of Lee's army as it redeployed after victory at Chancellorsville (May 1863), when he was attacked by 12,000 Union cavalry under Brigadier Alfred Pleasanton. Stuart saw off the assault and was soon in action again, screening Lee's flank manoeuvres at Gettysburg and attacking Federal lines of communication for seven days without relief. However, these operations had no bearing on the battles of the campaign. Cavalry were increasingly vulnerable.

Case study: Gettysburg

The Gettysburg campaign was a critical Southern invasion of the North

By 1863 the Confederacy began to rethink its defensive strategy. The siege of Vicksburg on the Mississippi (May 1863), the Federal sea blockade and war weariness in the population prompted Lee to seek a decisive victory inside Union territory. This, it was hoped, would undermine support for Lincoln, discourage those nations who supported the North, and compel both sides to reach a compromise peace. Accordingly, Lee marched 76,000 men of the Army of Northern Virginia north into Pennsylvania. There his troops found the countryside abundant with supplies. The Federal army (115,000) was taken by surprise (Lee having given them the slip from Fredericksburg by marching up the Shenandoah Valley), and, in order to protect Washington, had to interpose itself between Lee and the capital. Finding the Confederates was a key problem, and reconnaissance reports were often inaccurate. On 27 June, at Carlisle, Lee changed direction and headed east towards Harrisburg, whilst J. E. B. Stuart's cavalry swept through Maryland causing panic. However, Stuart's raiding deprived Lee of valuable reconnaissance troops. On 28 June, he was surprised that the Federal army was not still on the Potomac but only 25 miles away at Frederick in Maryland. General Joseph ('Fighting Joe') Hooker, the Federal commander, was replaced by Major-General George Meade in order to defeat the invasion. Meade tried to draw Lee into an attack. Lee, too, tried to tempt Meade into a costly attack. Nevertheless, cavalry on both sides, searching for their opponents, clashed north of Gettysburg on 30 June. With troops spread out on the line of march, the battle of Gettysburg began as a 'meeting engagement', units arriving piecemeal and being pitched into the fighting.

The battle of Gettysburg: the first day was inconclusive
As the Confederates brought up their leading two brigades, Brigadier General John Buford, commander of the 1st (Federal) Cavalry Division, rode his men forward and deployed his troopers in a dismounted role. The fire from their seven-shot Spencer repeating carbines was sufficient to halt the Confederate attack. Buford's tactics were successful because he combined mobility with firepower, but for decades cavalry would continue to be used in its traditional role attacking with cold steel. The Federals withdrew to a ridge to the south, overlooking the town. Although neither Meade, nor Lee, had wanted a battle at Gettysburg, there was little chance of disengaging. Meade sent Major General Winfield Scott Hancock to assume field command at the front, and Hancock organised the defence of the ridge. To the south east of the town stood the thickly wooded Culp's Hill which he garrisoned. To the south, and running southwards, were Cemetery Hill and Cemetery Ridge, which provided cover and a secure left flank. To prevent envelopment further left, Federal troops were also stationed at two knolls, Round Top and Little Round Top.

Ewell's attacks failed to achieve any result
As the Union troops began taking up their positions, Lee knew that he had an opportunity to take the high ground before the Union deployment was complete. Previously he would have turned to 'Stonewall' Jackson, but this corps was now commanded by Lieutenant General Richard Ewell, Jackson having been killed at Chancellorsville in May 1863. Lee issued orders for Ewell to attack 'if practicable', but Ewell decided that it was not. His troops were tired and had suffered in heavy in fighting around the town, and Ewell himself (who had lost his leg in battle at Second Manassas) was in agony. Instead, he probed and skirmished until nightfall. At midnight, Meade arrived on the battlefield and decided to continue with Hancock's defensive arrangement.

Troops continued to arrive and fill the gaps. Lee had lost his first opportunity.

The Confederate plan now depended on co-ordination and surprise
During the night, despite suffering from dysentery, Lee reconsidered the problem. Lieutenant General James Longstreet urged Lee to sweep around the Federal left flank and threaten Washington, forcing the Federals to fight on ground of the Confederates' choosing. But Lee would not risk marching to the flank without a protective screen of Stuart's cavalry, which at this point was still out of communication with Lee's headquarters. Instead, Lee opted to attack the left of the Federal position and roll up the line along Cemetery Ridge. To achieve surprise, Lieutenant General Ambrose Powell Hill's 3rd Corps was to feint in the centre and Ewell was to attack the northern position of Culp's Hill to absorb the Union reserves and exploit any opening. The attack depended on co-ordination by all three corps along a 2.5-mile (4-km) front.

The battle of Gettysburg: the second day (2 July 1863) was full of errors
Longstreet (1st Corps) was due to attack the Union flank around Little Round Top in the morning, but the attack didn't commence until 4pm. However, the Federal 3rd Corps, under General Dan Sickles, had advanced from the cover of the two knolls to a 'better position' without Meade's position. Indeed, the Little Round Top was completely undefended when a signaller reported Longstreet's advance. Brigadier General Governeur Warren, realising the danger the loss of this hill posed to the Union line, rushed troops to the summit, just as the Confederates reached the lower slopes. In the close country of rocks and trees, and extending across the notorious Peach Orchard, Devil's Den and the Wheatfield, a bloody and hard fought 'soldiers' battle' developed. Four hours of fighting failed to produce the expected breakthrough, but only as the firing died away did Ewell commence his attack in the north. The Federals were able to rush reinforcements to the new threat and Ewell was repulsed, clinging to a foothold on Culp's Hill at the end of the day. The Union's Army of the Potomac, so often dispirited and defeated in the South, was galvanised on its own territory and had checked the formidable Army of Northern Virginia.

The battle of Gettysburg: the third day (3 July 1863) was a disaster for Lee
Lee planned to resume the attack on the 3rd, using Longstreet and Ewell to act like pincers on each flank, before delivering a blow to the

centre. Meade had guessed that this was Lee's plan the night before, and he opened the day with a dawn attack (04.30) on Ewell's corps, ejecting him from the lower slopes of Culp's Hill. Longstreet, typically, delayed his attack, so Lee decided to reinforce A.P. Hill with Major General George Pickett's division (which had just arrived) and attack the Union centre. Longstreet tried to warn Lee that an attack in the centre was hopeless, but Lee pressed his assembled 15,000 men into action. Longstreet, again after much delay, bombarded the Union centre with 150 guns, the Federals replying with 80. The Federals expended 32,000 rounds, the Confederates 20,000: it was the biggest artillery bombardment of the war (not including sieges) but it was not as effective as they hoped. The Confederates ran short of long range ammunition and Pickett's men emerged from the trees below Seminary Ridge in Napoleonic style: lines behind their regimental flags, advancing the mile (1.6 km) across open ground to Cemetery Ridge. Blasted by canister and raked by rifle fire, the Confederates lost 7,000 killed and wounded. It is thought that 150 men penetrated the Federal defences on the ridge but, like Brigadier General Armistead who led them, they were killed. 'Pickett's Charge' was a powerful illustration of the devastating effects of modern weapons.

An analysis of the most significant battle of the war
Both armies remained on the defensive on the 4th. The North had lost 23,000 killed, wounded and missing, the South 27,000. The wounded were gathered in and transported south. The fine weather broke. Lee knew that he would be unable to dislodge Meade from the ridge so he quit the field at nightfall. Meade did not pursue and allowed Lee to escape across the Potomac, a decision that has aroused much controversy since. Despite the errors made, Lee's reputation was untarnished. He apologised to his troops for the debacle of Pickett's charge and was cheered by his men. Yet Lee's army had lost the air of invincibility they had enjoyed since 1862. The defeat at Gettysburg and the losses that Lee had sustained meant that another invasion of the North was unthinkable. The fall of Vicksburg and the loss of the whole Mississippi to Union forces under General Ulysses Grant came as another blow to the Confederacy as it made them vulnerable to encirclement. However, Gettysburg was the turning point.

The war in the west

Railways: The Union opened a second front along the Mississippi
Foraging inside Confederate territory, Grant took forts Henry and
Donelson, and combined with Major-General Don Carlos Buell to
defeat General Albert Sidney Johnston at Shiloh on 6 April 1862. In
that battle, the Federals had to give ground and the Sixth Division
(under Brigadier-General Benjamin Prentiss) was completely enveloped. However, on 7 April the reinforced Union Army of the Tennessee
rolled forwards. In 1863, with the fall of Vicksburg, Major-General
William Rosecrans tried to advance deeper south, but was checked at
Chickamauga (19–20 September 1863). Grant relieved the defeated
Union Army of Cumberland at Chattanooga and 20,000 troops were
switched to the western theatre by rail (under Joseph Hooker) from the
army of the Potomac, demonstrating the strategic importance of railways.

Sherman's campaign in Georgia was a notorious campaign of devastation
Grant, who had won the battle of Shiloh in 1862, assumed overall
command of Union forces in 1864. Despite a reputation for alcoholism,
Grant reasoned that the Federal army should continue to pin the
Confederates around Richmond, but use the abundance of manpower
to drive into the South. He sent General William Sherman on a 700-
mile (1,126 km) march from Dalton to Savannah in Georgia, employing
scorched earth tactics across a 50-mile front. Sherman's 110,000 men
seized railway lines and cut his opponents' tracks, rebuilding his own
routes where necessary. His troops lived off the land, and his foraging
parties secured supplies without regard to civilian welfare. Sherman
believed that 'war is hell', and it is alleged that therefore he 'made it so'.
Less prosaically, Grant was implementing economic warfare and the
psychological demoralisation he knew he needed to inflict on the resolve
of the South.

Mass casualties: Grant's campaign of 1864 showed that it was a war of attrition
Grant tried to wear down Lee in a six-week campaign in the late
summer of 1864. There were four major battles, Wilderness, Spotsylvania, North Anna and Cold Harbour. Grant had 105,000 men at the
beginning of the campaign and lost 55,000, whilst Lee lost 30,000 out
of his original force of 61,000. These massive casualty figures almost
broke the morale of both armies, but the North could replace its losses,
the South could not. Nevertheless, veteran Union troops refused to

expose themselves to effective fire and so would not press home an attack to make a battle decisive.

Changes in warfare

Technology: weapon systems had evolved
Whereas in 1861 most troops had been armed with muzzle-loading smooth-bore muskets (which were slow to load and fire – a trained soldier could fire three aimed shots a minute), by 1864 small-arms technology had advanced. Mass-produced percussion caps, using fulminate of mercury instead of gunpowder poured into an igniting pan, made misfires less likely. Percussion caps gradually replaced flintlock mechanisms. The M1842 percussion muzzle-loading smooth-bore musket was replaced by the Springfield and Enfield muzzle-loading rifle. These in turn were outclassed by the Spencer breech-loading rifle and the Sharps breech-loading rifle (1863), although only sharpshooters used these weapons. There were several types of manually operated machine guns but they were limited to use in sieges where ammunition supply was less of a problem. Despite the experience of many troops, there was evidence of the lack of training in the use of small arms, or perhaps the detrimental effects of combat. For example, 37,000 muskets were salvaged from the battlefield of Gettysburg, but 18,000 had been loaded twice or more. In the heat of the battle soldiers had either forgotten to fire or failed to clear their weapons of misfires. Ramrods had also sometimes been mistakenly fired while still in the barrel, rendering the weapon ineffective. However, few could doubt the courage of the troops. At Antietam, the 1st Texas regiment lost 82.3 per cent of its strength, at Gettysburg the 1st Minnesota 82 per cent. The 141st Pennsylvania lost 75.5 per cent in the same battle, while the 21st Georgia lost 76 per cent at Bull Run.

The Civil War produced trench warfare in the siege of Petersburg
The Confederate city of Petersburg was besieged by Union forces from 15 June 1864 to 2 April 1865. A 10-mile network of trenches, 55 redoubts and obstacles (sharpened *abattis* and *chevaux de frise*) protected the defenders. At the beginning of the siege, many of the redoubts and trenches were incomplete, but Major General William F. Smith, commander of Grant's XVIII Corps, decided to dig in after initial success on 15 June 1864. Two days later further Union night attacks succeeded in capturing two fortified hills, but the Confederate defenders cut down the second-

phase attack and the darkness caused confusion. Beauregard, the commander of the garrison, fell back on the outskirts of the town and was reinforced with Lee's Army of Northern Virginia. On 18 June a Federal daylight attack against the earthworks around the town failed with heavy losses (11,386 in two days); but Federal veterans were increasingly reluctant to attack. As a result, Grant decided to employ regular siege tactics. However, siege guns, including rail-mounted artillery, failed to end the stalemate.

Trench warfare and mine operations still resulted in heavy casualties
To break the deadlock, on 30 July 1864 the Federals detonated a huge mine consisting of 4 tons of explosives at the end of a 511 foot (152.4m) shaft. A gap 500 yards (472m) wide was blown in the defences, and Union troops poured into it but were unable to exploit their success. The Confederates recovered and counter-attacked, catching the Federals off balance. Penned into a narrow front, the Northern soldiers were cut down in large numbers. Those that tried to cross the open ground in daylight, back to their own lines, suffered heavy casualties. The Confederates had lost 1,000 men, but the Federals lost 4,000 without result. The siege continued, with Lee despatching Major General Jubal Early with 10,000 men up the Shenandoah Valley to draw off Union troops, and Grant trying unsuccessfully to cut railroad lines into the beleaguered cities of Petersburg and Richmond. Lee tried to break the Union siege in March 1865 by recapturing forts, but Hill's corps was repulsed. Thinly stretched, and at last appointed supreme commander, Lee decided to abandon Petersburg and preserve his field army. However, Federal troops harried the escape and swarmed over the skeleton force at Petersburg on 2 April 1865.

Domestic factors
The collapse of the South was the result of military and economic factors
As Lee withdrew from Petersburg, his dwindling force was cut in two at Appomattox and caught between Grant and the cavalry corps under Major General Philip Sheridan. The lack of industrial capacity in the South meant that they could not mass produce the firearms and munitions required to sustain the war effort. The blockade prevented supplies coming in from outside. The fact that the world viewed the conflict as an internal war meant that no foreign aid could be expected (as had been the case in the American War of Independence). Desertions, the exhaustion of Southern supplies, the hopeless strategic situation and the heavy casualty toll, compelled Lee to surrender at Appomattox

Court House on 9 April 1865. Local resistance continued for several weeks. The war had cost 620,000 lives. Lincoln's emancipation of the slaves on 1 January 1863 meant that there would be a social reconstruction of the South. Following Lincoln's assassination on 14 April 1865, Northern politicians (the 'radical republicans') treated the South as a defeated foreign country. They imposed one-party, military rule and Federal troops remained in the Southern states until April 1877.

The lessons of the American Civil War were not learned in Europe
Although European military officers had been present throughout the war, either as observers or advisers, there was a general feeling that the American Civil War was unrepresentative of modern war because it was felt that the untrained armies of North and South were unsuccessful where trained European professionals would have pressed on to victory. Despite the casualties sustained by artillery, machine guns and breech-loading rifles, military honour required professional soldiers to display courage. This often meant that officers were expected to lead by example and expose themselves to danger. The use of trenches was thought to be something to be confined to siege operations, or a last resort: men of honour resented grubbing into the earth like cowards. The Confederate Lieutenant-General John Bell Hood had warned that troops who stayed for too long behind breastworks 'became timid' and lacked the offensive spirit to win. Moreover, colonial wars, in which the Europeans were often committed in the nineteenth century, required that otherwise obsolete tactics were still useful, particularly when European troops often enjoyed superiority in firepower. As a result, the American Civil War was not regarded as the future of war, but as a unique conflict.

Tutorial

Progress questions
1. Compare the leadership of the armies of the North and South in the Civil War.
2. What changes in weapons technology were evident in the war?
3. Comment on the industrial capacity of the North and how it assisted in its victory.
4. How important was troop morale and inexperience in determining the outcomes of battles in 1861–63?

Seminar discussion

1. How far do you agree with the view that Confederate fighting spirit and Lee's leadership were doomed to failure against the industrial might of the Union?
2. Why did the European powers dismiss the lessons of the American Civil War?

Practical assignment

Try to summarise the main developments in warfare between 1815 and 1865 under the following headings: Citizen armies, Railways, Telegraph, Firepower, Machine guns.

Study tips

1. The American Civil War was exceptional because of the mass enlistment of American citizens, but note that, by the end of the war, the soldiers and their leaders were fighting with battlefield experience and no longer following European theories.
2. Try to picture the campaigns in your mind. Consulting a map of eastern America is helpful. By tracing the routes of the armies, you can see how important certain positions were.
3. Try to find out more about the leading generals of the war. Their attitude to war influenced their tactics, so Sherman and Lee provide a strong contrast.
4. The heavy losses in Civil War battles can sometimes give the impression that firepower had made attacks impossible, but many battles of the Civil War do not bear this out. Try to reach a balanced judgement.

7

The Wars of German Unification, 1864–71

One minute overview – The aggrandisement of Prussia under the direction of Otto von Bismarck reached its culmination with the unification of Germany in 1871. It was achieved through a combination of diplomacy and war, or 'blood and iron' as Bismarck put it. By engineering conflicts or playing on opportunities, the Prussian statesman defeated Denmark, Austria and France in the space of only eight years. The Prussians completed a series of military reforms and outclassed the French forces in the Franco-Prussian War of 1870-71. However, it was not simply a case of weapons superiority, for the French were often better armed and inflicted heavy casualties on the Germans. The German troops were well organised, were regularly supplied and enjoyed the moral advantage of advancing or attacking. In addition, their leaders enjoyed the support of efficient staff officers and a centralised command structure. Too often the French army was demoralised, was retreating or badly led. In the latter stages of the war, the Germans besieged Paris but found themselves under attack by guerrillas, the *franc-tireurs*.

In this chapter you will learn:

▶ what changes were made to Prussia's army and how Bismarck engineered conflict
▶ the reasons for Prussian victory in the Seven Weeks' War
▶ the developments of warfare in the Franco-Prussian War

Changes in the Prussian army and Bismarck's diplomacy

Prussian military reforms were far-reaching
In 1821 the chief adviser to the monarchy on military matters was changed from the Ministry of War to the Chief of the General Staff. In other words, a military officer replaced the civilian minister. As the largest single state in the German Confederation, it was clear that Prus-

sia could play a leading role in shaping the future of the region. However, Austria, which was a member of the German Confederation as well as a vast multiracial empire of its own, was eager to prevent the emergence of a powerful neighbour on its northern flank. In the first decades of the nineteenth century, Austria, Russia and Prussia had a common interest: the suppression of liberal, radical and revolutionary organisations. They all put down revolutionaries in the 'tolle Jahr' (mad year) of 1848. However, German intellectuals were also keen to see the establishment of a unified Germany. Whilst Austria was strong, and the Prussian monarchy refused to accept a 'crown of shame' from a popular assembly, this was impossible. In 1850 Austria reasserted its leadership of the German Confederation by restoring order in Hesse-Kassel, a state which Prussia regarded as a satellite. Although Prussia was forced to back down, Albrecht von Roon (War Minister, 1859) implemented military reforms to strengthen the state: namely universal military service and the adoption of the Dreyse 'needle-gun', a new rifle.

Leadership: von Moltke 'the elder' was one of Germany's best strategists
Helmuth von Moltke (1800–1891) was a strategist who commanded Prussian forces in the wars of German unification and who founded a general staff. Von Moltke began his career in a Danish cadet training school but transferred to Prussia in 1822. He took up mapmaking and surveying, the usual occupation of staff officers. Staff officers normally disseminated commands, kept track of armies on the move, and organised messages from headquarters to the troops on the ground. In 1835 he served briefly with the Turkish army but only commanded in battle once at the battle of Nezib in 1839. On his return to Prussia he took a great interest in technological developments such as railways and new rifled firearms. He became director of a railway in 1841 and was enthusiastic about their military potential. Under his direction, the Prussian army adopted rifles as the standard infantry weapon.

Von Moltke studied military history to address Prussia's weaknesses
Von Moltke was also a man of letters (he wrote 24 books) and his studies of military history made him realise that longer-range weapons would make possible enveloping forms of attack. This was a departure from the 'central position' strategy and linear tactics of the Napoleonic era. Von Moltke may have been influenced by a study of Cannae. The battle of 216 BC, between Hannibal's Carthaginians and the Romans, was a celebrated victory for Hannibal because he allowed the Romans to push his centre back so that his two wings could envelop and then

surround his enemy. The Romans lost 48,200 men in just one day. Von Moltke was aware of Prussia's military deficiencies (which were exposed by mobilisation in the 1850s) and worked with Albrecht von Roon to rectify them. Having larger numbers of men (which were necessary if weapons were more devastating and railways now made deployments over wider areas possible) was pointless unless they could be controlled/co-ordinated and equipped/fed.

Von Moltke's solutions to Prussia's problems
Von Moltke's solution (he became Chief of Staff in 1857) was to organise mobilisation using railway timetabling. Communications were speeded up using the telegraph. Speed of mobilisation was improved too. Von Roon's creation of more reservists meant that armies could be raised quickly on the outbreak of war, but the state would not have to pay for a vast and expensive 'standing army' in peacetime. Von Moltke also improved staff work. It was a centralised planning agency (drawing up plans for war in peacetime), but it could enable commanders to operate with some freedom of action once in the field. This was because von Moltke felt that 'no plan survives contact with the enemy'. He wanted his officers to be educated and daring, taking advantage of opportunities, not cautious and concerned by the rules of warfare and protocol. In the Danish war his subordinates did not execute operations according to his plan at first but he personally intervened and won victory.

Strategy and planning: von Moltke excelled at the enveloping form of attack
In the Seven Weeks' War (1866) von Moltke organised several converging corps to fight and envelop the Austrians. Forcing the Austrians to fight a defensive battle at Sadowa, his corps commanders crushed the enemy's attempted counter attacks. In the Franco-Prussian War (1870–71) he avoided repeating the encirclement strategy as a formula. Instead, he kept his corps moving along as narrow an axis as he could allow, encouraging his commanders to maintain contact with the French and support each other. Having compelled the French to give battle, von Moltke would then begin to encircle his enemy, using artillery to bombard the French troops in the centre. This was only possible because of efficient staff work and rapid communication. Von Moltke remained Chief of Staff of the German army until 1887. It was his skill that made the unification of Germany possible.

Bismarck combined diplomacy and war to unify Germany
Relations with Austria deteriorated in the 1850s. Austria was excluded

from an economic union in Germany in 1853, it lost Russian support after the Crimean War and various Prussian overtures to establish a federal German state under Prussian leadership were vetoed. Prince Otto von Bismarck was appointed Chancellor by Wilhelm I in 1862 when the monarchy faced a dispute with liberals over expenditure on the army. Bismarck realised that the liberal-nationalist spirit in the German states threatened to engulf Prussia. Moreover, Austria would remain an obstacle to Prussian hegemony in northern Germany. Bismarck used diplomacy and military force to forge a German state under Prussian leadership. By 1871 he had defeated Denmark, Austria and France and united Germany under the Prussian monarchy.

The Danish War was a one-sided conflict
In 1848 the German states became embroiled in a struggle with Denmark for the control of the duchies of Schleswig and Holstein. The London Protocol (1852) temporarily settled the dispute, but the Danes imposed their own constitution over the duchies. A succession crisis in the Danish monarchy gave Prussia the opportunity to champion the German cause with Austrian support. Denmark, believing it had British support, rejected a German candidate for rule in the duchies and Prussian troops attacked. Faced by the combined might of Prussia and Austria, the Danes initially tried to reach a diplomatic settlement, but Bismarck delayed until General von Wrangel had achieved a battlefield victory at Düppel, inside Denmark (March 1864). When an armistice expired on 26th June, the Danes were again defeated. The Treaty of Vienna brought the war to a close (October 1864) and by the Convention of Gastein, Austria and Prussia administered the two duchies. Nevertheless, relations between Prussia and Austria were tense.

Preparation and planning

There was diplomatic preparation for war between 1864 and 1865
Bismarck rushed troops to the Russian border when a revolt broke out in the Russian province of Poland in 1863. His co-operation with the Russians won over the Tsar. Alexander II saw Prussia as a useful ally against his rival Austria. In 1865 Bismarck visited Napoleon III at Biarritz to discuss the future of Germany and he secured French neutrality in the event of an Austro-Prussian war. In January 1866 the Italians offered to buy Venetia, but the Austrians rejected the offer. Bismarck secured an Italian alliance in April 1866 with the proviso that Prussia should initiate a conflict within three months so that the Italians could

secure Venetia. Mobilisation began in Prussia, Austria and Italy, and Bismarck put forward the idea of a federal German state knowing that it would be rejected, thus providing him with a *casus belli* (cause of war). The Austrians rejected both the proposal and offers of mediation by the other powers, thereby isolating themselves. Austrian interference in Prussian-held Holstein prompted Bismarck to send troops into the duchy. However, unable to provoke Austria into firing the first shot, Bismarck proposed that the German Diet (assembly of states) be dissolved. He then ordered Prussian troops into Hanover, Saxony and Hesse-Kassel on 15–16 June 1866. Austria declared war in defence of the status quo. Bismarck had not been wholly successful in his diplomacy, but he had engineered a war and had divided the Austrians on two fronts.

The Prussian plan was for a quick victory

Von Moltke had developed a mobilisation scheme which could raise 400,000 men from each region (doubling the numbers of troops raised before the reforms in 1860). These troops could be transported by road and rail to form three armies. What was remarkable was the way that von Moltke applied precise calculations to the formation, transport and arrival of divisions using timetables and telegraph. The Prussian General Staff became an élite of highly trained officers who would implement these plans. However, von Moltke also realised the trains and telegraph could not affect the events on the battlefield directly. As his three armies converged on the Austrians, commanders would still have to make independent judgements and orders would still have to be delivered via officers on horseback.

Technology: the needle-gun and Prussian artillery illustrate strengths and weaknesses

The chief advantage in the Prussian army was the 'needle-gun' rifle. This weapon was designed in 1827 by von Dreyse (a Frenchman) and adopted by the Prussian army in 1848. The cartridge was inserted into the breech and closed by a 'bolt-action'. This differed from other armies which loaded the Minié-bullet cartridge down the muzzle (in British service from 1851). Curiously, the Prussian army had not adopted the breech-loading 6-pounder cannon, created by Krupps (a German firm) in 1851, nor the British Armstrong and Whitworth rifled cannon (used in the American Civil War). Consequently, when the Prussians faced the Austrians, they possessed only shorter-range smooth-bore artillery which they had to push forward to engage their enemies.

Leadership and staff work: the Seven Weeks' War

The Prussians carried out a successful envelopment at Langensalza
The success of von Moltke's envelopment by converging armies was first demonstrated against the Hanoverians. On the Austrian declaration of war on 15 June, the Prussians transported their troops by rail and converged on the slow moving and single Hanoverian force. At Langen-salza, 27 June 1866, the Prussians surrounded them and forced their surrender. This example shows that far from being obsolete, pre-battle manoeuvre was essential to the success of military operations. Indeed, manoeuvre offered a swift solution to the blood-letting seen in the American Civil War. The Prussians mobilised rapidly using their railways and efficient staff work as planned.

Strategy: the advance to Sadowa (Königratz) was by envelopment
Three Prussian armies, numbering 221,000 men, invaded Bohemia, with the object of destroying the 205,000-strong Austrian army under General Ludwig von Benedek. Advanced Prussian units drove back detached Austrian corps, the needle-guns proving their worth. Austrians troops were compelled to load and fire standing up, but the breech-loading mechanism gave Prussian troops the option of firing from the prone position. Advancing Austrian troops suffered heavily from close range Prussian artillery. On 3 July von Moltke received definite information on the location of the Austrian main body and launched his three corps in a converging, concentric envelopment. However, whilst the Army of the Elbe and the First Army moved together, the Second Army remained stationary because the telegraph had broken down. Consequently, only two thirds of the Prussian army arrived in front of the Austrian army. Benedek remained on the defensive, but his artillery, ably commanded by General Anton Mollinary of IV Corps, halted the Prussian attack so effectively that Wilhelm I wondered if the Prussians were losing the battle. However, the belated arrival of Second Army and a flank attack by the Army of the Elbe broke the Austrians. The needle-guns cut down their Austrian opponents and Benedek refused to send in the reserves. They lost 65,000 for Prussian losses of 10,000. Benedek escaped with part of his force intact and Prussian cavalry were reluctant to pursue in the face of the Austrian artillery. Bismarck was anxious for a rapid settlement and had to restrain the king and the army from pressing on to Vienna.

The Italian contribution to the war was limited
The Italians were defeated by the Austrians at Custozza (24 June 1866) and at sea in the battle of Lissa. However, by the terms of the Peace of Prague, Austria lost Venetia to France who handed it on to Italy.

The causes of the Franco-Prussian War were based on military rivalry
Bismarck's main reason for ending the Austrian War was to prevent the French from intervening. Napoleon III had expressed interest in acquiring the Rhineland and therefore influence over the Catholic southern German states. Publication of these French designs turned Germans in the Rhine area against France. Bismarck concluded military agreements with the defeated states of Germany, giving Prussia control of their armed forces in wartime and rights of access to their railway networks. The French army was a formidable obstacle to Bismarck's plans to control southern Germany, and a threat to the Prussian state. The French had defeated the Russians in the Crimea in 1856, and launched a successful punitive expedition against Syria and Lebanon in 1860 following the massacre of Christians there. They had been unable to defeat Austria in 1859 and 23,000 French troops under General Forey had captured Mexico in 1863, only to be withdrawn (and the puppet regime overthrown) in 1867. Bismarck tried to engineer a war that would bring in the other German states against the French, but his first attempt, the Luxemburg Crisis of 1867, failed. However, French objections to a Prussian candidate for the Spanish throne led to a French ultimatum. Bismarck engineered the Prussian King's reply to give maximum offence and France declared war on 19 July 1870.

The development of warfare in the Franco-Prussian War, 1870–71

The technology and organisation of the protagonists were unequal
Von Moltke's military machine swung into action once more, mobilising 500,000 German troops from across the states and transporting them to the battlefronts in trains. By contrast, the French army could muster 224,000 and railways were used to move civilian refugees out of the theatre of operations. Nevertheless, the French army was confident: Leboeuf, the War Minister, had told the Cabinet in 1869 the French army was 'ready to the last gaiter button'. The French army was equipped with the Chassepot rifle, a long-range needle-operated rifle. The German Dreyse had a design problem. It had a poor gas seal

which meant that it had to be fired from the hip, but could still go off and injure the firer. Fouling was also still a problem. Residue from each round fired tended to build up in the barrel, making a breech explosion more likely. The Chassepot rectified this problem by inserting a rubber ring in the breech. This weapon had a greater range than older patterns of muzzle-loaders and targets could be hit at 1,600 yards (1,463m) if fired in groups. The French were also armed with the Reffye *mitrailleuse* (machine gun). Twenty-five rotating barrels could fire between 75 and 125 bullets a minute at ranges of 500 to 1,250 yards (455–1,137m) but the French chose to employ it as artillery rather than in intimate support of the infantry. The key change in the Prussian army was the artillery arm. Learning from Sadowa, the German forces now employed rifled and breech-loading artillery and heavier calibres.

The invasion: the French army's problems were based on poor organisation
According to Michael Howard, the French army relied a little too heavily on improvisation. At Metz, for example, millions of rounds of Chassepot ammunition failed to be distributed because there was no staff to organise it. Leboeuf expected there to be 385,000 men in his Army of the Rhine, but two weeks into the mobilisation there were only 202,448. Napoleon III was to take personal command, but he was sick, and the French army was issued with vague ideas about an offensive. There was a complete lack of proper intelligence gathering, so the direction and strength of the German invasion could not be determined. Worse still, there was no co-ordination between divisions, which might cross each other's path and hold up everyone else. A division could take several hours to pass a single point. There were delays too, because the French army adopted a routine it had learnt on campaign in Africa, that of concentrating all the division in one place for the night rather than bivouacking along the line of march, or as battalions or brigades. At Saarbrücken, 2 August 1870, six French divisions went into the attack without any prior reconnaissance and drove off a single German regiment, but it lulled them into a false sense of security. The French army failed to destroy the railway station, telegraph (which sent information about the French movements for days) or mine any of the bridges.

Figure 4. The Franco-Prussian War, 187–71

Technology and tactics

The Battle of Spicheren demonstrated comparative weapon characteristics

Von Moltke's army corps marched with a front of over 100 miles, along avenues of advance that would converge at the crucial moment. He avoided repetition of the envelopment manoeuvre used in the Austrian war, but planned to bring the French to battle and envelop their flanks. However, his aim of enveloping the French in northern Alsace was dashed when the First Army commander, Steinmetz, and the two Bavarian Corps seemed to have their own ideas about how the war should be fought. This may have been because an isolated French division was routed at Weissembourg on 4 August. Von Moltke diverted his Second Army to support the First Army and they converged at Saarbrücken. General Charles Frossard, the commander of the French 2nd Corps, occupied the heights and valleys to the west of the town, around the village of Spicheren. General von Kameke (14th Division commander in VII of the German First Army) launched a frontal attack at the French corps. As the battle raged, Frossard did not receive any reinforcements, despite their proximity, whilst Prussian commanders used their initiative and 'marched to the sound of the guns'. The German forces won because their artillery outranged and outnumbered the French cannon, although the Chassepot rifles had pinned down or repulsed German infantry formations. In an attack on a feature called the Rotherberg, German troops had been initially pinned down at its rocky base, but were encouraged up the slopes by their officers and captured the plateau at the top. French infantry counter-attacks could not throw them off, but their artillery prevented reserves being brought up to them. Prussian hussars, following the conventional practice of pursuing an enemy, were slaughtered as they tried to make their way up a sunken lane.

The results of the battle highlighted the power of German artillery
Frossard was only forced to give up his position in the evening because he lacked support and the Germans began to edge around his left flank (at the village of Forbach). However, an important psychology had developed. Frossard believed he had been defeated, but the Germans did not. What was already clear was that the concentration of forces by the Germans, the effectiveness of massed rifle fire in checking attacks, and the reliance on German artillery to suppress the French Chassepot riflemen was the pattern of the war that followed.

Tactics: Battle of Froeschwiller caught the French by surprise
The German Third Army crossed the frontier to engage the French 1st Corps (under Marshal Patrice MacMahon), knowing that its support at Belfort (7th Corps under Felix Douay) was far too distant to help MacMahon. The French 1st Corps was dangerously dispersed, as the division at Weissembourg discovered on 4 August, because supplies were inadequate and the troops had to forage from the local area. MacMahon could count on 48,000 men to defend the hills above the Sauerbach river, near Froeschwiller. The French were so confident that their position was secure that no vedettes were posted beyond the river, the bridges were not destroyed and no trenches were dug. The most

important concern was that some of the soldiers had not eaten properly for four days, and they set about cooking when the first German cavalry appeared on 5 August. Nevertheless, the German forces were drawn into battle, to quote Michael Howard, 'like a workman whose clothes have been caught in the cogs of a machine'. In the northern portion of the field, Bavarians were engaged in exchanging fire across open ground near the village of Langensulzbach. In the south, German artillery silenced the French guns and, in the centre, 14 batteries of German artillery bombarded the hills.

The closing stages of the battle illustrated the weakness of cavalry
The impetuous General von Kirchbach ordered the German V Corps to attack prematurely and they were repulsed. However, the French could not hold out indefinitely. Despite initial success, even counter-attacks by the thinly held French right, they were outnumbered and pressed back. In this emergency General Lartigue, who commanded this sector, launched nine squadrons of cavalry against the Prussian infantry, hoping to throw them back. Unlike the Napoleonic era, the infantry did not form squares. They lined the walls and hedges of the vineyards and took shelter in the village of Morsbronn, and shot down the French horsemen in large numbers. Gradually, two huge pincers gripped the French position, but it was the collapse of the French right which ended the battle. To prevent envelopment, MacMahon repeated Lartigue's cavalry charge with a brigade of cuirassiers but, once again, they were cut down without even reaching the Prussians. Even French artillerymen were being shot down by German infantrymen and they fell back. The reserve infantry attempted a charge, but they fell so thickly that eyewitnesses, noting the blue jackets, described the area as being like a field of flax. The Prussians lost 10,500 men, but half of MacMahon's force, 11,000, lay killed and wounded.

There were several lessons to be drawn from the early battles
Defects in both sides were revealed by these opening battles, but the two sides drew different conclusions. The French artillery was less effective and the shell fuses they used were unreliable. The German shells exploded on impact (percussion fuse), unless the ground was very soft. French troops, subjected to the heavy shelling of Prussian guns, were remarkably courageous, but the psychological effect of having to remain inactive under seemingly indiscriminate bombardment eroded their morale. German infantry needed to adopt 'open order' formations, but their reservists tended to huddle together for moral support

and were cut down by the French breech-loaders. French reservists were little better: some had arrived at Froeschwiller not knowing how to load a Chassepot rifle. The use of cavalry was clearly changing. They were essential to reconnaissance, but hopelessly vulnerable to artillery and infantry fire. The damage that had been done to MacMahon's force compelled him to pull back 150 miles (240 km) to Châlons on the Marne.

Leadership: Bezaine

The Battle of Vionville, 16 August 1870, cut off Bezaine's retreat westwards
Marshal Bezaine, defeated at Spicheren, tried to move his army back across the Moselle at Metz, but baggage wagons got congested in the town with its two bridges, forcing him to turn and fight off a German attack on 14 August, later named the Battle of Borny. An army in retreat can only get away from its pursuers if it is able to check them in a battle and 'break clean' or, alternatively, screen its withdrawal with deception. Bezaine did neither. His divisions were delayed and congested along the road westwards from Metz to Verdun. German cavalry had crossed the Moselle river to the south, and engaged the flank guard of the French, coming close to closing the Verdun road at Vionville altogether. Pausing along the line of retreat, the French were then attacked by two German Corps, the III and X, at Vionville, 8 miles south-west of Metz. The Germans were outnumbered, but cleared the woodland that lay in front of the French, then, in a 15,000-strong infantry attack across open ground, seized a key hill feature. The German infantry suffered heavy casualties from *mitrailleuse* machine guns. The fall of the hill, which had been hastily fortified, was the signal for the withdrawal of the French back towards Metz. Interestingly, a German cavalry charge (the approach of which was concealed in 'dead ground') was successful against a French battery, leading military theorists to the conclusion that cavalry was not an anachronism on the battlefield. Nevertheless, von Bredow's cavalry suffered 380 casualties out of 800.

The Battle of Gravelotte, 18 August 1870, encircled Bezaine at Metz
The Prussians reinforced the troops on the western side of the Moselle. They drew up, 188,332 strong (with 732 guns), facing eastwards. Bezaine, commanding 112,800 men and 520 guns, was in a strong position on heights above a stream valley (the Mance), anchored on the village of Gravelotte and a number of fortified farms in his centre. The Germans thus intended to turn the French right flank, and began

marching northwards to the village of St Privat. However, they also attacked in the centre, suffering huge losses from French troops concealed in woods or protected by trenches. Once again, Steinmetz disobeyed von Moltke who wanted an envelopment of the town of Metz from the north. Despite the confusion in the German attack, Bezaine missed the opportunity for a successful counter-attack and the envelopment of his right continued. The Prussian guards were savaged by Chassepot fire from St Privat, so that they formed a ragged skirmish line about 600 yards from the village, unable to get any further forward. It is estimated that 8,000 were killed or wounded, most of those in a period of only 20 minutes. The arrival of the XII (Saxon) Corps, and especially their artillery, reduced the French garrison. The French decided to withdraw, but a covering force of cavalry was cut down before it had covered 50 yards. As the French pulled out, leaving a few units in the village, the Germans surged in. In the centre, the Germans also recovered and the French retreated back into Metz. It was a key moment in the war, as the morale of Bezaine's army began to fail. Moreover, the French now had one of their armies bottled up in Metz.

Leadership: von Moltke

An attempt to relieve Metz led to the battle of Sedan
To relieve Metz and achieve victory, Napoleon III joined MacMahon and the reconstructed Army of Châlons, intending to march to the Belgian border before turning south to join Bezaine's break-out. Concentred together, the two armies would defeat the Germans in the area south of Sedan. Von Moltke received information on the new threat through the Paris newspapers, and despatched the Third Army and the Army of the Meuse to meet it. The rains descended again, just as they had done at the start of the campaign, the roads were narrow and it was not an easy task to select the right routes for the armies. General Pierre de Failly was attacked at Beaumont and his withdrawal marked the end of Napoleon III's plan to link up with Metz. Instead, MacMahon positioned the Army of Châlons inside Sedan. The marshy valley of the Meuse protected its southern flank, and a pause here would give the tired and demoralised troops a respite. Even on 31 August the German artillery crowned the hills in a semi-circle to the south. MacMahon thought only of sending out a reconnaissance to the east and west, but this gave von Moltke more time to envelop the French completely. Morale was low, even amongst the French officers.

There was little enthusiasm for the imperial cause. Troops marching past Napoleon III had remained ominously silent, and the reservist *Garde Mobile* in Paris, when called on to shout '*Vive l'Empereur*', called back,'*Un, deux, trois, merde!*'

The turning point: the Battle of Sedan

Sedan, 1 September 1870, was a classic German envelopment attack
The battle began prematurely as the 1st Bavarian Corps crossed the Meuse and took the village of Bezailles. In the fighting, French civilians had assisted the French soldiers, which so infuriated the Bavarians that they shot many of the civilians they took prisoner. This would mark a dramatic shift in the war, where civilians increasingly joined the war as guerrillas against the invaders. German artillery now began to pound the French positions around the town. MacMahon was wounded. General Ducrot knew that the Germans were about to surround the French army and he gave orders for an immediate break out to the west. The orders were then countermanded by General Wimpffen who claimed that he was in command. In the confusion, orders were lost, the German shelling increased and at 1300 hours the French 7th Corps collapsed and fled into the shelter of the town. Ducrot realised that the villages of Floing and Calvaire d'Illy had to be held to provide an escape route for the army. It was too late. Troops allocated to Calvaire had failed to arrive at all (they were perhaps diverted to the north), and Floing was in German hands, although Chassepot fire had prevented them getting further forward. The fall of Calvaire threatened to split the French positions in the west and north completely in two. Ducrot's infantry were unable to proceed far against 90 German guns, and even the troops he rallied fell back into the cover of woodland.

Tactics: the cavalry charge at Floing was a desperate attempt to avoid defeat
In front of Floing all the French guns had been silenced, and the infantry had suffered badly. As German infantry began to deploy on the lower slopes of the French position, in front of Floing, Ducrot called on General Margueritte's cavalry to charge through the Germans and break them. As Margueritte went forward to reconnoitre the ground, he was shot in the face and his troopers swore revenge. General Gallifet took personal command and this splendid and courageous force rode over a ridge, straight into the fire of German artillery and breech-loading rifles. The survivors divided north and south of the village. Some managed to break out to the west, others were cut down or rounded up.

Ducrot, desperate, asked Gallifet and those that had made it back to the French lines if they could repeat the manoeuvre. The reply has gone down in history: 'As often as you like, *mon général*, so long as there's one of us left.' The second charge went in and they were cut to pieces. It is said that Gallifet and a handful of troopers were allowed to pass the German infantry who ceased fire and saluted them. It was the end. Units gave up, and the last batteries were silenced. Napoleon III ordered a white flag to fly over the town. They had lost 17,000, the Germans 9,000. More humiliating was the capture of 104,000 French soldiers and the Emperor himself.

The results of Sedan were political as well as military
The fall of Sedan marked the fall of the Second Empire. It was a turning point in the balance of power in Europe, from France to Prussia. An uprising in Paris overthrew the Bonapartists on 4 September. Two weeks later, the Germans arrived on the outskirts of Paris. The reasons for the French failure at Sedan included: poor security about troop movements (which had appeared in the press), insufficient artillery, confusion in the chain of command, the absence of a clear strategy, and low morale amongst the French troops. The opening battles of the war demonstrated that cavalry could not be used in its traditional 'shock effect' role. The superiority of Prussian artillery was also evident. However, the German troops also faced supply problems the further away from the railheads they advanced. There was disharmony between the commanders, particularly the Bavarians and the Prussian chief of staff von Moltke.

The siege of Paris extended the war for several months
Paris, although completely surrounded, held out behind its ring of forts from 19 September to 28 January 1871. Leon Gambetta, the new Republican leader, escaped Paris in a hot air balloon, but the republican government (Government of National Defence) was cut off. There was consideration of a break out, but politically it was felt that the fall of Paris would mean the fall of France. However, the Army of the Loire, as it was termed, was unable to break through the German cordon to relieve the city. General Chanzy was defeated at Le Mans, General Faidherbe was defeated at St Quentin and General Bourbaki failed to relieve Belfort. This force was raised using territorial arrangements and the legislation of 1793, but there was an acute shortage of officers and proper training. Large bodies of men tended to move slowly and were bigger targets for the Prussian gunners. On 14 October

it was decreed that any person, from France or overseas, could serve in the Auxiliary Army, a law which encouraged Garibaldi to join in the war against the Germans. However, the election of officers, supply problems and indiscipline meant the new forces were no match for the trained professionals of the Prussian army. There was initially some confidence that, if the Germans broke through the Parisian forts manned by sailors, then the people would engage in street fighting. A number of sorties from Paris failed to dislodge the besiegers and food supplies began to run down. Revolutionary elements were soon disillusioned with the efforts of the republican government, and the 300,000 *gardes nationales* and volunteer units were unreliable. In the sortie of 19 January they fired on their own side.

The franc-tireurs were guerrillas operating in the provinces
Gambetta urged that, to defeat the Germans (and perhaps rescue French honour for a better bargaining position), all efforts must be made to 'harass' the enemy. This was a call to arms to the whole French people, and a number of small groups, totalling 57,300, sprang up with the intention of waging a guerrilla war. The idea was already there, of course. The Prussians had hanged civilians who had fired on them as they crossed the Moselle as early as 15 August 1870. When Metz surrendered on 27 October 1870, it was even more imperative to launch attacks. Sharpshooters used the cover of rural lanes, but the German response was to hunt them down. If *franc-tireurs* fired from houses, the houses were burnt down. Bismarck told Jules Favre, the republican Minister of the Interior, that they were treating the *franc-tireurs* like murderers. The French people themselves were angered at the indiscipline and behaviour of these freebooters, but some fought well in a defensive action at Châteaudun on 18 October 1870. The republican government also decreed that local authorities support the war effort, and the defence of their territory. Roadblocks, earthworks and volunteers troops were organised. Everywhere the German forces went they were met by ambushes. However, the German response was simply to punish all civilians they had contact with.

Results: the Paris Commune and German unification
When the government at Bordeaux eventually decided to accept peace terms, Parisians objected to a German victory parade through the city they had defended (even though the Germans had entered the outskirts of the city). On 18 March 1871 rioting broke out when local forces refused to surrender their weapons to the 'Bordeaux troops', and they

hanged two generals. Adolphe Thiers withdrew his troops, but the Parisians established their own revolutionary committee called the Commune. With German troops looking on, Gallifet and MacMahon fought through the streets against the revolutionaries between 21 and 28 May 1871. The Parisians shot their hostages, and streets were destroyed by street battles which left a legacy of bitterness for 30 years. The Germans were unified by a declaration in the Palace of Versailles on 18 January 1871. Their army remained in occupation of France until 1873.

Conclusion

The effects of industrialisation were evident in warfare in the 1860s and '70s. Railways had been used for mobilisation and deployment in the wars of German unification. New weapons, manufactured on a large scale, were having a deadly effect on the battlefield. Strasbourg was devastated by an artillery bombardment. By the end of the war of 1870–1, the fighting took on the character of a people's war as *franc-tireurs* ambushed German troops. Nevertheless, von Moltke's brilliant planning and organisation seemed to point to the continuing advantage of the attack and the value of decisive, rapid operations. As a result, all the European powers adopted the organisation of a general staff and began to analyse ways of achieving the efficient mobilisation for a rapid victory.

Tutorial

Progress questions

1. Account for the rapid defeat of Austria in 1866.
2. What was the effect of technology on the war of 1870–71?
3. Why did the French army find itself trapped at Metz and Sedan in 1870?
4. How effective were the *franc-tireurs*?

Seminar discussion

1. Comment on the following: 'von Moltke's skill lay not in his predetermined plans, but in his flexibility and staff work'.
2. How seriously did the European powers take the cavalry's function for providing security and reconnaissance in 1870–71?

Practical assignment

Examine a map of the campaign area. Note that the early battles were fought in the hilly and forested country on the French-German border. Trace the movements of the armies onto a sketch-map to gain a better understanding of why the relief operation for Metz, and then Paris, failed.

Study tips

1. Note that organisation, especially logistics, is as important in determining the outcome of a battle or war as technology.
2. Look back at the Napoleonic era to gain a better understanding of why the French used their cavalry and machine guns in the way they did. Note that the uniforms of the French army were still resonant of the Napoleonic period, such was the faith in its modes of warfare.
3. Notice that guerrilla warfare was not effective against the German occupation, but it represented an outburst of civilian anger. It created a feeling of bitterness not unlike the Peninsular War of 1808–1814.
4. List the key deficiencies of the French army, and the strengths of the German army as a summary of this chapter. Make comparative notes with the American Civil War.

8

Minor Wars: China, Japan, the Muslim World, the Indian States and the Zulus

One minute overview – Non-European modes of warfare offer an interesting contrast to the west and the wars of the wider world remind us that Europeans did not possess a monopoly on developments in warfare. Chinese modes of warfare were archaic, unless they could match the firepower of their opponents. The Japanese decided not to reject Western methods, but to embrace them and they achieved success against China in 1894–5. The Muslim world, which had expanded in previous centuries, found itself on the defensive in South Asia, the Balkans and North Africa. South Asian states were often better armed than their British opponents, but they failed to combine at the crucial time. Exceptional leadership and an aggressive philosophy of attack, even against superior numbers, often gave the British battlefield success. The Zulus achieved a remarkable conquest over other African peoples with their militarised social structure, but they were unable to prevail against modern firearms. Europeans, whilst often outnumbered and outgunned, were able to organise themselves for sustained campaigning overseas when their opponents could not. However, the success of the Western powers was by no means guaranteed and they suffered a number of setbacks.

In this chapter you will learn:

► Chinese modes of warfare
► Japanese modernisation
► the armies of the Muslim world
► the modes of warfare of the Indian states
► the Zulu Mfecane and Cape Frontier Wars

Chinese modes of warfare in the Chinese Wars, 1839–42 and 1859–60

Quality of troops: the Chinese army was a relic of previous eras
The Chinese army, a million strong, still retained a style of warfare

from the medieval period and its army consisted of several elements. During the Chinese Wars, the mounted arm were the Tartar cavalry, known as the Bannermen, who were hereditary soldiers. Some fought on foot, but the majority of the eight divisions or 'eight banners' fought from the saddle. They carried matchlocks and bows, but, despite this obsolescence, they were skilled in their use. Amongst the other infantry weapons, the Chinese chose to use halberds, pikes, spears and stinkpots. The Militia tended to fight from fortresses and some of them manned artillery. Chain mail armour was still worn, and a colourful and imposing livery. The matchlock musketeers gained the respect of the British for their courage. The method of loading was to insert gunpowder and a musket ball, then strike the butt against the ground to charge the weapon. This loading drill was in fact faster than the British or Indian troops and their rate of fire was consequently that much greater. The Chinese angered the British with their ruses of war: around Canton, in 1840, the Chinese poisoned the wells, and they delivered a consignment of poisoned tea via pirates. This tactic backfired, since the pirates sold the tea to Chinese civilians, many of whom died.

The Chinese navy was outclassed by the Royal Navy
A considerable part of the Chinese Wars was fought at sea or in the river estuaries of the Chinese coast. Faced with anchored British frigates, the Chinese used fire rafts, floating them into the British ships. At Canton in 1840 they released no fewer than 18 rafts or old fishing boats, chained together in twos, in a night attack. They failed to damage any of the British ships, although two Royal Navy vessels collided when they tried to get out of the way. Indeed, the flotsam provided the navy with firewood for a month. The main Chinese ship was the war junk, a traditional Chinese vessel armed with a variety of cannon. They were simply outclassed by the Royal Navy. On 3 November 1839, a flotilla of war junks opened fire on the 28-gun frigate *Volage* and a sloop called *Hyacinth*. In a matter of minutes one junk had exploded, three were sunk and several others were taking in water. Overwhelmed by the British firepower, the Chinese used wrecks to block rivers, but these were by passed by skilful sailing. Perhaps the most unexpected form of attack though was the use of rockets, or the deployment of monkeys with fireworks on their backs. There was an expectation that the monkeys would climb into the rigging of the British ships and set fire to them. Chinese tradition placed a great deal of emphasis on scaring the opponent with psychological warfare, but pulling faces, waving flags and banging gongs amused rather than terrified the British forces.

The Chinese War: the British expected the Chinese to come to terms

The Chinese, or Opium, War began in 1839 when Chinese officials tried to close down and destroy the import of opium. Angered by the destruction of British property, the threats to British nationals (by the internment of the traders of Canton) and the blank refusal to trade with Britain, the government supported the local commander Captain Elliot as he took action against the Chinese. After the initial naval engagement at Canton, British and Indian troops were sent to capture the island of Chusan, hoping that this would end the conflict. An eight-minute naval bombardment and musketry from two British divisions compelled the defenders to surrender.

The British possessed superior firepower but there were other problems

However, camped outside the town near malarial swamps, the 3,000 British troops lost 450 dead and as many as one third were unfit for duty. Even food supplies were inadequate. The Cameronians had rations delivered from India in dirty sacks and boxes. Of 900 men, only 110 were fit for duty a month later. With no sign of Chinese willingness to negotiate, the Royal Navy's first iron steamer *Nemesis* bombarded the Bogue Forts at the mouth of the Pearl River on 7 January 1841. One thousand five hundred British troops captured the forts by storming their walls and ditches. Such was the effect of British musketry and naval gunfire that the British lost only 38 men wounded and the Chinese lost between 300 and 400 killed. Attacking the forts and Chinese squadrons along the river in turn, Captain Elliot made his way up to Canton. Major-General Sir Hugh Gough's Indian troops scaled the hills above the city to attack the forts. As 700 men (mainly the 37th Madras Native Infantry) paused before the final one, a huge downpour coincided with a charge by 10,000 Chinese militia. In the rain none of the muskets could be fired and Chinese had the advantage with their long spears. They did not press home their attack, and, as the rain paused, the musketry resumed and both sides pulled back. However, the conclusion of a peace deal at this point only convinced the Chinese that the Europeans couldn't fight on land and that they could be defeated by the Militia.

The Chinese War spread inland

Both sides disowned the temporary truce. The Chinese Emperor Daoguang despatched an 'army of extermination' to Canton, while Captain Elliot, observing the build up of Chinese troops around him, made a preventive strike. The same pattern was repeated: fire rafts and river barricades from the Chinese, naval bombardments and landings by the British. On 21 May1841, 71 war junks were destroyed and 60 shore batteries seized. The Emperor simply refused to accept the loss of Canton, and argued that the Chinese had, in fact, won. Sir Henry Pottinger replaced Elliot in the summer of 1841 with orders to defeat the Chinese. The navy brought its fleet up to 25 warships, 14 steamers and numerous support vessels under the command of Admiral William Parker. Parker set out drilling his gunners to perfection. Gough was the commander of the 10,000 land forces and he was popular. At 62, he had seen active service all over the world and was wounded twice in the Peninsular War. He was personally brave, chivalrous, but spoke a 'soldiers language' in a broad limerick accent. Two thousand British infantry were sent to capture Amoy with its garrison of 9,000 and did so with a loss of two dead and 15 wounded. They then went on to take Chusan (involving an attack on the fort of Tinghai), where Gough was hit in the shoulder. Ningpo fell on 13 October. However, the Emperor's cousin, I-ching, was appointed to defeat the 'barbarians' who were now committed to a land engagement.

Leadership: Chinese miscalculation led to their utter defeat
I-ching was not a military commander, but the director of the Imperial Gardens and Hunting Parks. Nevertheless, he was a meticulous civilian planner. He concentrated 12,000 Bannermen and 33,000 Militia at Soochow, expecting victory. However, the junior officers were all scholars, not soldiers, and there was no organised chain of command. I-ching organised a competition to see which scribe could come up with the best victory proclamation. There were tea parties, feasts and poetry readings. Then the supplies began to run out. The Militia were exhausted by their marches in heavy rain and hungry. In the attack on Ningpo, I-Ching retained 60 per cent of the army as bodyguard units for the general staff. The time for the attack was chosen by an oracle (the Tiger Hour of the Tiger Month or 0300, 10 March 1842) and it began with a hopeless charge of 700 knife-wielding Szechwan Militia. At Chen-Hai, a simultaneous attack failed when the reserve commander failed to commit his troops: he was in an opium-induced stupor. The Chinese sent red booby-trapped boxes down river, but only two unwary sailors opened them and were killed. A Chinese 'marine' commander, ordered to recapture Chusan, sailed his seasick troops about without fighting and sent false reports of his victories. The war then descended into guerrilla activity. Isolated Indian sepoys, caught in brothels and alehouses, were captured and executed. At Chapu, fearing

rape and slaughter, the Chinese garrison slit the throats of their own wives and children, or drowned them in ponds and wells. Unable to explain their defeats, the Manchu troops suspected 'inner allies' and set about murdering 'suspects'. Suicides increased amongst civilians and soldiers.

The Treaty of Nanking, 1842, marked an uneasy peace until 1856
The attempt to seize Chinese sailors sailing in the *Arrow* under a British flag led to a breakdown in Sino-British relations in 1856. Sir John Bowring, Governor of Hong Kong (which had been acquired under the Treaty of Nanking), ordered the destruction of Chinese government buildings in Canton as a punishment. The Chinese responded by destroying European factories in the city. A party of Chinese troops also disguised themselves to get aboard a British steamer and killed the 11 crew before scuttling the vessel. Admiral Seymour retaliated by setting fire to the western suburbs of Canton. Issuing rewards for the deaths of 'red-haired barbarians' in 1857, the Chinese government encouraged the Chinese bakers of Hong Kong to poison the British residents with arsenic; it failed. The war then followed a pattern of small groups of British sailors and marines bombarding then storming forts and flotillas of junks. Large forces were not available because of the mutiny in India, so the war was not fully prosecuted until 1859.

The British were repulsed at Taku Forts in 1859, but defeated China in 1860
On 25 June 1859 a British flotilla under Rear-Admiral Sir James Hope was surprised by concealed heavy guns during a bombardment of the Taku Forts on the Peiho River. The British ships had burst through iron and wood barriers in the river, but the Chinese held their fire until the British ships were close inshore. A joint British and French landing force of 1,000 men then attempted to take the forts, but they became bogged down in thick river mud and raked by gunfire from the ramparts. The following year Lieutenant General Sir James Hope Grant led 11,000 British troops, alongside 6,000 Frenchmen under General Charles Montauban, to take the forts. Major General Sir Robert Napier made a flanking march and repulsed a charge of 4,000 Tartar cavalry. Grant bridged all the creeks leading to the forts and deployed his artillery. After a swift bombardment, an assault was made in the teeth of Chinese gunfire. Ladders were brought to the walls, but the Chinese fought hard at close quarters. Eventually, the fort fell. A series of engagements in the open, such as the battle of Pa-Le-Chiao (September 1860), marked the Anglo-French progress to Peking and

the defeat of the Chinese. The resulting Treaty of Peking was an important shift in the balance of power in the Far East. Russia seized Chinese
territory in the north, and the European powers gradually imposed
'spheres of influence' over the river valleys and coasts. The French occupied Indo-China in 1885 and the British invaded the Chinese colony of
Tibet in 1904. Japan joined the European powers and defeated the
Chinese in a short war in 1894–95, although it was forced to relinquish
Port Arthur by pressure from the Continental powers.

Industrial development: Japanese modernisation

In the early nineteenth century, Japanese military tradition was still
based on a feudal structure. The provincial warlord or *Shogun* was also a
governor. His military forces were essential retainers for the warlord
and a handful of samurai warriors. Strict codes of conduct and fighting
merged in Japanese society. However, after the visit of Commodore
Perry's modern warships of the United States in 1853, and the bombardment and storming of forts at Kagoshima and Shimonsekei by the British navy and the Royal Marines Light Infantry in 1863 (following
attacks on Europeans), the Japanese embarked on a rapid programme
of modernisation. A national army was formed in 1873 and conscription
introduced. In 1875 the Japanese invaded Formosa and engineered a
conflict with Korea in 1876. Lacking natural resources to sustain the
modernisation of the rest of Japan, military, naval and civilian leaders
alike began to look for islands and mainland colonies, but there was
also a desire to sustain national prestige in the light of European
encroachments elsewhere in Asia. The Japanese purchased British ships
and sought to emulate British naval success. However, in copying the
West, the Japanese also tried to retain their traditional martial values.
Officers were expected to carry samurai swords and obey without question. Death by suicide, *hari kari*, was preferred to dishonour. This code
gave the Japanese army a fighting spirit and discipline that enabled
them to defeat larger Chinese forces in the Sino-Japanese War of 1894–5.

The armies of the Muslim world

The quality of troops in the Muslim world was variable
Islam was a sustaining force for the Muslim states, stretching from the
Indian subcontinent to the coast of North Africa, in the face of
European encroachments. For some, the prospect of dying in the right-
eous cause of armed resistance to the infidel, thereby gaining access to

paradise, was irresistible. It gave them reckless courage and fighting spirit. However, there was great variation in the quality of troops.

The First Afghan War, 1838–42, ended inconclusively for the British
The Afghans fought the British in 1838–42, when Lord Auckland feared that the Russians meant to occupy the country close to British India's borders. Although the Persian army with its Russian advisors withdrew after an unsuccessful siege of Heart, British forces marched through Sind, via the Bolan Pass, into Afghanistan. Concentrating two armies at Kandahar, Lieutenant General Sir John Keane attacked the fortress of Ghanzi, not with siege artillery, but by blowing the Kabul Gate with a charge of gunpowder. Kabul fell, but resentment of the new ruler Shah Shuja was only kept at bay by the payment of subsidies. In late 1841 a British brigade returned to India, weakening the small army of occupation. On 2 November, rioting broke out in Kabul against the British presence, but Major General William Elphinstone did not act against the mobs. The political envoy, William Macnaghten, tried to play one Afghan leader off against another, but was murdered. Elphinstone agreed to evacuate Afghanistan from 6 January 1842, but 4,500 troops and 12,000 camp-followers were starved and massacred in their retreat through the snowy passes. A last stand was made by the remnants of the 44th Foot and the Bengal Horse Artillery at Gandamack on 13 January 1842. Initially it was thought that there had been only one survivor, Dr Brydon, who rode as far as the British garrison at Jellalabad. Sir Robert Sale defended this little post for six months until relieved by Major General Sir George Pollock. Pollock advanced on Kabul and relieved the other garrisons that had held out and a number of hostages.

The Afghan army was a mixture of ancient and modern styles
There was no army in the European sense in Afghanistan, but a tribal structure or Jagadir system ensured that chiefs could command the loyalty of followers, especially if they belonged to the same clan. The responsibility for pay and supply fell on the Jagadir commander or *Sirdar*, although, in theory, being in the field for a long period was supposed to mean 'central government' support. In practice this rarely happened. Afghans fought as individuals on foot, often skirmishing using long-barrelled Jezail muskets from behind hard cover. These Jezails outranged the British weapons and volley firing had little effect on Afghans concealed on rocky hillsides. Pollock managed to drive off bodies of Afghans when he secured the high ground around them. The

richer of Afghan society were mounted in the Persian fashion, clad in chain mail and helmets with lances or swords. They were less effective as they were confined to valley floors.

The Persian army in the war of 1856 was unsuccessful
The Persians, having failed to take Heart from the Afghans in 1838, declared that it was formally annexed on 25 October 1856. Negotiations having failed, the British landed a small force that captured the fort at Reshire, and bombarded the port of Bushire. Four thousand five hundred British and Indian troops were attacked on 27 January 1857 by 7,000 Persians who had adopted European tactics. When the 3rd Bombay Cavalry and Poona Horse charged, the Persian infantry formed 'squares'. The squares were broken and the Persians fled, leaving 700 dead on the battlefield. The British lost 10 killed and 62 wounded. This battle, named Koosh-ab, suggests that, in its traditional role of shock action and pursuit, cavalry was still formidable. The Persian troops lacked the discipline and training needed to sustain a square in the face of a determined cavalry attack. Moreover, the Persians had to abandon their positions at Mohamrah and Ahwaz because of the fear of British naval firepower. The Persians had some regular troops, some dressed in Turkish or European fashion, but the irregular forces were either undisciplined cavalry (who were, nevertheless, proficient with their weapons), or the Tuffekdjis infantry. Artillery was mixed, making supply difficult and mountings were poor. One unusual, but ineffective weapon was the *zamburek*, a cannon mounted on a camel saddle that could be fired when the animal lay down. Carrying its own 50 rounds of ammunition, the camel-borne artillery was capable of making vast distances across the central and southern deserts. Leadership, however, was very weak. The Persian officers were eager to talk of their prowess but neglected their troops.

The Ottoman Army in the Crimean War was plagued with internal problems
The Ottoman Army suffered many of the same problems as the Persian, but with the added complication of its multiracial composition. In the Balkans, at the opening of the Crimean War (1854-56), the defenders of Silistria were made up of Turkish regulars, well-armed Egyptians, less well-armed Albanians and irregular cavalry called Bashi-Bazouks. They built ramparts of earth and dug-outs to protect themselves from the Russian bombardment. They raided the Russian trenches, hoping to disrupt the siege operations, but the British advisers to the commander Mustapha Pasha were shocked when irregulars tried to terrify the

Russians with decapitated heads of Russian dead on the ramparts. Severed ears were also sought out as trophies and they delighted in slitting the throats of the wounded. In the area around Kars and Ezerum, the corruption of Turkish officers added to the difficulties of the British commander Colonel William Fenwick Williams. The dead would not be recorded so that their pay could be pocketed. At Kurekdere on 7 August 1855 a force of 40,000 Ottomans was defeated by a Russian force half its size because of a confused chain of command and cowardice by some of the officers. Williams was left to defend the towns with 14,600 men armed with flintlocks and in rags. The 2,000 cavalry were mounted on horses in an equally bad condition. Williams noted that musketry training was almost unknown in the Ottoman army. However, the individual Turkish soldiers were brave and stoical. Many fell dead at their post, exhausted by the fighting. They endured months of siege at Kars until Williams' force was decimated by disease and starvation, and consequently capitulated. In an act reminiscent of warfare a century before, Williams was permitted to march his survivors out of the town with 'military honour', flags flying and drums beating.

Tactics: the French army adapted their tactics in North Africa
The French invasion of Algeria in 1830 was provoked by a diplomatic incident where the Bey of Algiers struck the French Consul in the face with a fly-whisk. However, relations between the two states had been bad since the French refused to pay for supplies to Napoleon's army in Egypt, and the French Bourbon regime was desperate for prestige to support its tottering authority at home. The French army relied on Napoleonic tactics: manoeuvre of large formations around a 'front' marked by outposts. The Algerians, who fought as mounted troops, launched raids on these posts, and slipped away to avoid major battles. General Thomas Bugeaud, who took command of the French forces in Algeria in 1841, adopted the raid or *Razzia* and abandoned many of the fixed posts to reinforce mobile columns. The *Razzias* were designed to wage an economic and psychological war on the Algerian population. Crops were destroyed, and villages razed. There were no capitals to capture so the only alternative was to take grain, herds and flocks which supplied the fighters. French officers enjoyed devolved command. In 1842 General Changarnier launched 200 cavalry with the support of an infantry battalion against a column of Algerian civilians who were protected by 1,500 horsemen. The attack was rapid and resulted in the capture of 2,000 camels and 80,000 other livestock. Similarly, the Duke of Aumale's column was able to attack and defeat the Algerian

leader Abd el-Kader at Smala on 14th May 1843. However, these tactics worked because the French possessed larger numbers of men who could be sustained in the field. A force of 108,000 French opposed a core of 10,000 Algerian horsemen with a supporting irregular force of 40,000. Abd el-Kader surrendered in 1847. Bugeaud also used these tactics in Morocco, defeating the Sultan's army at Isly on 14 August 1844.

The Indian states

Alliances: the Maratha Confederacy was a powerful aggressor to the British
The Marathas, powerful confederate states in central India, had given the British considerable difficulties in the second half of the eighteenth century. An advance on Seringapatam in 1791, a Maratha capital, was abandoned when an epidemic occurred amongst bullocks, the mainstay of their transport system and therefore their supplies. In 1792, and again in 1799, the British were more successful and utilised divisions amongst the Marathas themselves to secure their lines of communication and local numerical superiority. Moreover, rivalry between the states of the Marathas, Mysore and Hyderabad made it easier for the British to deal with each of these opponents in turn. In 1803 eager to extend British control and therefore security in the subcontinent, particularly against the marauding and bandit Pindari horsemen, Sir Arthur Wellesley (later the Duke of Wellington) advanced once more on Seringapatam. He planned the movements meticulously, and deployed 60,000 men across a wide front.

Leadership: Wellesley at the Battle of Assaye, 1803
At Assaye, 23 September 1803, Wellesley achieved his aim of a decisive victory. With 4,500 men, 17 guns and 5,000 unreliable Indian cavalry, he took on and defeated a force of 30,000 cavalry, 10,000 infantry (directed by French officers) and 100 guns. The victory was all the more remarkable in that Wellesley went on to the attack, and much of the fighting was a confused hand-to-hand struggle as the British infantry stormed straight into the Maratha artillery. The bayonet charge had given the British troops a psychological advantage too, helping them to overcome losses of 25 per cent to their force. It is interesting that, in this same period, Napoleon's battles receive so much attention, when Wellesley faced far greater odds and still won. His belief was that victory in India could only be secured by rapid movement and taking the offensive. At Argaon, 29 November 1803, Maratha artillery repulsed the first British attack, but Wellesley attacked again, more

closely supported by light cannon. Although he frequently lacked intelligence on the movements of his opponents, he retained the initiative. The Marathas possessed well-trained and mounted artillery, but Dowlutt Rao was forced to accept peace in December 1803. Lack of funds and confusion in the chain of command had not helped his army in the latter stages of the campaign.

The British used horse artillery successfully in the operations of General Lake
General Gerard Lake, Wellseley's commander operating independently in the north, was also successful against the Marathas at Dehli, 11 September 1803, Laswari, 1st November 1803 and at Farruckhabad on 17 November 1804. Since 1793 the British army had used horse artillery and Lake benefited from the introduction (in 1800) of a brigade of horse artillery in the Bengal army of the East India Company in his operations against Maratha cavalry. However, shortages of artillery cost Lake a battle at Bharatpur in 1805. The victor, the Maharaja of Indore, was forced to surrender when he was outmanoeuvred and driven out of his own territory in 1806.

Tactics: the Indian armies adopted European techniques
In the eighteenth century French officers had been willing to assist Indian rulers to adapt to the western modes of warfare in order to defeat the British or their Indian rivals. The Nizam of Hyderabad, Tipu Sultan of Mysore and Marathas all adopted European formations, artillery and weapons. French engineers also helped design and upgrade fortresses, such as the one at Seringapatam. At the same time, the British recruited local soldiers, or Sepoys (a corruption of the Persian Sipahis). The Army of the East India Company was dominated by Indian soldiers. They were dressed and equipped in a largely European fashion, and frequently drawn from castes with a military tradition. As the demands on the army grew, so it developed in size. In 1763 it had been 18,200 strong, but in 1805 it had reached 154,000. The British used Indian troops in Mauritius (1810), and the East Indies (1810). There were problems in trying to defeat the guerrilla forces of Ceylon's kingdom of Kandy, partly the result of logistical problems, disease and the inhospitable climate. However, Ceylon was finally conquered in 1815 by the concentration of independent columns. At Vellore the interference with Indian traditions and ornamentation led to a Mutiny in 1806. The murder of British soldiers in a hospital provoked the fury of the 69th Foot. Sir Rollo Gillespie of the 19th Light Dragoons joined the British infantry who were hard pressed on the

ramparts of the town's fort. They cleared the walls and blew in a defended gate before setting on the mutineers at close quarters. It had shown that there were limits to the employment of Indians in British service.

Quality of troops: both sides had fighting spirit in the war in Nepal, 1814–16
The expansion of the Kingdom of Nepal had begun in the 1760s, but incursions into East India Company territory provoked a British expeditionary force to enter Nepal in four columns in November 1814. The mountainous terrain proved a greater obstacle to movement than expected. The Gurkhas often fought from hill forts and stockades, such as Kalunga. British attacks were repulsed, but the Gurkhas were impressed by the British care of their wounded and the British were equally in awe of the courage of the hill men. The Gurkhas' preferred weapon was the *kukri* knife, but a charge at Makwanpur, 28 February 1816, was beaten off with heavy casualties. As the British neared Katmandu, the Nepalese sued for peace. However, impressed by the prowess of the British, especially in bayonet fighting, and encouraged by the anglophile monarch Jung Behadur, the Gurkhas joined the British army and the East India Company's army, marking the beginning of decades of loyal service.

Strategy: offensive action produced victory in the Third Maratha War
Plagued by the Pindari horsemen in the central plains of India, the British Governor General, the Earl of Moira, formed two armies, the Grand Army and the Army of the Deccan. His aim was to crush the bandits who roamed in forces of 10–12,000, plundering to supply themselves. Whilst the Pindaris were easily crushed or rounded up, the Maratha states resented the British interference and declared war in November 1817. Colonel C. B. Burr, with a small garrison at Poona (2,000), routed the Peshwa Baji Rao II and his 18,000 cavalry, 8,000 infantry and 14 guns on 5 November 1817. At Nagpore, Lieutenant Colonel H. S. Scott and 1,300 Indian sepoys successfully held off the 18,000-strong forces of the Bonsla Raja until relieved by the Army of the Deccan. At Corygaum 900 British and Indian troops under Captain Staunton held off the Peshwa, who had recovered, on 1 January 1818, although they suffered heavy casualties. The Peshwa's army broke up and dispersed as a British column arrived to attack them. Finally, the army of Indore, mustering 30,000 horse, 5,000 infantry and 100 guns, faced the British Army of the Deccan in open battle at Mahidpur (23 December 1817). General Sir Thomas Hislop

commanded only 5,500 men but, to conceal the disparity of numbers, he attacked as soon as he made contact with the Marathas. The Maratha horse fled but the infantry and the gunners fell where they stood. Once again, a bayonet charge by the British and Indian infantry had decided the day, with losses of 800.

Sind was annexed by rapid manoeuvre against great odds in 1843
Raiding by Baluchis threatened the security of the Indian border satellite state, Sind, and the possibility of large Baluchi forces assembling after an attack on a British Residency, prompted Sir Charles Napier to attack the Baluchi *amirs* with only 2,800 men. The armies met at Miani on 17 February, the Baluchis discharging matchlocks and pistols before charging home. The British received them with musketry and then bayonets at close quarters. The 9th Bengal and Scinde Horse turned the Baluchi flank and their men began to stream away. Many of the chiefs surrendered but Napier continued his advance to Dubba, where his 5,000-strong army charged 20,000 Baluchis who had entrenched their line on 24 March 1843. The shock effect of Napier's attack worked, and in clearing the enemy he lost only 265 men (most of them from the British 22nd Foot who were expected to lead the Indian regiments by example). The Baluchis resorted to guerrilla tactics from their hill villages. Napier took men of the 13th and the 39th Foot, mounted them on camels and set off in pursuit of the guerrillas, but sporadic fighting continued until 1847.

Leadership: Gough's attacks were costly in Gwalior and the First Sikh War
In the war against Gwalior in December 1843 Sir Hugh Gough's small force attacked, head-on, as soon as it made contact with 17,000 Marathas at Maharajapore. These troops were all European trained and entrenched, and Gough succeeded in capturing 56 guns with the loss of 797 men on 29 December. At Punniar a second British column attacked a force of 12,000 on the same day, with the same result. The defeats were enough to convince the last Maratha state to sue for peace.

The Sikh War: Moodkee, 18 December 1845, was another costly victory
When an old ally of the British, Ranjit Singh, died in 1839, more ambitious leaders, Tej and Lal Singh, decided to take advantage of the British setbacks in Afghanistan to assert their power over the north-west of India. On 11 December 1845, the Khalsa (Sikh army) crossed the Sutlej into British territory. Sikhs did not have a nation state, being followers of a religion, but they inhabited the Punjab, or 'Land of Five

Rivers'. The Khalsa was the most formidable of all the 'native' armies of the subcontinent with strong military traditions in its society, but there were internal divisions in the army, and some doubted the wisdom of the invasion. Gough, marching to intercept the invasion, put little faith in reconnaissance and preferred to go straight into a frontal attack, whatever the odds. His 12,000 men were tired after a long march when they were surprised by the arrival of the Khalsa at Moodkee. Gough's cavalry drove off the Sikh irregular horse on the flanks, but he sent the infantry straight ahead into the fire of Sikh artillery. He suffered 800 casualties but took several guns and won the field by nightfall.

Quality of troops

The Sikh War: British troops demonstrated their tenacity in the latter stages

On 21 December Gough pushed forward and encountered an entrenched Sikh army, between 35,000 and 50,000 strong, at Feroze-shah. Bringing up his reserves, Gough increased his strength to 18,000 but attacked the trenches and guns frontally. In the darkness a portion of the trenches had been taken, but it was decided to wait until daylight. The next day Gough renewed the attack and cleared the position, only to be confronted by another Sikh army under Tej Singh. However, not knowing how exhausted the British were, or how short of ammunition, Tej Singh marched his forces away. Whilst he waited for reinforcements, the casualties having been regarded as unnecessarily high, Gough despatched a force under Sir Harry Smith to protect his line of commu-nications. Smith encountered a force twice the size of his own, entrenched at Aliwal. Smith attacked and the 16th Lancers made a cavalry charge on the right flank, which broke through the Sikh lines. Unable to flee because of the river Sutlej at their backs, the Sikhs were routed and lost all their artillery. Finally, Gough attacked the Sikh bridgehead head-on at Sobraon (February 1846) even though the 35,000 defenders were protected by trenches and 67 guns. Again suffer-ing heavy casualties (2,383 killed and wounded), Gough's men carried the position and the Sikhs fled, many drowning in the river as they tried to escape. Lahore was captured within a few days and the war was brought to a close.

The Second Sikh War, 1848–49: Sikh troops were courageous and skilful

Rebellion against British influence sparked the beginning of the Second Sikh War, and attempts to use loyal Sikh troops to suppress an uprising at Multan in the opening stages failed. Gough went on to the offensive at Chillianwalla on 13 January 1849, attacking frontally through jungle and over broken ground. With over 2,000 casualties, the British cleared the Sikh positions, but a retirement to reorganise gave the Sikhs the chance to recover some of their guns. The Sikhs fell back, reinforced with Afghan cavalry to a strength of 60,000. The British, also reinforced, could muster 24,000. At the battle of Gujerat the British artillery for once got the upper hand and almost silenced the Sikh guns. Cavalry drove in both flanks and the infantry slogged away at the centre, achieving a complete victory at a light cost (800 killed and wounded). The battle was a turning point. The Punjab, the last obstacle to British control of the subcontinent, was annexed. The war had shown that, with European training and weapons, Asian states could conduct operations that seriously threatened the British. The artillery was the most formidable arm of the Khalsa: 11,000 of its 71,000 regular troops were gunners. Moreover, Sikh artillery fired 'prepared rounds', ball and propellant in one case, which enabled them to fire more rapidly than the British. Khalsa infantry battalions were organised and drilled along French lines, and wore uniforms copied from the British, except for their own distinctive headdress. The only exceptions were the socially élite irregular cavalry and the religious zealots or Akhalis who fought half-naked on foot with swords and matchlocks.

The Indian Mutiny, 1857–58

The Indian Mutiny, an uprising of much of the Army of Bengal abetted by civilians and opportunists, required the largest deployment of British troops between the Crimean War and the South African War of 1899–1902. In this war the British suffered heavily from the effects of disease and climate, the majority of the fighting occurring at the height of the hot season. Moreover, the British were frequently outnumbered and outgunned, their artillery often having fallen into the hands of the mutineers. However, relatively small forces, assisted by the loyal Indian troops of the Bengal and Madras presidencies, as well as Gurkhas and allied princely states, defeated less well-organised mutineers.

The early stages of the Mutiny were marked by atrocities
Many British regiments were in the Crimea, in China, or in occupation of the Punjab when Sepoys mutinied against the introduction of a new cartridge at Meerut on 10th May 1857. The new cartridge for the Enfield rifle was rumoured to be coated in pig and cow fat and, as the end had to be bitten off to load the weapon, the result would be ritual defilement of Hindus and Muslims. This potent issue was really only

the spark in a much deeper problem of relations between the officers and their men and suspicions about reforms. However, the first rebellious regiments murdered their officers and set fire to buildings. British women were also killed in the mêlée. This set the tone for the rest of the conflict, as British troops were driven by a desire for revenge. In Delhi, to which the mutineers flocked as the symbol of old Mughal authority, British men and women were killed. The massacre of the garrison at Cawnpore, which had capitulated after a one-sided siege, was notorious because men had been shot down as they boarded boats and surviving women and children were butchered, their bodies being thrown down a well. Lucknow was besieged, the Residency being held despite fierce bombardments, mining and sniping. Sir Henry Lawrence, who organised the defence, inspired confidence in all his garrison of 1,720 men as well as the 1,280 non-combatants even though he was wounded. When Lawrence died of his wounds, his place was taken by Colonel John Inglis.

The relief of Cawnpore and Lucknow were temporary successes
The survival and relief of the Lucknow garrison was regarded as a symbol of the survival of the prestige of the British Empire. Almost all of the defenders felt that there were high expectations of their behaviour. Sir Henry Havelock assembled a relief force for Cawnpore which left Allahabad on 7 July 1857. They fought three battles at Fatehpur (12 July), Aong (15 July) and Cawnpore (16 July), and marched 126 miles in incredible heat, only to find the grisly evidence of the massacres. The British reluctance to take prisoners in light of the atrocities made the mutineers fight with renewed tenacity. Havelock tried to break through to Lucknow but, despite victory at Bithur (16 August), he was twice forced to turn back. Setting out for a third time on 21 September, Havelock fought his way to the besieged garrison at the Residency, losing 535 men of his 2,500-strong force. However, Havelock was unable to break out.

Successful operations on the Delhi Ridge: the turning point of the Mutiny
British troops and loyal Indian units trickled through and reinforced a small besieging force on the ridge outside Delhi. At times, this group was so heavily engaged in beating off mutineers from Delhi that it seemed that they were the ones under siege. Artillery fire, raids by mounted mutineers, disease and heat killed or maimed many of them. Brigadier John Nicholson, the charismatic frontier commander, arrived and immediately put new heart into the attack. Breaches were made in

the walls of the city and a daring band of seven men blew in the Kashmir Gate whilst under point blank fire. The besieging force stormed in, though greatly outnumbered, and spent six days fighting through the streets. Delhi fell and William Hodson, a commander of an irregular cavalry force, captured (almost single-handedly) the last Mughal emperor, Bahadur Shah. The fall of Delhi was a turning point in that it released troops for other operations and broke the symbolic heart of the rebellion.

Campbell's careful planning and methodical approach brought victory in Oudh
Agra was recaptured and the new commander-in-chief, Sir Colin Campbell, arrived and reorganised supply and transport before advancing on Lucknow. He stormed the rebel strongpoint at Sikander Bagh and his troops gave no quarter in revenge for Cawnpore. Lucknow's garrison was then relieved and evacuated, but Havelock died from dysentery on 24 November 1857. A small British force was defeated in front of Cawnpore by Tantia Topi in November, but Campbell recovered the town with a victory on 6 December. He then advanced again on Lucknow, more slowly, and meticulously laid siege to the rebel strongholds which all fell by 16 March 1858. The rebels in Oudh turned to guerrilla warfare, but they were unable to sustain their campaign for long.

There were mopping operations in central India
Isolated rebellions in central India, some led by the famous Rani of Jhansi, were countered by the 'flying columns' of Major General Sir Hugh Rose. Janhsi was eventually besieged and Rose defeated Tantia Topi's relief force on 1 April 1858, and defeated his forces again in pursuit at Kunch (1 May) and Kalpi (22 May). Rose marched rapidly to defeat the army of Gwalior, which had joined Tantia Topi, and the Rani was killed on 17 June at Kotah-ki-serai. The Tantia Topi was eventually captured on 7 April 1859 and hanged. The Mutiny had been crushed.

The Zulu Mfecane and Cape Frontier Wars

Quality of troops: the Zulus inflicted the Mfecane on south-eastern Africa
Under King Dinigiswayo in the early nineteenth century the Nguni peoples reorganised their warrior units along age lines, and gave them distinctive regimental identification. Young men were placed under royal households, located at strategic points throughout the kingdom. This practice helped foster an identity beyond the local clan and gave

the king more centralised authority. Loyalty to the king was inculcated as part of the regimental *esprit de corps*. The warriors were physically fit and had an intimate knowledge of their own lands through hunting. They could cover 50 miles in one day, and they moved at a jog trot rather than a walk. They were trained to fight in impis, an army grouping, but could disperse into smaller units. Iron discipline was enforced. Under Shaka, Dinigiswayo's successor from 1816, a standing army was established with warriors living in military settlements, training and drilling constantly. His own clan of Zulu gradually absorbed all the peoples of the Nguni, and, by 1828, all the territories between the Drakensberg mountains and the Indian Ocean. Shaka's campaign of expansion, driven by population growth, droughts and land hunger, was known as the Mfecane, or 'crushing', because of its ruthless suppression of neighbouring peoples and the flight of hundreds of thousands of other Africans.

Technology: the Battle of Blood River, 1838, illustrated the power of firearms

Shaka was assassinated by his followers when his rule became autocratic and warfare drained the resources of the Zulu state, but the Zulu military state survived. When Afrikaner settlers arrived from the Cape in the Great Trek, they contested the lands of the Zulus. Attempting to negotiate land, the Afrikaner leader, Piet Retief, was murdered. Isolated homesteaders were massacred and 600 were killed at Weenan. The most important engagement was the battle of Blood River on 16 December 1838, where settlers under the leadership of Andreas Pretorius formed a *laager* of wagons. In their efforts to get close enough to the Boers to use their short stabbing spears, the assegais, the impi was hemmed in between two banks along the river bed. The Boers poured fire into the attackers and inflicted perhaps as many as 3,000 casualties for no losses. The battle was a turning point for South Africa, as the Boers (farmers) established two republics in the interior. However, they were ousted by the British from Natal in 1846 (lands which had been cleared of inhabitants by the Mfecane). What is curious is that the Zulus, unlike many other Africans who had come into contact with European firearms, did not adopt muskets and rifles as their preferred weapon. It is thought that thousands of rifles made their way into Zululand, but the Zulus retained their faith in the power of the assegai and close-quarter battle, despite the defeat at Blood River.

The Cape Frontier Wars were protracted

As white settlers arrived in the Cape Colony, the indigenous Xhosa peoples fought a series of wars known at the time as the Kaffir Wars (derived from the Arabic for unbeliever). The British, who also fought the Dutch pioneers of the colony in the Napoleonic Wars, often employed locally-raised African and settler forces to augment small garrisons of regular troops. In the Fourth and Fifth Cape Frontier Wars (1811–12, 1817–19), the Xhosa were driven back to the Great Fish River. The Xhosa and the Basutos favoured ambushes and made extensive use of acquired firearms, but they were often defeated by mounted riflemen. These men, including the Cape Mounted Rifles (officially formed in 1827), could move rapidly across the vast distances of southern Africa and fight either as dismounted troops or from the saddle. They were made up of both white and black troopers. Along the frontier a variety of forts or defended posts sprang up, protected by grenade-dischargers, swivel guns or any available ordnance. These posts acted as ideal supply bases to keep the mounted units in the field. The Boers, who clashed with the British, were defeated at Bloomplaats in 1848, but they were more effective against the Africans. Their favoured tactic was to ride ahead of the tribal force, dismount and fire, then remount to ride to a safe distance before repeating the manoeuvre. The Xhosa themselves initially relied on throwing javelins, each soldier carrying seven and moving in organised units but, armed with firearms, they stood their ground in ambushes or concentrated on attacking supply columns.

Conclusion

Although colonial wars are often studied together, regardless of period, it is clear that Europeans did not always possess all the advantages on the battlefield. Their weapons were not always superior. For example, the Afghan Jezails outranged the British muskets in 1839–42. In the Indian Mutiny, the sepoys often had more artillery. The Indian gunners, like other arms, were trained by the British and were highly skilled. In many Asian and African campaigns the Europeans were usually heavily outnumbered. The Europeans pressed home their attacks with determination and sought a complete victory, often with permanent occupation. This differed from Asian and African ideas of military objectives, where the aim was to compel the opponent to seek terms. British troops were also prepared to take heavy casualties, their discipline, motivation and training overcoming the instinctive desire for self-preservation. Europeans were also well organised and able to sustain armies in the field permanently. Their sea power gave them the chance to reinforce and resupply forces thousands of miles from their homelands, and imperial colonies developed robust defences of their own.

Tutorial

Progress questions
1. Why were Chinese methods of warfare so ineffective against the British in the mid-nineteenth century?
2. How successfully did non-European states adapt to European modes of warfare?
3. To what extent did British and French forces adopt African or Asian modes of warfare in the period 1830–1858?
4. What importance can be attached to fighting spirit, and the willingness to take the offensive against overwhelming odds, in explaining British and French success in the wider world?

Seminar discussion
1. What is the importance of technology in explaining the success of British and French forces in wars across the world between 1830 and 1860?
2. What were the advantages and disadvantages of employing Africans and Asians in European armies?

Practical assignment
Write an essay accounting for the successes and failures of British and European armies in the wider world between 1814 and 1859. Limit your essay to 1,500 words.

Study tips
1. Note how the Sikh Wars and Indian Mutiny are examples of the similar forces at war, which means we have to seek explanations for their outcomes which are not based on technology or organisation.
2. Notice how failure to modernise affected the Chinese and some Muslim States, but do not assume that modernisation guaranteed success. Look at the failures of Europeans and the Indian states that adopted European modes of war.
3. Be aware that facing the climate and terrain of colonial wars was as important as facing an opponent.

9

Minor Wars: Colonial Wars in Africa, America and Asia, 1873–1899

One minute overview – The Europeans and the United States spent much of the last third of the nineteenth century fighting non-Europeans in a series of colonial wars. These episodes provide a useful insight into changes in warfare or, indeed, regression in tactics, because Western powers faced a variety of terrains and enemies. Many have assumed that technological superiority made Western success a foregone conclusion, but there were a number of setbacks where all the other factors of warfare were evident, such as leadership, concentration of force, surprise and tactical skill. Nevertheless, the technology gap was widening. Machine guns and rifled artillery appeared on colonial battlefields and caused heavy casualties where non-European powers failed to adapt. However, guerrilla forces were able to harass conventional forces. The Europeans responded by destroying the fabric of property and agriculture that could support guerrillas, such as villages, livestock and crops.

In this chapter you will learn:

► how Wolseley's logistical planning ensured the success of British colonial campaigns
► how the United States and Russia opened up their hinterlands with military force
► how the British adapted militarily to opponents in Africa and Asia
► how Samori defended central West Africa against French incursions
► the contrast between the battle of Adowa and Omdurman as examples of firepower

Wolseley's campaigns: the importance of logistics

Wolseley prepared carefully for the Ashanti Campaign, 1873–74
Sir Garnet Wolseley earned a reputation for dashing, quick victories from his Red River Campaign in Canada in 1870. He manoeuvred so

successfully that no major engagement was needed against rebellious
Indians. In 1873 he was selected to lead a punitive campaign against
the aggressive and hitherto undefeated Ashanti (Asante) of the West
African coast. Wolseley was meticulous in his planning, creating a
national catchphrase: 'all Sir Garnet', meaning well planned and ready.
He was called 'Britain's only general', because of his reputation for courage and success (he had been wounded several times in his battles as a
young officer in Burma and the Crimea). In the Ashanti campaign,
each of the 2,200 soldiers was given quinine to guard against malaria,
light cotton clothing (designed by Wolseley) instead of traditional wool
serge uniforms, and a pocket book of field discipline. Stores and equipment were carefully assembled and the force advanced through thick
undergrowth in a skirmish line, firing into the bush when Ashanti
warriors drew near. The Ashanti themselves were well armed but
tended to saw off the barrels of their weapons to make them easier to
carry. They used fire to make a shock effect, rather than to inflict
casualties, and they usually fired from the hip. Traditional weapons
were also used. Wolseley took the Ashanti capital, Kumasi, and
destroyed it, carefully withdrawing when terms of surrender were
extracted from the chieftain, Kofi Karikari. The success of this operation earned Wolseley public acclaim and assisted in his promotion. It
was in stark contrast to the problems the British army had faced in the
Crimea.

The wars of imperial expansion in America

The Indian Wars in the United States were a struggle for territory
Land hunger, population growth and prospectors drove forward the
frontiers of the United States. In the early nineteenth century there had
already been a series of wars across the south, but the discovery of gold
in California marked the beginning of a struggle for land. At first, the
Americans had an impossible task. The land frontier extended 6,000
miles and the army was only 16,000 strong in 1849. Even armed with
Minié-firing rifles the infantry, supported by howitzers and cavalry,
could not hope to control or defeat 75,000 Plains Indians, nor the
290,000 Native Americans who lived beyond. Indian tribes, however,
were frequently engaged in war with each other. They were dependent
on the annual migrations of vast herds of buffalo for their food supply
and they were outgunned, if not outnumbered. They also had different
modes of fighting. The Apaches of the southwest generally fought on

foot in the hills and valleys, in a guerrilla style. The Sioux (numbering only about 4,000 braves) and the Comanches were superb horsemen. Their allies were the Cheyennes, Arapaho and Kiowas. They were opposed by the Crow, the Pawnee and the Shoshones. A number of other tribes were devastated by disease, or adopted Western culture and posed no threat to the US army or the Plains Indians. There were frequent skirmishes across the region between the 1820s and the 1880s.

The nature of the Indian Wars was marked by bitterness and atrocities
The US army sought to protect the main arteries that were followed by settlers with forts. These also acted as bases for cavalry patrols deep into hostile territory. The army spent much of the early nineteenth century in a police role, intervening occasionally in disputes over land and livestock, and were virtually withdrawn altogether during the Civil War. The wave of settlers encroached on Indian lands even where boundaries were agreed, and the construction of the transcontinental railroad in the 1860s split the migration routes of the buffalo in half. By the mid-70s, the herds were in decline. However, several tribes, including the Sioux, agreed to a treaty over land, in return for the safe passage of settlers in 1851; thus the army secured its objectives by diplomatic means. Nevertheless, successive breaches of the agreements led to a number of wars, such as the Rogue River War (1855–6), the Cour d'Alene War (1858), the Wichita Expedition (1858) or the Paiute War (1860). The bitterness that ensued encouraged the practice of murder, mutilation and the established tradition of scalping by Indians. The capture or killing of women and children drove the whites to equal acts of savagery. The worst was perhaps the Battle of Sand Creek, 29 November 1864, where Colonel John Chivington, seeking revenge for the murder of miners and settlers, killed Indian men, women and children (who thought they were under government protection).

The War of 1876 was caused by a legacy of bitterness
In 1865 the US army was able to reoccupy abandoned forts and posts. They were better armed than before and more mobile cavalry detachments (usually fighting dismounted) replaced the less mobile infantry. In the decade after the civil war there were some 200 separate skirmishes or battles. In 1868 Red Cloud of the Sioux signed the Fort Laramie Treaty and secured exclusive control of the Black Powder country and the Black Hills of Dakota. However, many in the army felt that the concessions had been too great, particularly as the Fetterman Massacre, the ambush and annihilation of 81 cavalrymen (21 Decem-

ber 1866), had not been avenged. In 1874 gold was discovered in the Black Hills, and as prospectors poured into Sioux territory the younger warrior leaders led raids against the whites. Offers to purchase the land were rejected and demands that Indians move onto reservations were ignored. The army sent three converging columns into Sioux territory, preceded by a reconnaissance force under Lieutenant Colonel George Armstrong Custer.

Custer's Last Stand, 25 June 1876, was an exceptional defeat
Custer failed to wait for the arrival of the main bodies of the army, characteristically hoping to win any glory for himself. He fatally divided his regiment, the 7th Cavalry, into four columns. Major Reno was ordered to follow the Little Big Horn river and attack the Indian camp, Captain Benteen was ordered to patrol to the southwest, while Custer took two columns in a flanking ride to the north. Reno was charged by a mass of Indian horsemen and was compelled to fall back, first to a small copse and then to a hill above the river. Custer, finding the main Indian camp where all the branches of the Sioux had concentrated, soon found himself charged by the main body of the Indian cavalry. As Lieutenant J. Calhoun's two troops were completely overwhelmed, the trail of bodies towards the summit of a hill suggests Custer's men dismounted and tried to make a fighting withdrawal to a commanding position. But the warrior leader Gall had made an attack with only a part of the Sioux force. Before Custer could reach the summit, he was overwhelmed by a flank attack by Crazy Horse. The entire column was wiped out. Part of the reason for the disaster was Custer's overconfidence and lack of sufficient reconnaissance. However, the Indians were in fact better armed. Alongside their traditional close-quarter weapons, – clubs, spears and tomahawks – they carried Winchester repeating rifles. Custer's command carried the single-shot Springfield carbine, with twenty rounds of ammunition but no sabres for close-quarter battle. They lost 262 dead and 59 wounded, 7 fatally.

The demise of the Indian tribes was perhaps inevitable
The demand for revenge after Little Big Horn led to a series of skirmishes, attacks on tribal villages and, harried through a harsh winter, the erosion of Sioux warrior numbers through attrition. New forts controlled Sioux and Cheyenne territory. Gradually the Sioux gave up and accepted the reservations set aside for them. Sitting Bull, the mastermind of the 1876 concentration, finally surrendered in 1881, having fled to Canada. In the south the Apache leader Geronimo was

also forced to capitulate in 1886. In 1890, many Indians adopted the cult of the Ghost Dance, where Ghost shirts were supposed to give protection against white men's bullets and the world could be renewed through the annihilation of the whites. Attempting to contain the uprising, the army tried to arrest the leaders and a skirmish developed at Wounded Knee. Suspecting treachery, the army responded to an ambush at close quarters with volleys of rifle and machine-gun fire, killing 150 (including women caught in the crossfire) for a loss of 25. It was the last gasp of the Indian Wars.

The wars of imperial expansion in Russia

The Russian annexation of Central Asia began with the disaster of 1839–40
General Perovsky's attempt to capture the Khanate of Khiva in 1839 failed even before his 5,200-strong army reached the city. Security was maintained by the diplomatic bluff that his troops were an escort to a 'scientific mission' to the Aral Sea, but the British, chief rivals for influence over the khanate, knew of the expedition three months before it left its base at Orenburg. Perovsky calculated that travelling in the winter would avoid the heat of the desert and provide fresh water supplies for the horses. However, terrible weather conditions killed off the 10,000 camels and turned his troops into frostbitten fugitives and they staggered back along their 1,000-mile invasion route. Snow buried the fodder and fuel and obliterated the route. The cold prevented basic hygiene from being maintained and disease took its toll. The 4,500 survivors didn't return to their base until the following May, suffering from scurvy and snow-blindness.

The Russians found it hard to win the war in the Caucasus
Russian attempts to secure the range of mountains between the Caspian and the Black Seas, ostensibly to create a defendable southern frontier, can be traced back to the reign of Peter the Great in the eighteenth century. Russia defeated the Persians in the war of 1827–8, and General Paskiewich drove the Turks out of the southern Caucasus in 1829. However, Circassian tribesmen conducted an effective guerrilla war from the mountains and valleys of the west, and Daghestanis fought in the unconquered portion of the east. In 1836 the veteran of the Greek War of Independence, David Urquart, supplied the guerrillas with weapons and ammunition as well as moral support. The main Russian shock arm, the Cossack cavalry, were ineffective against the Circassian

horsemen who were better armed. The guerrillas had an intimate knowledge of the terrain. The Russians then despatched columns of infantry with artillery support, destroying crops and villages along their line of advance. The Circassian cavalry were unable to break the Russian squares that were formed, and so they retreated into the mountains, choosing to ambush. However, they were vulnerable to artillery fire unless they remained in small and dispersed formations. The Daghestani leader, Imam Shamyl, was able to sustain his campaign in a similar way for thirty years, whilst he kept to the mountains and valleys. Nevertheless, he was unable to capitalise on the Russian commitment to the Crimean War through lack of troops and his forces were overwhelmed at Vedeno in 1859. Shamyl was at large for months until captured. He died at Mecca, revered for his *jihad* (holy war).

The fall of the central Asian Khanates was achieved with small forces
In the 1860s, with the Caucasus finally subdued, the Russians began to encroach on the central Asian khanates. Chimkent fell in 1864, Tashkent in 1865 and Samarkand in 1868: all to Major General Cherniaev, the 'Lion of Tashkent'. Whilst frequently outnumbered, the Russians possessed better field artillery and often made appeals to the elders and merchants of the city-states before their attacks, finding allies amongst the commercially minded élites. The khanates themselves were bitterly divided, just at the point of the Russian advance. At Tashkent, which could muster up to 10,000 men but had a garrison of 30,000, Cherniaev attacked with just 1,900 and 12 guns. A storming had the advantage of seizing the initiative, particularly when no siege could be sustained and a withdrawal would be a humiliation. The moral effect was dramatic: 39 Cossacks charged and routed 5,000 Tashkent cavalry. Fires kept the defenders at bay at night, and the foothold gained in the city was extended at daybreak on 16 June 1865, forcing a capitulation. To win over the hearts and minds of the population, taxation was suspended for a year and conscription abandoned. Bokhara's cavalry collapsed after a demonstration on the Syr Daria when shells hit their city of Samarkand. Whilst General Kaufman pursued the Bokharan army 100 miles deeper inside their territory, a second Bokharan force descended on the small garrison left at Samarkand. Retreating to the citadel, the Russians determined to sell their lives dearly, but Kaufman rode back and arrived in time to save them with his army of 3,000 men. Kaufman then attacked the territory of Yakub Beg, Kashgaria, on the Chinese border and defeated a force twice their number on 25 June at Kuldja.

The war against the Turcomans was the most serious of Central Asia
With the fall of Khiva in 1873, the only remaining force in the region
was the Turcoman population. These nomads lived by the traditions of
raiding, often providing slaves to the city states, or plundering caravans.
They were so effective that areas of northern Persia and Afghanistan
had been denuded of settled populations altogether. Swooping from the
desert, they managed to evade battle but checked a Russian force under
General Lomakin at Geok Tepe on 9 September 1879, driving them
into the desert. The flamboyant Russian commander Skobelev, 'the
Garibaldi of the Pan-Slavs', counter-attacked the Turcoman fortress at
Geok Tepe in January 1881. He besieged it with 7,000 infantrymen and
60 guns. However, his artillery made little impression on the deep mud
walls, designed by a Turcoman who had studied Russian fortifications.
On 24 January, at night, two tons of explosive were detonated beneath
the walls and an infantry assault went in. After a fierce hand-to-hand
struggle the 10,000 defending troops and the 40,000 civilians began to
retreat into the desert. However, the pursuit of the Russian cavalry,
mainly Cossacks, was described as a vengeful massacre as 8,000 were
killed, including women and children. A further 6,500 defenders lay
dead in the fortress. Skobelev encouraged the slaughter and rapine that
occurred, hoping to terrorise the Turcomans into submission in the
future. Skobelev was recalled to Minsk, but he died of a heart attack
the following year.

The Russo-Turkish War, 1877–78, highlighted problems in the Russian army
The massacre of 12,000 Bulgarian Christians by Muslim Bashi-Bazouk
irregulars gave the Russians the motive to invade the Ottoman Empire
in April 1877. However, their progress was slow. The Turkish fortress at
Plevna held up the Russian advance for five months and there were
35,000 Russian casualties through artillery fire and costly assaults.
Russian railways were unable to supply the troops directly because the
Russian lines were a different gauge to those in the Balkans. Many of
the supplies rotted as they waited for trains at the Romanian border. In
Anatolia progress was also slow because Muslim guerrillas in the
Caucasus harried the Russian supply columns. When Plevna fell, the
Balkan campaign developed quickly and Skobelev won a decisive
victory at the Shipka Pass in Bulgaria. The Russians, advancing on
Constantinople in February 1878, were threatened with British intervention and concluded a hasty peace treaty called San Stefano. The
war demonstrated that railways could bring troops and supplies rapidly
to a nation's frontier, but left a problem of supplying the army beyond

the railhead. Sieges were also still important to the outcome of a campaign.

Wars of British imperial expansion: the Zulu War, 1879

The opening of the war: disaster at Isandhlwana and success at Rorkes Drift
Plans to confederate the states of southern Africa were threatened by the continued existence of the powerful Zulus, so an invasion was launched in January 1879 under the command of Lord Chelmsford. Against Chelmsford's 16,000 (including 9,000 very unreliable levies), the Zulus could field an army of 50,000. The British plan was to converge on the Zulu capital, Ulundi, in three columns, but this left them vulnerable to attack without any mutual support. Cetesweyo, the Zulu king, concentrated 20,000 against the main column, but sent a strong force to the southern border. Chelmsford, meanwhile, left a garrison of 822 British and 431 Africans to guard his camp at Isandhlwana, while he pressed forward with the main body. On 22 January the Zulus encircled and swept towards the camp, but were kept pinned down until ammunition began to run out. The camp was overrun and the defenders slaughtered. Later a force of 4,500 Zulus attacked the mission station at Rorkes Drift, defended by a company of the 2/24th Foot. Improvised defences and fire discipline enabled the small garrison to defeat the Zulus and 11 Victoria Crosses were awarded for courage.

The British army secured victory at Ulundi, July 1879
The Zulus besieged Eshowe, but were defeated at Gingindlovu on 2 April by Chelmsford's relief column. The Zulus scored only minor successes, such as the destruction of a wagon train on the Intombe River on 12 March, but they managed to inflict heavy losses on the cavalry of Colonel Evelyn Wood's command on 28th March. Wood's men beat off Zulu charges the following day at Khambula. The British lost 18 killed and wounded (all fatally), but the Zulus lost 800. On 4 July Chelmsford's main force of 4,165 British and 1,152 Africans, advanced on the king's *kraal* at Ulundi in a giant square formation. The Zulus, 20,000 strong, attacked the square but fell back without even reaching it, and cavalry pursued them from the field. Six thousand Zulus were killed. The presence of Africans amongst the invasion force was evidence of the inter-tribal hostility of the region. In the 1880s tribal warfare developed to the extent that Zululand was annexed. The

British and other European powers enlisted Black Africans into police and military forces across Africa throughout the period.

The Second Afghan War, 1878–80 and the North-West Frontier

Hoping to forestall a Russian invasion, the British tried to establish a Resident (to exercise influence) in Kabul. The ruler, Shere Ali, refused to admit the envoy and war broke out on 20 November 1878. The invasion force of 35,000 men aimed to secure the Khyber Pass, Jelalabad and Kandahar before advancing on the Afghan capital after the winter. The southern column, under General Sir Donald Stewart, reached Kandahar unopposed, but Major General Frederick Roberts had to fight his way through the Afghans at Peiwar Kotal, where he carried out a flanking attack on 2 December 1878. Lieutenant General Sir Sam Browne was unable to capture the fortress of Ali Masjid, but defeated the escaping garrison nevertheless. Shere Ali died in February 1879, and his successor, Yakub Khan, surrendered in May as British troops reached the capital. However, the Resident and his escort were massacred on 5 September by rebellious Afghan troops, compelling the British, who had withdrawn their forces, to re-enter the country. Roberts captured Kabul but had to fight off a major assault at Sherpur Cantonment on 23 December 1879, his 7,000 men defeating 100,000 Afghans. Roberts' men, protected by walls and earthworks, suffered the loss of only two men. A new Amir was instated, and Roberts, having punished the rebels who had massacred the Resident's bodyguard, prepared to withdraw.

Tactics: Afghans and Pathans evolved tactics to combat the British
The Afghans were capable of defeating the British under the right circumstances. In March 1879, at Deh Surruck, the Shinwarri Afghans were charged by the 13th Bengal Lancers (an Indian regiment), but, in spite of the orthodoxy of the day which suggested tribesmen could not stand against cavalry, the Shinwarris gave a volley at close range and then formed groups of four men, back to back. The Lancers charged several times, but eventually had to withdraw, covered by the 17th Foot. Afghan tribesmen, like the Pathans of the North-West Frontier, more typically preferred sniping or the killing of sentries at night. They tried to hold the high ground or carry out ambushes in rocky defiles. British tactics evolved to 'crown the heights' (secure the highest points) to

protect columns of troops in the valleys. Small parties had to fight their way up to and down from their eyries as the column moved along below. Much of the fighting therefore consisted of long-range shooting, or close quarter hand to hand fighting with knives and bayonets. There were over 40 campaigns along the North-West Frontier between 1868 and 1898 to pacify the tribesmen.

The British defeated at Maiwand, and Roberts marched to relieve Kandahar
To support the local ruler of Kandahar, the Wali Ali Khan, the British despatched a brigade of 2,600 men. However, when another claimant to the throne, Ayub Khan, advanced to attack Kandahar, the Wali's men fled, leaving the small British and Indian force under Brigadier General G. S. Burrows' brigade to fight alone at Maiwand. Outnumbered and shelled by Afghan artillery, the force was overwhelmed. The 66th, the only British infantry regiment present, made a 'last stand' whilst the survivors retreated to the walls of Kandahar. Roberts, hearing of the catastrophe, created a mobile column of 10,000 men to march to the rescue. They marched through 300 miles of desert and mountain with a minimum of baggage. They left the artillery behind and relied only on mountain guns (which could be dismantled and carried on mules). Three weeks later, the column arrived and immediately went into battle, defeating Ayub Khan at Kandahar on 1 September 1880. The Afghans were able to inflict defeat on Burrows' force when they possessed superior firepower and numbers, but they could not sustain conventional warfare. What persuaded the British to evacuate Afghanistan in 1880, as in 1842, was the cost of maintaining control of the country. Guerrilla warfare enabled the tribal groups to avoid defeat, if not helping them to achieve victory. The British were plagued by frequent guerrilla uprisings along the North-West Frontier which, although suppressed, were never really ended.

Wars in Africa

The First Anglo-Boer War, 1880–1
Tactics: the British were defeated at Majuba Hill
The Transvaal rebelled against British rule in 1880 (they had reluctantly accepted annexation in 1877), but the Boers took the British by surprise. Two hundred Boers attacked a British column at Bronkhurst Spruit on 20 December 1880. In just 15 minutes 57 British soldiers were killed, 100 were wounded (20 fatally) and each of them had an average

of five wounds. The battle was part of a lost age. The British, in red coats, played the national anthem before the action. The Boers assisted the British wounded after the shooting stopped and the band played *Rule Britannia* as the wrecked column marched off. Sir George Pomeroy Colley marched 1,200 men to relieve besieged posts in the Transvaal, but found his way blocked by 2,000 Boer marksmen at Laing's Nek on 28 January 1881. Colley launched a frontal attack, the 58th Regiment even carried its colours into battle, but the attack was stopped dead by rifle fire. On 26 February, Colley took possession of Majuba Hill, overlooking the Boers at Laing's Nek, although he had no artillery to shell them with. The Boers assaulted the hill the following morning. The Boers moved as individual riflemen, taking up fire positions behind any natural cover and firing to protect the movement of their friends. The British, conspicuous in their red coats, were easy targets. Two hundred and eighty five British soldiers and sailors were killed and wounded, out of a total force of 365 men. The survivors fled down the slopes of the hill. Colley was killed. The war concluded with negotiations, but it had shown that British tactics, still reminiscent of Waterloo, were obsolete against the firepower and field craft of the Boers.

Egypt and the Sudan, 1882–1885

Leadership: Wolseley used deception to secure the Suez Canal

A nationalist revolt by Arabi Pasha, a colonel of the Egyptian army, led to the death of 50 Europeans in Cairo and a potential threat to the Suez Canal. As a British and French naval squadron assembled off the port of Alexandria, Egyptians fortified their coastal gun emplacements. Admiral Seymour shelled the coastal forts when they refused to surrender on 11 July 1882. On 14 July, sailors and marines went ashore to restore order in Alexandria. An expeditionary force of 16,400 men was transported by steam ships to Egypt from Britain, and they were joined by 7,600 from Mediterranean garrisons and 7,000 from India. Lieutenant General Sir Garnet Wolseley built up forces at Alexandria as a feint, landing a second force to secure Ismailia on the Suez Canal on 18 August. The strategic objective achieved, Wolseley then concentrated more troops at Ismailia and advanced on Cairo, taking the Sweetwater Canal (for freshwater for the base at Ismailia) and the railway line to the capital for efficient re-supply. Arabi's forces tried to dislodge the British from Kassassin at night on 28 August and on 9 September, but they were repulsed by infantry fire and a moonlit cavalry charge.

The Battle of Tel el Kebir, 13 September 1882, demonstrated British discipline
The Egyptians constructed a defensive position at Tel el Kebir, 6 miles
west of Kassassin, and manned it with 20,000 regular troops, 2,000
tribesmen and 75 guns. Wolsley reconnoitred the position carefully
over several days, noting that the bulk of the Egyptian troops withdrew
to camp at night. He decided on a bold night attack, artillery being
taken forward to fire only at the moment the element of surprise was
lost. Two prongs went forward, and the Highland Brigade managed to
get within 150 yards without detection. Fierce skirmishing and bayonet
fighting took place in the entrenchments, but by 6am the Egyptians
were routed. The British lost 57 killed and 382 wounded, but Egyptian
losses were over 2,000. In less than one month Wolseley had landed,
fought a decisive battle and captured Egypt. The organisation and efficiency of the operation had been remarkable, further enhancing the
reputation of this officer.

The Sudan operations of 1883–84 were marked by the continued use of the 'square'
The collapse of Egyptian power was the signal for an uprising in its
colony, the Sudan. Led by the charismatic Muslim leader Mohammed
Ahmed Ibn Seyyid Abdullah, or 'the Mahdi', a Sudanese army quickly
defeated Egyptian forces in the region. An Egyptian army, 10,000
strong was despatched from Khartoum, under General William Hicks
but, drawn into the desert, this demoralised and thirsty force was
surprised and annihilated at Kashgil on 3–5 November 1883. Egyptian
columns were also repulsed or cut to pieces at Tamanieb (2 December
1883) and El Teb (4 February 1884). General Charles Gordon was sent
to evacuate the Egyptians from Khartoum, but refused to leave. A British force, under Major General Sir Gerald Graham, advanced from
Suakin in a 'brigade square' formation (to protect the baggage of the
column) and on 29 February defeated a Sudanese force at El Teb.
However, at Tamai on 13 March 1884 Sudanese warriors broke into one
of the two British squares and a fierce hand-to-hand battle took place.
It was clear that a larger expedition was required if Gordon, now cut
off in Khartoum, was to be relieved and the rebellion suppressed.

Quality of troops: the Mahdi's army was enthusiastic but poorly armed
The Mahdi's messianic message united 56 tribes of the Sudan and they
possessed different fighting styles. The Hadendowa was the name given
to all the Beja tribesmen, popularly referred to as 'Fuzzy-Wuzzy'
because of their hair styles, and they preferred to charge with a long
knife. These men were known for their exceptional courage, and their

preference for close quarter fighting and stealth earned them the respect of the British soldiers. The rest of the army was divided into four 'flags' to which local emirs led their clan through regional loyalty. The 'flags' were divided into four 'rub', each consisting of separate units of spearmen, riflemen, horsemen and swordsmen. Independent units, called *Jihadiyya*, were also divided into 'standards' and sub-units. After the Mahdi's death his successor, the Khalifa, formed a personal bodyguard or Mulazimiiyya, about 10–12,000 strong, divided into 'rubs' or 'standards' too. The tactic of the army was the shock effect of the charge, covering the ground to the enemy as fast as possible. Muskets and sawn-off rifles, javelins, leaf-bladed spears, straight-bladed slashing swords (*kashkaras*) and tripod-supported elephant guns all demanded that the army fight at close quarters. The Sudanese artillery was limited, particularly because of shortages in ammunition. At Tofrek, 20 March 1885, Hadendowa hid among bushes and rocks, then rose up when close to the British lines, leading to a hand-to-hand struggle. The Mahdists were eventually driven off. At the battle of Omdurman, 2 September 1898, one Sudanese unit concealed itself in a dried riverbed and some, when charged by cavalry, lay down to swing their swords against the horses' legs. The practice of playing dead in order to make surprise attacks encouraged the British to shoot at any Sudanese lying down.

Wolseley's relief expedition of 1885 arrived too late to save Khartoum
Wolseley set about the relief of Gordon with his usual attention to detail, setting out with 6,000 troops up the Nile. When messages came from Gordon that Khartoum could not hold out much longer, Wolseley despatched a 'flying column' consisting principally of the Camel Corps (British cavalrymen mounted on camels), across the desert under Major-General Herbert Stewart. The Desert Column, as it became known, was attacked at Abu Klea near Metemmeh on 17th January 1885. One thousand four hundred British troops were formed in a square, but the 10,000 Mahdists briefly succeeded in breaking into the formation. The Mahdists fled with 1,100 casualties. Meanwhile the River Column sent out a flotilla of river steamers, but they arrived two days too late. Wolseley withdrew his exhausted men. The expedition finally drew to a close when efforts to build a railway to Berber from the coast provoked more Mahdists attacks, another charge being beaten off with some difficulty at Tofrek.

The guerrilla resistance of Samori Touré

Perhaps the most successful resistance in Africa was that of Samori Touré, a mercenary fighter of the upper Niger. Islam was the unifying cause of his followers, but his military organisation ensured obedience across a territory that, by the 1870s, stretched from the Niger to Sierra Leone. He divided the region into ten provinces, each of which maintained an army of 4–5,000 *sofas* (warriors) who worked in agriculture for half the year and spent the other half training, giving Samori a permanent military establishment. This was a distinct advantage over other African armies which could not be sustained in the field for want of supplies or agricultural labour. Samori supplemented the *sofas* with an élite corps in each province of 500 men. The tactic they evolved in battle was to advance in an arc formation with a reserve, a similar arrangement for many West African forces (and, indeed, the Zulus). Finance for this standing army was raised through taxation and through profits from slavery. Samori also acquired 8,000 repeating rifles. Realising that the French army was superior in tactics, firepower and discipline in open battle, Samori adopted guerrilla tactics. Ambush and a scorched-earth policy made it more difficult for the French to come to grips with his forces, and Samori remained defiant of the French for twenty years. At Kong, in 1895, Samori's guerrillas defeated a French force that was low on supplies and isolated. Samori was eventually captured in his own camp by French cavalry in 1898.

Miscalculation and comparable firepower: Adowa, 1 March 1896

An influx of breech-loading weapons into Ethiopia persuaded the ruler, Menelik, to abandon the traditional spear phalanx attack and adopt looser formations that combined firepower and envelopment. General Oreste Baratieri of the Italian army had invaded Ethiopia, a long-standing rival for influence over the coastal provinces of Eritrea and Somaliland (in Italian hands). Baratieri was in the process of withdrawing to Eritrea, when the 100,000-strong Ethiopian army drew up 4 miles away. Baratieri had 20,000 men, half of them Ascaris (Africans in Italian service) armed with single-shot breech-loaders, and 56 guns, all of the light 'mountain' type. At least 70,000 of the Ethiopians had breech-loaders and most of the 46 artillery pieces were modern French Hotchkiss guns. They also had a number of machine guns. Both the Italians and the Ethiopians were short of rations, but just as Menelik began to consider breaking up the army in search of food, Baratieri attacked.

The defeat was due to Italian errors

The Italians were divided into three groups. Baratieri aimed to secure the high ground in front of his fortified camp, whilst a brigade marched to the north to cover the flank. However, due to confusion in the orders, the main body advanced beyond the heights it was supposed to occupy and the northern brigade and the reserve were no longer able to support it. For several hours the Ethiopians hurled themselves against the Italian Ascaris, gradually enveloping them. The Italians in the centre were thus forced to withdraw. The northern brigade was surrounded and cut off, and was almost annihilated. The Ethiopians had lost 7-10,000 and the Italians 4,829 killed, 500 wounded and 1,900 taken prisoner. The battle demonstrated that, armed with modern weapons and outnumbering the Europeans, the African forces could be successful. However, the discipline and defensive posture of the Italians meant that, whilst outgunned, they could still inflict heavy casualties on the Ethiopians. Menelik's men had still relied on a head-on assault, until their numbers naturally spilled around the Italian flanks. If Baratieri had not attacked, then the Ethiopians would have withdrawn through lack of supplies.

Courageous charges against discipline and firepower: Omdurman, 1898

The British decided to reoccupy the Sudan in 1896 when other European powers seemed to threaten the security of the region. Major-General Herbert Horatio Kitchener prepared the re-conquest in meticulous detail. He began with the recapture of the Dongola province, defeating a Sudanese force at Firket (7 June 1896). He then set about the construction of a railway across the desert to avoid having to stretch his communications along the Nile. British troops reinforced his Egyptian army in January 1898 and on 8 April Kitchener attacked the entrenched camp of Uthman Diqna (or Osman Digna) at Atbara. Clearing the position in two hours, Kitchener paused for more reinforcements, bringing his army to 26,000 men. On 1 September Kitchener arranged his forces in a defensive square, supported by gunboats on the Nile, within sight of the Khalifa's base at Omdurman. The next morning the Dervishes attacked but were unable to get to close quarters, being mown down by rifle, artillery and machine-gun fire. The British were firing at ranges above 1,000 yards, yet inflicted casualties of 10,000 dead (the number of wounded is unknown). When Kitchener advanced, two 'flags' of the Khalifa's army, which had remained in reserve, then attacked but they were cut down, mainly by Sudanese soldiers in British service. The 21st Lancers charged into a hidden ravine filled with Dervishes, but managed to extract themselves after close quarter fighting. The total British losses were 48 killed and 434 wounded.

Conclusions

Technology: European firepower and other factors
The writer Hilaire Belloc once remarked that the secret of the European success was: 'whatever happens, we have got the Maxim gun, and they have not'. However, Douglas Porch argues that the Europeans conquered African and Asian states not through firepower alone but through superior tactics, organisation and discipline. If combined with clear chains of command, decisive leadership and secure logistics, the Europeans were able to mount, execute and conclude operations using relatively small numbers of men. In some cases, the Europeans forged alliances with African and Asian rulers, at other times they incorporated them into their armies. The British, for example, fielded an Indian Army of circa 87,000 British soldiers and 153,000 Indian Sepoys in 1887.

Technology changed in the late nineteenth century
Breech-loaders became the standard firearm of all European forces by the 1880s. The introduction of smokeless powder meant that troops could fire from concealed positions. The rifle was now a reliable weapon system. There were no difficulties in firing in bad weather as the mechanism was housed inside a metal breech. Bullets were propelled by a charge contained in a metal cartridge case and the complete cartridge (with a percussion cap in the base) could be manufactured in factories and simply shipped out with the army. Heavy calibre bullets could inflict terrible injuries, but the soft-nosed dumdum bullet experiment (which was shown to have the same effect on the human body as an explosion) was banned internationally in the early 1900s. Nevertheless, machine guns also accompanied the European armies, greatly increasing their ability to dominate the battlefield.

Strategy and tactics lagged behind the changes in technology
The destructiveness of weapons had increased but tactics in the field remained wedded to the doctrines of the mid-nineteenth century. There was a strong emphasis on offence: Europeans were expected to overawe their enemies rapidly, to sustain the image of the superior white man. Where small garrisons were besieged, small expeditions were mounted to relieve them, again with an emphasis on speed and

mobility. In the Matabele Rebellion of 1893 the British South Africa Company and the British Bechuanaland Border Police, mounted with Maxim machine guns, defeated large numbers of tribesmen. The presence of Maxim guns was enough to discourage rebellion after the first skirmishes in Nigeria in 1903, and sustained rifle and machine-gun fire dispersed the almost feudal Tibetan army in 1904.

The responses of the indigenous populations
Not all indigenous peoples chose to resist. However, those that did fight found that their own modes of warfare were inadequate. In north Africa wars were rarely pursued to conquer or destroy the enemy. Fights were opportunities to prove individual prowess and status. The courage of individuals was the measure of their fitness as warriors. The Mashona and Matabele were so bewildered by the European methods that they turned to religion to explain their predicament. In the 1896 rising, the Matabele believed Oracles that told them the bullets of the white man would turn to water. The Pathans of the North-West Frontier, who rose in rebellion in 1897-98, were also told by Mullahs that the bullets would be harmless and the shells would turn to stone. The Ethiopians, and Samori's guerrillas, were more successful because of their acquisition of modern weapons, but even then it was a lack of logistical organisation to the same level as the Europeans which rendered them vulnerable. The battle of Omdurman epitomised the contrast: not even 50,000 undoubtedly brave warriors with artillery and at least 15,000 firearms could prevail against 20,000 well-sited and well-armed British and Sudanese soldiers.

Tutorial

Progress questions
1. Why did Sir Garnet Wolseley earn a reputation for efficiency?
2. Why did the North American Indians resist whites so fiercely in the 1870s?
3. What problems did the Russians encounter in Central Asia and the Caucasus?
4. To what extent were the outcomes of Isandhlwana, Maiwand and Majuba Hill due to errors of leadership?

Seminar discussion

1. How were non-Europeans sometimes able to win colonial battles?
2. How important was mobility compared to firepower for Western and non-European forces in the period 1873–1899?

Practical assignment

Draw up a comparative list of British, French, Russian and American colonial wars. What common problems did they face? How did they overcome them? Were there similarities in the responses to these colonial forces? Write a short paragraph concluding how these campaigns affected Western modes of warfare.

Study tips

1. Note that the exceptional battles, Isandhlwana, Rorkes Drift, Custer's Last Stand, Omdurman and Adowa, have often been remembered at the expense of more typical actions.
2. When assessing colonial campaigns, bear in mind the climate and terrain, which had a considerable effect on the performance of the troops involved.
3. Note that contemporaries often explained military success in terms of racial superiority. Racial groups, including Europeans, were thought to have different martial characteristics, but these were often deeply held beliefs about the way in which they viewed the world and how they should conduct themselves in war.

10

The South African War, 1899–1902 and the Russo-Japanese War, 1904–5

One minute overview – The South African War began as the 'last of the gentleman's wars' and ended in a bitter and protracted guerrilla war that characterised many of the conflicts of the twentieth century. The British were forced to adapt to the firepower and marksmanship of the Boers, devolving command to more junior levels and improving field craft. Moreover, when the Boers were forced to adopt guerrilla tactics, the British had to find new ways of defeating them, primarily by removing the resources that could sustain their mobile commandoes. Trenches, barbed wire and machine guns gave the war a modern appearance, but there was still a heavy reliance on cavalry and mounted infantry to cover the large distances in South Africa. A dispersed war was also fought in Manchuria, but here the two armies were 'conventional'. The Russians were tenacious in defence, the Japanese no less determined in the attack. Each of the battles of the Russo-Japanese War produced heavy casualties. However, none of the European powers lost their faith in the importance of mobility and the attack, developed over the previous decades.

In this chapter you will learn:

▶ the problems the British faced at the beginning of the South African War
▶ the Boer strategy and how it failed in conventional warfare
▶ the success of the British conventional offensive
▶ the effectiveness of the Boers' guerrilla tactics
▶ measures the British used to defeat the guerrillas
▶ the Japanese tactics in the Russo-Japanese War
▶ technological change by 1900

The problems the British faced at the beginning of the South African War

The causes of the war concerned regional supremacy
The discovery of gold on the Witwatersrand in the Transvaal in 1886 gradually changed the country from a rural backwater into a wealthy state. Thousands of foreign workers, or Uitlanders, on the Rand were denied political rights because the Transvaal Afrikaners feared they would be outnumbered. This, and the punitive taxation of the mine owners' profits and materials, prompted Cecil Rhodes to try to overthrow the Transvaal government in 1895. The Jameson Raid, where a column of 500 volunteers was defeated by a Boer commando at Doornkop, caused a marked deterioration in relations between Britain and the Transvaal. Sir Alfred Milner, the High Commissioner of Cape Colony from 1897, believed that unless the Transvaal was incorporated into a British dominated South Africa its wealth would enable it to eventually replace British power in the region. Milner provoked the Transvaal into a declaration of war on 11 October 1899, but the British army was at a disadvantage for the first few months.

The British army had several problems in southern Africa
The British garrison in southern Africa was small. At Kimberly there was a garrison of 2,600 men, but only 600 were regular troops. Mafek-

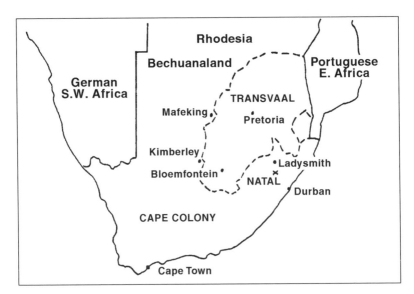

Figure 5. The South African War, 1899-1902

ing could muster 1,200 police, and Major General Penn Symons, the commander of forces in Natal, had a field force of just 4,500 men. The largest force consisted of the 13,000 regulars and 1,800 local volunteers under General Sir George White. Until 10,000 men from India and the Mediterranean and an army corps from Britain could arrive, these small detachments had to contain a Boer army of 50,000 men. Moreover, there was a shortage of heavy calibre artillery. Many of the colonial wars in Africa and Asia had not required heavy ordnance and the British were forced to press 4.7-inch naval guns into service, with special mountings designed by Captain Percy Scott. Another problem was artillery ammunition. New high explosive Lydite shells were less effective than anticipated.

The Boer strategy and how it failed in conventional warfare

Strategy: the Boer invasion was designed to achieve a quick victory
The decision to take the offensive before British reinforcements could arrive was a sound one, but the numerical advantage was lost when many Boers were tied down in sieges of Mafeking, Kimberley and Ladysmith. Relatively few Boers were despatched to Cape Colony to raise Afrikaners there and to threaten the rail links at De Aar and Naauwpoort. Commandant-General Piet Joubert led 21,000 Boers against the Natal forces. It seems that the Boers expected a short war and a decisive battle, like the battle of Majuba Hill, that would persuade the British to sue for peace. The Boers certainly had international sympathy, holding out against the British Empire. A number of volunteers from Ireland, Germany, Russia and America joined the Boers during the conflict.

Technology and tactics
The Battle of Talana Hill demonstrated the effects of modern firepower
While White concentrated his force at Ladysmith, Penn Symons advanced 45 miles north-east to Dundee with 4,500 men. He was surprised by a bombardment of his camp on 20 October 1899 from Talana Hill, which he attacked. Penn Symons was mortally wounded and his troops were cut down in large numbers as they pushed up the slopes. The British fell back on Ladysmith to avoid being surrounded. The Boers were not only crack shots but were armed with modern German Mauser or Mannlicher rifles, a magazine weapon which

enabled each rifleman to maintain a high rate of fire. From 1885, smoke-less powder in cartridges meant that it was far harder to locate the enemy. The Boers' use of cover and concealment meant that the British could not even see those that shot them down. The Boers also possessed machine guns, such as the Nordenfeldt, or the Vickers-Maxim auto-matic gun (nicknamed the 'pom-pom' because of its sound). The British army carried the magazine-fed Lee Metford rifle, but there was still little appreciation that the weapon could be used as effectively in a snip-ing role as in its preferred 'volley firing' function. British officers were keen to retain control of the fire of their men and the volley was thought to have a morale effect that individual fire did not. The British also felt that getting to close quarters, if possible using the bayonet, added to this morale effect.

The Battles of Elandslaagte and Nicholson's Nek were setbacks for Britain
A Boer commando, led by J. M. Kock, tried to raid the railway settle-ment of Elandlaagte but Colonel Ian Hamilton arrived by rail and drove off the Boers on 21 October, Kock being mortally wounded. The arrival of Boer reinforcements compelled Hamilton to withdraw. Hoping to avoid encirclement, White carried out a night march to outflank the Boers at Nicholson's Nek. The attack, on 30 October, was badly co-ordinated, hundreds were taken prisoner, and White fell back into Ladysmith where a siege began on 2 November 1899.

Strategy: the sieges were a waste of Boer resources
At Kimberley 7,000 Boers lethargically besieged a garrison under Colonel R .G. Kekewich, although this commander had to put up with the impatient criticisms of Cecil Rhodes throughout the investment. To the north Colonel Robert Baden-Powell organised the defence of the railway town of Mafeking. The relief of this tiny garrison did not arrive until May 1900, but Baden-Powell's spirited and ingenious defence gained world renown. Deception was used, artillery and ammunition manufactured. Morale was sustained by their own newspapers, and by concert parties. Black people were used as sentries and labourers, but some were expelled when food supplies ran low. At Ladysmith, the chief problem was food. Horses and mules were eaten as '*chevril*' and dry biscuits were fried in axle grease. Factories were created to turn out horsemeat sausages, paste and soup. Mealie meal and reduced sugar rations kept the men alive. The perimeter became a network of dug-outs and trenches, but casualties from the 16,000 Boer shells fired during the siege were relatively light. With 10–12,000 surrounding the

town, the Boers could have launched attacks, but concern to reduce casualties meant they opted for victory through starvation of the garrison. They poisoned the water supply with dead horses so that, when the water purifiers gave out, cases of enteric fever and dysentery increased. The British managed to raid and disable some Boer guns early on and also repulsed a Boer attempt to capture the commanding heights of Caesars' Camp and Wagon Hill on 6 January 1900. The sieges were the Boers' biggest error, for they locked up valuable troops and allowed time for British reinforcements to arrive.

Methuen's advance to the Modder River was unsuccessful
With White and his troops confined to Ladysmith, command devolved to General Sir Redvers Buller. Buller hoped to strike through the Orange Free State and on to Pretoria, but the presence of Boers in Natal and the need to relieve Ladysmith took priority. Yet to contain the threat to the Cape, Buller was forced to divide his forces. The Cape frontier was to be guarded by a force under Lieutenant General Sir William Gatacre (nicknamed 'back acher'). The cavalry division, under Major General John French, was held in reserve at Colesberg. Lieutenant General Lord Methuen (with 13,000) was ordered to relieve Kimberley and Buller took the remainder to relieve Ladysmith. Methuen found that the Boers, over a distance of 75 miles, would hold a position just long enough to inflict heavy casualties and then withdraw, which they did at Belmont (23 November 1899) and Graspan (25 November). Expecting the Boers to fall back again, Methuen was faced by more determined and effective resistance on the Modder River on 28 November. The Transvaal leader Koos de la Rey and some of his men bolstered the flagging Free Staters, bringing their force up to 3,500 men. De la Rey posted his men in shallow trenches at the base of a hill, rather than on the summits where they were vulnerable to British artillery fire. The lower positions also gave the rifle fire more effect: the flatter trajectories would be more likely to hit British soldiers than fire that was directed downwards. Consequently, when the British artillery shelled the hillsides, it fell beyond the Boer positions. The British infantry advanced, only to be hit by a wall of fire. The Boers then withdrew at night.

Black Week was the low point of the British campaigns
Methuen pursued the Boers to another position at Magersfontein. The Boers once again entrenched themselves and, as the British infantry attacked on 11 December 1899, they were pinned down by rifle fire, the

Boers having marked out the ranges for their weapons in advance. Nine hundred and forty eight British soldiers became casualties, and the Boers lost 280. Methuen was compelled to withdraw to the Modder River. On 10 December Gatacre had advanced on the Boers at Storm-berg with 3,000 men in a night attack. The guides lost their way and at dawn the British were forced to fall back from a position overlooked by several hills. Six hundred men were left behind in the confusion and were captured. Buller didn't deploy his full force of 20,000 men in his thrust at Colenso on 15 December, thinking that a two-day bombard-ment of the Boers on the heights above the Tugela River would be suffi-ciently demoralising. The 8,000 Boers, under Louis Botha, had plenty of time to prepare for Buller's attack. Botha filled the river bed with barbed wire, entrenched his burghers, and ordered them to remain concealed throughout the shelling.

Tactics: the battle of Colenso demonstrated the contrast of Boer and British tactics
Buller planned the assault of the Tugela Hills with three prongs. On the left, General Hart's Irish Brigade advanced towards a ford but, hemmed in by a loop in the river and misled by a local guide, they were cut to pieces by Boer rifle and machine-gun fire on the opposite bank. Buller sent forward Major General Lyttleton's brigade to support the extraction of Hart, but they arrived too late to save the Irishmen. Within 40 minutes 400 of them lay dead and wounded. On the right, Colonel Lord Dundonald's mounted brigade was unable to capture Hlangwane Hill, a key position which could have turned the Boer flank. In the centre, General Hildyard's 2nd Brigade were ordered to cross the Tugela at Colenso. As they advanced, Colonel C. J. Long took forward his guns to within 600 yards of the river, expecting to shell the hilltops beyond. Instead the Boers were entrenched along the river and they shot down the gunners in a matter of minutes. Attempts to rescue the guns failed. When the 2nd Brigade attacked they cleared Colenso and crossed the river, making use of cover and advancing in short rushes as they progressed but at this critical moment Buller, who could not see the crossing, decided to withdraw and prevent needless loss of life.

The organisation of the state for war
The result of Black Week was the mobilisation of the British war effort
The British immediately realised that changes were required. Field Marshal Lord Roberts was appointed commander of the forces in

South Africa, and the highly efficient Lord Kitchener was made his Chief of Staff. More reinforcements were despatched, especially much needed cavalry. Drawn from the existing volunteer structure in Britain, 8,000 cavalry, many of them styled Imperial Yeomanry, were sent from Britain in early 1900. Volunteers also filled infantry companies for service in South Africa. Australia, Canada and New Zealand sent contingents to show Imperial solidarity. Buller, who was later criticised for suggesting White should surrender Ladysmith, was replaced but still commanded the largest force then in South Africa. With news that John French had successfully checked the Boers' advance into Cape Colony, Buller devolved command to Sir Charles Warren to carry out a flanking manoeuvre on the Tugela. The whole of his force had swelled to 30,000 men, but again only a portion was to be committed to battle. Warren successfully crossed the Tugela River and began to occupy the heights beyond. The key position was Spion Kop. However, the three-day movement of the 17-mile long column gave the Boers plenty of time to meet the new threat. Nevertheless, Warren successfully tricked the Boers by leaving a camp standing, bugles being sounded as usual, while he slipped away and occupied much of the high ground across the river.

The Battle of Spion Kop, 23 January 1900, was a costly defeat
With the element of surprise lost, Colonel Dundonald successfully launched a cavalry strike on the Boers' extreme right flank, only to be recalled by Warren when the move could have been exploited. Dundonald's men, with the South African Light Horse, made some progress against entrenched Boers on Bastion Hill, but Warren opted for a two-day bombardment to destroy Boer morale before making another assault. However, as casualties mounted, Warren was compelled to seize Spion Kop in a night attack. The seven-hour ascent achieved complete surprise, but the 1,800 troops barely had time to scratch a shallow trench before daylight. At dawn they realised that they were not at the summit. The Boers overlooked and enfiladed the British position and for eleven hours they poured fire into the shallow trench. The dead were used to form a parapet and, where possible, the British launched charges to clear the Boers from their front. The commander, General Woodgate, was shot in the face. On his own initiative, Major General Lyttleton attacked up the eastern face of Spion Kop with the King's Royal Rifles but by accident they were shelled by their own side. The Boers fell back, but the attack was then called off. Lieutenant Colonel Thornycroft, who had assumed command on the hill, decided to evacuate the hill at nightfall. Two hundred and forty three were

killed and 500 wounded, many of them fatally. Although these figures pale into insignificance in the light of the First World War, at the time they were regarded as horrific for such a small action.

Vaal Krantz, 5 February 1900, failed to achieve a breakthrough
Buller made another attempt to break through the Tugela hills by seizing the ridge of Vaal Krantz, 3 miles east of Spion Kop. On 5 February 1900 a number of pontoon bridges were thrown across the Tugela River. The thinly held Boer line (about 4,000 strong under Ben Viljoen) was alerted to the attack despite a diversionary bombardment to the west. Lyttleton's brigade crossed open ground to the foot of Vaal Krantz, but Buller held back crucial reserves. Although a Boer counter-attack was beaten off on 6 February, Buller decided to withdraw Lyttleton's brigade.

Strategy: the success of the British conventional offensive

Roberts reorganised the commissariat in Cape Colony and created more mounted units (even converting some foot soldiers to MI, or mounted infantry). He advanced to the Modder River, brushing aside the army of Piet Cronje by sending the cavalry, still under John French, on a wide flanking ride on Cronje's left. Cronje kept his forces at Magersfontein, but French relieved Kimberley and the besiegers fell back. Roberts then launched a diversionary attack at Jacobsdal, south of Magersfontein, and Cronje was uncertain whether he was being outflanked or about to be attacked in front. With French somewhere to his rear, Cronje fell back on Bloemfontein, but the 400 wagons with the wives and children that accompanied the Boer army of 5,000 slowed his movements. Moving eastwards, French cut off his line of retreat across the Modder River and Cronje was forced to take up a defensive position at Paardeberg on 17 February 1900. Cronje was encircled and shelled. He could not break out with all the families and capitulated on 27 February 1900. Boer commandos in the western Cape were thwarted by Kitchener's mobile columns (which occupied the towns). Attempts to defend Bloemfontein failed when the Boers were outflanked at Poplar Grove on 7 March. With 2,000 Boers drawn towards Roberts' offensive in the Free State, Buller renewed his attack on the Tugela. From 17 to 27 February, Buller systematically took one hill after another. Infantry went forward under the cover of artillery fire. They used cover more effectively and command was devolved to more junior officers who could organise assaults at low level. The Boers grew disheartened and abandoned their posts. Ladysmith was relieved.

The effectiveness of the Boers' guerrilla tactics

Although Roberts captured the capitals and all the territory of the Boer republics, some of the Boer leaders resolved not to give up. Louis Botha and President Steyn formed commandoes in the Transvaal, whilst Christiaan de Wet operated in the Orange River Colony. Roberts and Buller returned to Britain, whilst Kitchener was left with the 'mopping up of fugitives'. However, it was soon apparent that the British faced determined opponents. Railways were wrecked, bridges blown up, posts attacked. Supply convoys were ambushed. Operating as mounted formations of varying size, the commandoes simply fled into the vast expanses of the Veldt if the British assembled larger forces. They lived on the generosity of the Boer populations, or from what they could steal from the British. Although only half of the available Boers were active at any one time, there were as many as 60,000 men that could be called upon. Against them, Kitchener had about 200,000. The Boers' chief problem was the relatively small effect they could have on the British, but they hoped to avoid defeat by simply wearing the British down until a settlement could be reached or the British evacuated their territory. Ammunition and rifles were taken from the British when it became impossible to obtain supplies for the Mausers. Horses too were in short supply so that, by the end of the war, half of the Boers were fighting as dismounted men. However, not all the Boers were keen to continue the war as 'bitter-enders'. By the end, half of the Boer forces still in the field were fighting on the British side.

Tactics: the measures the British used to defeat the guerrillas
At first Kitchener deployed slow-moving columns across South Africa to pursue the commandos, but they were easily eluded. 80,000 mounted infantry were now operating across the region, but the Boers split up when pursued and reformed for local attacks. Kitchener then began to divide the veldt into zones with barbed wire fences and blockhouses, manned with small detachments. Railways supplied the blockhouses and armoured trains steamed along the lines, sweeping the darkness with searchlights. Eventually 8,000 mutually supporting blockhouses, constructed of tin, turf and stone, were built. Four thousand miles of barbed-wire fences were set up. In each of the zones 'drives' were

carried out: long lines of troops swept across the countryside to flush out commandoes or drive them into the fences and blockhouses. In February 1902 9,000 men, each one 12 yards apart, marched 20 miles a day along a front of 54 miles.

The media's reaction to Kitchener's 'scorched earth' policy

To deny the Boers their supplies, crops were burnt, livestock slaughtered and Boer farms blown up or burnt down. The Boer women and children, and their African workers, were herded into 'concentration' camps, but poor facilities and sanitation accounted for thousands of lives. Criticism of the camps led to a suspension of the policy in 1901. Eventually the Boers agreed terms offered by the British, including political concessions and freedom from any reprisals for having participated in the war. Indeed, the British agreed to £3 million of compensation for war damage. British deaths in the war totalled 21,000 (13,000 from disease) and 52,000 were wounded or fell sick. The Boers lost in the region of 65,000, but only 4,000 of these had fallen in action. The Afrikaners developed a strong sense of nationalism as a result of the war. In Britain there had been some dissent in the media with a minority calling Kitchener's tactics 'The Methods of Barbarism'.

Reforms of the British Army were made in light of the war

The Boer War had revealed some shortcomings in the army, which began to be rectified even before the conflict was over. Improvements were sought in field artillery and ammunition that had been deficient at the outbreak of the war, more dispersed tactics for infantry and a greater attention to the use of hard cover or the digging of 'shell scrapes' (shallow hollows in the ground) as protection from rifle and machine-gun fire. Cavalry continued to function as a mounted fighting force (there had been a shortage of mounted men to cover the vast distances in South Africa), but they were now expected to spend as much time in a dismounted role using rifles. In Britain Haldane (War Secretary) created a General Staff and provided for an expeditionary force of six infantry divsions and one cavalry division that could be mobilised at short notice. In addition, in 1908 Haldane converted the part-time Volunteers, Militia and Yeomanry into the Territorial Force with Officer Training Corps at universities. In the Royal Navy John Fisher revolutionised tactics and training and supervised the launching of a new battleship, HMS *Dreadnought*, in 1906. This vessel, with its ten 12-inch guns and speed of 21 knots, rendered all others obsolete and sparked a naval race amongst the European powers.

The Russo-Japanese War

The war was caused by Japanese fears for their security and military ambition
When Russia began to secure concessions from the Chinese in
Manchuria and looked as if it was about to seize Korea, Japan decided
to retaliate. This region it regarded as its own sphere of influence, and
vital to the country's future survival because of its resources. The Japanese viewed Korea as a security zone for itself, but the construction of a
Russian railway in Manchuria appeared to threaten Japanese interests.
Moreover, the Russians had, with international support, ejected the
Japanese from the strategic harbour of Port Arthur after the Sino-Japanese War (1894–95). When the Russians took it for themselves in 1898,
the Japanese allied themselves to Russia's chief rival in Asia, Great Britain (in 1902).

The Japanese tactics in the siege of Port Arthur were costly
With so few resources compared to the giant Russian Empire, Japan
launched a surprise attack, without a declaration of war, on Port
Arthur on 8 February 1904. The torpedo boats disabled and destroyed
a number of Russian ships of its Pacific Fleet, but the 90,000-strong
invasion force, which landed 27 miles (43 km) north of the port, was
held up for two months by General Stoessel and his 30,000. In that
time the Russian engineers reinforced the defences. On 30 July the
Russians withdrew into the town, behind a formidable network of inter-
locking strongpoints, trenches and gun emplacements. Their force
totalled 40,000 with 500 guns, but few supplies. Searchlights lit up the
landscape at night for the Russian gunners. General Maresuki Nogi
launched three separate frontal assaults on the positions with his infantry between 19 August and 26 November. The Japanese soldiers were
brave and seemingly indifferent to casualties, charging across open
ground covered with barbed wire into machine-gun and magazine-
rifle fire. They regularly sustained losses of 15 per cent. In the intervening periods the Japanese shelled the Russian positions with quick-firing
guns, and the 11-inch howitzer (capable of hurling a 500-lb/227-kg
shell over 5 miles/8km). Mines were dug and explosives created craters
that became new objectives in costly fighting. The Japanese sustained
10,000 casualties in 15 hours during the third *banzai* (charge) on 26
November. Nogi therefore directed all his efforts to the capture of '203
Metre Hill', which commanded the harbour and would allow Japanese
gunners to destroy the remaining Russian ships and the town.

Technology and tactics

The capture of the vital '203 Metre Hill' was achieved after prolonged siege warfare
The Japanese built zig-zag saps (trenches) to within a few yards of the
revetted Russian trenches. The Russians had constructed thick roofs to
withstand artillery fire, with loop holes to fire from. From 27 November
the Japanese began their assault. Hand grenades were used extensively
in attacks and counter-attacks. The Japanese used paraffin, poured into
Russian emplacements and then ignited, to flush out the defenders but
they were swept away by fire from mutually supporting positions. The
Japanese then bombarded the hill with 4,000 11-inch shells, but the
battered Russian garrison continued to hold on. Japanese diversionary
attacks and artillery fire isolated the Russians and prevented reserves
reaching them. They had suffered 4,000 casualties when the final
assault came on 6 December 1904. Fresh Japanese soldiers overwhelmed
the exhausted defenders in the early hours of the morning. The Japanese
immediately began to direct their fire on the ships in the harbour and
the port fell on 2 January 1905. The attack on '203 Metre Hill' had cost
Nogi 8,000 men. Both commanders suffered personal setbacks: Stoessel
was undeservedly found guilty of dereliction of duty and sentenced to
death by the Russian army, although this was later commuted to life
imprisonment. Nogi tried to commit suicide when he was told his only
son had been killed leading the attack on the hill. The Russians had
suffered 31,000 casualties in the siege, and the Japanese total was
60,000 with another 34,000 sick. A total of 20,000 Japanese died of
beri-beri.

Strategy: the Battle of Mukden was vast
The Japanese strategy was to secure Port Arthur and to win a decisive,
quick victory. Their resources would not permit them to sustain a long
war, and their lines of communication, across the Japan Sea, meant
that naval supremacy was essential. The Japanese army was 300,000
strong with a further 400,000 reserves, but the Russians had to bring
reinforcements, munitions and supplies along the 5,500 miles of single-
track Trans-Siberian Railway. Their forces in the theatre of operations
were only 83,000, rising to 250,000 by the end of 1904. The battle of
Telissu (June 1904) had lasted two days but produced little result. Two
further engagements were fought, Laioyang (August 1904), which
lasted two weeks, and Sha-Ho (October 1904), which lasted 12 days.
The casualty lists were extending with each encounter, and General
Kuropatkin, the Russian commander, decided to withdraw to Mukden.

The Russians' 276,000 men, 1,200 guns and 54 machines guns faced the Japanese who were approximately 207,000 strong with 1,000 guns and 254 machine guns. Their fronts extended 40 miles.

Tactics: Mukden was an inconclusive struggle
The battle, which lasted from 23 February to 9 March, was fought in heavy snows and freezing temperatures. The Japanese infantry would open fire half a mile from the position they were to attack. Small groups would run forward in short bursts then fall to the ground to fire on a hand signal. Strict discipline was maintained. A battalion would take three hours to get within a quarter of a mile of the objective and then launch a fierce charge. This tactic worked against the Russian right, and, having defeated a Russian counter-attack, the Russians were compelled to make an orderly withdrawal. The Japanese lost 70,000, the Russians 20,000.

Leadership and strategy: the Russians were defeated
Mukden was not a decisive battle, and the Japanese had not achieved their rapid victory over the Russians at Port Arthur as they had hoped. They were harassed by naval raids from the port until its capitulation, and there was a fear that their own resources would run out before the Russians were defeated. However, the stretched Russian supply lines revealed that this enormous empire could not sustain operations on the periphery effectively. The Japanese utilised their naval strength to defeat the Russian navy and were not drawn into the interior. However, the Russians lacked decisive leadership. Admiral Marakov, the best Russian naval officer in the region, was killed when his vessel struck a mine. General Kuropatkin was efficient but cautious. By contrast, Generals Oyama and Nogi were bold and prepared to take risks. The Japanese enjoyed artillery and numerical superiority throughout much of the campaign, but the courage and tactical skill of the Japanese troops were matched by the doggedness of the individual Russian soldier in defence. Domestic unrest in Russia and the loss of the Russian Baltic fleet at Tsushima eventually persuaded the Russians to sue for peace in September 1905.

Analysis of the Russo-Japanese War
The war showed that modern industrialised powers that brought to bear large field armies would be compelled to forgo manoeuvre in the face of overwhelming firepower. The advantage had shifted to the defensive, since troops who dug in sufficiently well, protected by

barbed wire and artillery fire, would be able to defeat infantry and cavalry attacks. Flanks, the only vulnerable point, were continually extended and incorporated into the defensive scheme. Only the vastness of Manchuria prevented the development of a battlefield that resembled the Western Front of the First World War, although the fighting around Port Arthur had all the hallmarks of that type of warfare.

Changes in warfare by 1900

Strategy: there was continuing faith in mobile warfare
The growth of Western imperialism provoked anti-colonial resistance around the world. To deal with ill-armed, if numerous, insurgents small mobile forces had to be deployed. These operations put an emphasis on the need for bold, decisive attacks, to snuff out rebellion and discourage further resistance. The British handbook *Small Wars*, published in 1896 by Colonel C. E. Callwell, urged British troops to inflict casualties and act with resolution, especially early on. This would prevent the insurgency degenerating into a protracted guerrilla war. General Louis Lyautey produced a paper for the French army called *Colonial Rule of the Army* (1900) in which he advocated the total occupation and sound administration of colonies, rather than resorting to punitive campaigns against people on the margins of the empire. These campaigns antagonised their opponents, with their raids on property and livestock, and were expensive. Lyautey concluded that these operations were therefore self-defeating. He favoured the incorporation of subject peoples in the imperial system. The Western powers used colonial troops throughout their period of imperial occupation.

Citizen armies and mass movements of resistance were more common
Where, perhaps, many insurrections in Europe in previous centuries had been spontaneous and un-coordinated, a number of revolutionary movements with 'professional' activists developed in the later nineteenth century. In 1848 many cities in Europe had been affected by revolutions, and troops had been called in to restore order. In 1905 in Russia a defeat had coincided with domestic unrest to produce an explosion of rioting which again troops had to suppress. Across Europe assassins and revolutionary socialist parties emerged, often aligned to Marxist doctrine. The antithesis of this movement was patriotism. European peoples were enthusiastic supporters of their armed forces. The armies had fostered national pride with successful imperial expansion and

they were seen as the vehicles for national security in an uncertain world. Most European countries favoured conscription to give them mass armies. To sustain the cost, many European citizens served relatively short periods in the armed forces before becoming reservists, subject to being called up in a national emergency. Thus the future battlefield was not only extending laterally but also rearward, involving millions of people. The spread of military service produced an increasingly militant notion of nationalism amongst Europeans. There was also a growing faith in militarism, looking for military-style solutions to social issues or diplomatic problems. Thus two diametrically opposed philosophies had developed by 1900: revolutionary socialism and nationalistic militarism.

The continuing faith in quick victories and nationalism
The European rail network offered strategists the chance to mobilise mass armies and deploy them rapidly. Moltke's railway timetables were perfected until the German army was confident it could mobilise vast numbers and place them in the field in just 24 hours. The Napoleonic concept of rapid and decisive victories, which had been reinforced by Moltke's successes in 1870–1, encouraged the German General Staff to believe that they could achieve a quick victory against any continental power, particularly their chief rivals France and Russia. There was also a social scientific development: pride in national identity had been fostered throughout the late nineteenth century by states eager to weld their citizens together. By the 1890s nationalistic beliefs had combined with 'scientific' studies into national and racial characteristics. Imperial domination of non-Europeans only heightened this conviction. In Germany the idea that Germans were possessed of warrior attributes was popularised. The writer Bernhardi argued that war was the only real test of manhood and was therefore to be welcomed.

Aggressive nationalism was not confined to Germany
In France there was a national longing for *revanche*, a war to recover the lost territories of Alsace and Lorraine from Germany. In Russia Pan-Slavism developed, which was a feeling of ethnic solidarity against the Germanic races of Austria and Germany. In the Balkans national humiliation caused by Ottoman occupation led to two short wars in 1912 and 1913, but the aggrandisement of Serbia, and its ability to inflict defeat on the Ottoman Empire, only served to fuel its nationalistic chauvinism against the Austro-Hungarian Empire. In Austrian lands there were many thousands of Serbian people, and there was a strong sense

of injustice against the rulers of Vienna. In the wars of the future, nationalism was an important part of sustaining morale in the civilian population. Armies were seen as the extension of the nation and, as colonial wars had proven, civilian populations expected their armies to win as a point of national honour.

There were signs of disquiet with militarism
In Russia there was a growth in revolutionary and terrorist organisations opposed to the Tsarist regime and the army that sustained it. Elsewhere in Europe socialist groups began to form, espousing the doctrines of class war and revolution. Although their supporters were still in a minority, there was popular support in France for a Jewish officer wrongly accused of spying. Captain Dreyfus was dismissed from the army, but the secretive and overbearing righteousness of the military, and the unequivocal support of the government and the Catholic Church, angered moderate liberals and more radical socialists alike. In France the Dreyfus case led to bitter social division. In Germany the mistreatment of civilians at Zabern in 1913, and the dismissal of any case against the army in the courts, led to widespread anger amongst liberals and democratic groups.

Fortresses were designed to cope with heavier artillery fire
Fortress design had evolved from the mid-century. Rings of smaller fortresses, well beyond the city they were designed to protect, had long replaced the old curtain walls and bastions on the city perimeter. In the Franco-Prussian War the Germans had found it necessary to tackle the fortresses that ringed Paris, 10,000 yards out, and this demanded sufficient heavy artillery to reduce them. When smaller works and gun emplacements were located between the main fortresses, a whole network of almost continuous field fortifications could be found. Iron and steel plate were added to the earth that made up fortress walls, and concrete provided a rapid and effective strengthening. German artillery had fired 1,000 shells from a range of 800 yards (728m) to breach the walls of Belfort in 1871, but the French had continued to defend the walls and the ruins for 105 days. The French therefore placed a great deal of faith in the power of fortifications from the 1880s. They discovered that 6–10 feet of concrete, steel and earth provided impregnable protection.

The changing design of artillery made it more powerful and faster
Larger-calibre guns were designed which could fire 15,000 yards

(13,650m), and field guns could fire 9,000 yards (8,190m), in the expectation that envelopment of fortresses and shelling from a distance might destroy them without the need for costly assaults. In 1862 the Siemens brothers had invented the hydraulic system of recoil for Krupps breech-loading guns. This system was soon copied by other armies as it meant that guns could be kept aligned on their target and thus fire more rapidly. The French '75', designed in 1897, was a field gun that combined explosive and charge in one round and could support infantry attacks with very high rates of fire.

Communications improved
The first telephones were patented in 1875 and, by 1885, German artillery officers were experimenting using telephone lines to control artillery fire from observations well ahead of the gun line. Sir William Preece sent the first wireless signal in 1892, a feat perfected by Guglielmo Marconi in 1895. By 1901 it was possible to send wireless messages over 3,000 miles.

Powered flight made better reconnaissance possible
The Wright brothers' success in flying their aircraft on 17 December 1903 provoked considerable interest in the military applications of flying machines. The Western powers began experimenting with rifle fire from aircraft and bombing using lead darts. In 1911 the Italians used aircraft in Libya during fighting against Turkish troops. The role of these flimsy machines was still limited by weather, visibility and their vulnerability. However, aircraft could be more effective in reconnaissance than combat sorties.

Tutorial

Progress questions
1. What were the special characteristics of the Boer forces in the South African War?
2. Why did the British win the South African War?
3. What 'low level' infantry tactics did the Japanese and the British employ at the turn of the century?
4. Why did European and non-European armies retain the use of cavalry after 1900?

Seminar discussion

1. Why did it take so long for the British to defeat the Boers in 1899-1902?
2. What had changed, and what had remained the same, in warfare between the 1850s and the 1890s?

Practical assignment

Assess the Boer war and Russo-Japanese war as 'modern' wars. Why were experts able to draw different lessons from these conflicts and the wars of the late nineteenth century? What had happened to the balance between firepower and mobility in the early 1900s?

Study tips

1. Be aware of the difficulties the Europeans had with being able to predict the shape of future wars. In 1898 the British had defeated the charges of the Dervishes at Omdurman, but a year later they were the victims of effective fire in the battles of Black Week. Sieges, such as the one at Port Arthur, had always been costly struggles where attackers emerged from trenches but this was not thought to be typical of 'open' battles.
2. Notice how technology was providing better weapons but mobility was still limited to horses and railways. Motor vehicles were unable to perform well without sturdy roads.
3. Both the British success in South Africa and the Japanese victory in Manchuria were dependent on naval supremacy. This point is often overlooked.
4. As in previous chapters, it is important to consult a map, especially one showing physical features, in order to understand the movements of the armies. Kuropatkin, Nogi, Roberts and Buller all made railways the axes of the movements.

11

The First World War: mobility and defence

One minute overview – The First World War, or the Great War as it was known to contemporaries, was the first total war. Although there was a strong public expectation of quick victory, many military men such as Lord Kitchener in Britain knew from the outset that this would be a long war. When the opening battles of 1914 degenerated into trench stalemate on the Western Front, alternatives were sought in the Near East where Britain could 'knock away the props' of Germany by defeating her allies. Although Britain retained her naval supremacy and achieved remarkable successes in Africa, the siege warfare in France and Belgium cost thousands of lives. Provided with more munitions and fresh troops, the British army tried to break through on the Somme. Here, valuable lessons were learnt, but at a terrible price. France's attack philosophy in 1914 was a costly failure and it suffered heavy casualties at Verdun. The Germans, disappointed by the failure of the Schlieffen Plan, decided to remain on the defensive in the west and attack in the east. Huge quantities of men and materials were involved in the war: it was a conflict on an unprecedented scale.

In this chapter you will learn:

▶ why there was stalemate on the Western Front
▶ why the Eastern Front remained a theatre of manoeuvre
▶ how the Allies tried to break the stalemate on the Western Front
▶ what alternatives were sought to the Western Front in other theatres
▶ the importance of Verdun and the Battle of the Somme

The Western Front, 1914–15

Strategy: the Schlieffen Plan enjoyed some early success
The German high command was fearful of fighting a war on two fronts, France in the west and her ally, Russia, in the east. While Austria held

the south, and token German forces faced the slow build-up of the Russians, the bulk of the German army was to make an enveloping attack on Paris by swinging in a great arc through neutral Belgium. The Kaiser knew that this would inevitably bring Britain into the war, but he believed the British possessed too small an army to make any difference. German mobilisation was rapid and, by 5 August 1914, German artillery was shelling the 12 Belgian forts of Liège. Covering a front of 15 miles, machine-gun fire dispersed the German cavalry that tried to sweep around them, and the German gunners were unable to prevent the repulse of infantry attacks. At night searchlights and flares lit up the advancing troops. However, the great strength of the German army was its 3,500 heavy guns, many of them 21-cm calibre. The most infamous was 'Big Bertha', a 42-cm gun capable of firing a one-ton shell a distance of 16,000 yards (14,560m). It weighed 75 tons, had a crew of 280 men and fired ten rounds an hour. Under this bombardment, the Liège forts were ripped open or surrendered. They had held up the Germans for almost two weeks, but fortresses were unable to halt an army with heavy artillery.

The Schlieffen Plan was flawed, and failed
The German war plan failed to achieve its objective for several reasons. Mobilised soldiers could be rushed to the front in trains but then had to march or ride into battle. German soldiers were soon exhausted by the effort of fighting and marching across France and Belgium. The reliance on lines of communication for ammunition and supplies confined the advance to certain roads, and army corps had to follow separate avenues to avoid congestion. When corps were held up, others had to conform to their new alignment. Consequently the offensive began to slow down and turn to the east of Paris. The largest force was supposed to be on the right wing, but this had been weakened when the Russians mobilised more quickly than expected. When the Germans met stiff resistance from the British, stubborn defensive actions and civilian attacks from the Belgians and aggressive thrusts from the French, they lost confidence in the Schlieffen Plan altogether.

Quality of troops: the British army performed well at Mons
The BEF (British Expeditionary Force), numbering 100,000 men, was commanded by Sir John French and its task was to 'support and co-operate with the French army'. Its size was its greatest weakness; although the British did not know it, the main effort of the German army was to be placed against it. Von Moltke, the German Chief of

Figure 6. The Western Front, 1914–18.

Staff, aimed to swing his armies through Flanders, across the rivers Meuse and Somme, to envelop Paris. At Mons on 23 August 1914, the BEF demonstrated its firepower was out of all proportion to its size, as it inflicted over 5,000 casualties on the advancing German First Army. German officers complained that the British were all armed with machine guns, but in fact the marksmanship and rapid-fire drills of individual British soldiers was the reality. Riflemen could fire 15 aimed rounds a minute. Moreover, they had learnt their lessons from South Africa. Their uniforms were designed to blend in with their surroundings and they fought using all available cover. However, to avoid being overwhelmed, it was necessary to fall back in line with their French allies, as General Lanzerac was being pushed back.

The British withdrew to Le Cateau
The fighting withdrawal inevitably cost lives and so at Le Cateau the

Commander of II Corps, Sir Horace Smith-Dorrien, decided to give the Germans a 'stopping blow'. The centre of the line easily checked the German attacks, but once again there was a risk of being outflanked. The battle and the extraction cost the BEF 7,200 men, but it created breathing space. The 'Retreat from Mons' continued, but without the immediate risk of envelopment which had characterised its first few days. News that the German armies had swung south before reaching Paris seemed to offer the chance of a counter-attack. The French did so, checking the German armies on the Marne. However, the Germans began to dig in along the river Aisne, and in order to outflank them it was necessary for the BEF to march north to Ypres.

Tactics: French tactical thinking had put too much emphasis on the attack
The French troops were dressed in a conspicuous uniform of blue and red in 1914, and their strategic plan similarly tried to capture the spirit of Napoleonic warfare by emphasising the attack. The French Plan XVII was designed to drive into Alsace and Lorraine, the two terri-tories lost in the Franco-Prussian War, but the attempted envelopment by the Germans to the north soon caused this plan to be abandoned. Unlike the British, who used firepower in defensive positions, the French attempted to send their men forward with the bayonet. This resulted in heavy casualties.

The effect of artillery and the scale of armies were apparent from the outset
The British suffered their heaviest losses from German artillery fire in the early battles of 1914, and the number of head injuries eventually produced the shrapnel helmet to replace the cloth caps previously worn. The Germans possessed 160 guns per corps, whilst the French had 126 and the British 154. Austria-Hungary had 130 guns per corps and the Russians 90. This concentration of artillery was capable of neutralising the advantage that larger armies may have brought, where the strengths were as follows: in the west Germany had 1,485,000 against the French 1,150,000, the Belgians 117,000 and the British 100,000. In the east, Germany had 400,000 alongside the Austrian 1,100,000 against Russian forces of 1,300,000. In the south, Austria fielded 200,000 against the Serbians' 190,000.

Lines of trenches extended across Belgium and France
Both sides tried to outflank each other in the so-called 'Race to the Sea', but lines of trenches marked the consolidation of the troops and soon a network extended 500 km from Switzerland to the English Channel. To

break the, as yet, thin line, the Germans launched an attack at Ypres against the depleted BEF. On 31 October, the Germans almost broke through, but there were desperate counter-attacks where even support troops (grooms, cooks, transport men) were rushed into the firing line. The London Scottish, the first Territorial battalion in action, defended Messines Ridge alongside the regulars, an indication that the war would require more of its citizens to hold the front. The main German attack was delivered on 11 November, and a gaping hole in the line was plugged by a courageous charge by the Oxford and Buckinghamshire Light Infantry. The BEF suffered heavy casualties: 58,000 died between Mons and First Ypres. The size of a battalion before the fighting was 1,000 men, but after Ypres the average number of original survivors was 30. Units were reinforced, but the figures give some idea of the scale of sacrifice made by the professional soldiers of the British army. The Germans had also suffered terribly. They called Ypres *Kindermord*: 'massacre of the innocents'.

The fighting on the Eastern Front

Strategy: the Russian invasion of East Prussia was hasty
The German 8th Army was ordered to hold the Russians in the east, but the Austrian forces in Gallicia decided not to depend on German co-operation, and advanced into Poland. The Russians were prompted to take offensive action earlier than expected because the French were pleading for a diversion. However, there was little coherence in the offensive, except a vague intention to advance on Berlin and Vienna. Russian troops were also inadequately supplied and their horse-drawn transport was confined to narrow roads. General Pavel Rennenkampf began his attack on the Germans in East Prussia by establishing the First Army on the right (Gumbinnen) and the Second Army on the left, south of the Masurian Lakes. However, the distances between the armies meant that co-ordination and mutual support were impossible. Worse, the commander of the Second Army, General Alexander Samsonov, was a personal enemy of Rennenkampf.

The Battle of Tannenburg, 26–29 August 1914, was a Russian disaster
At Gumbinnen the First Army was defeated by the Germans under General Max von Prittwitz. However, the Germans withdrew, a decision that cost Prittwitz his job. Samsonov, encouraged by the apparent Russian victory, advanced into East Prussia on 21 August 1914. Rations began to run low when the exhausted troops entered the forested coun-

try around Tannenburg. Ludendorff and Hindenburg, who replaced Prittwitz, left a defensive screen of six cavalry divisions opposite First Army and marched (or moved by rail) the bulk of the German Eighth Army onto the Russians' flanks. Part of their success was attributed to being able to read unencoded Russian wireless messages. By the 26th, the Russians were enveloped and their centre was compelled to surrender *en masse*; 90,000 were taken prisoner, 30,000 Russians had become casualties and 500 guns had been captured.

The war in the east remained mobile
The Austrians continued to penetrate Poland (whilst the Germans fought at Tannenburg), but the Russians enveloped them at Rava Ruska. Two German corps were then diverted from the Western Front to take up positions on the Austrian left as they fell back to the Carpathian mountains. The German forces in East Prussia also marched south so that by 29 September they could threaten Warsaw. The Russians counter-attacked and forced the Germans to withdraw by overlapping their flanks. The huge distances meant that fighting on the Eastern Front did not remain as static as in the west. Cavalry, or rather mounted infantry, continued to play a key role in reconnaissance, or as screens for troop movements. The Germans, thwarted in the west, decided to switch more troops to the eastern theatre during 1915. The Austrians also managed to crack Russian codes early on which gave them an advantage if they obtained any radio or telephone traffic.

Attempts to break the stalemate on the Western Front

Trench warfare: the German Army remained on the defensive
In the west the trench systems continued to develop over a four-year period. Even when objectives were taken, new defences were erected in the rear. By the end of the war deep belts of barbed wire and successive lines of trenches several miles deep characterised the front. The Germans, occupying French and Belgian soil, decided to remain on the defensive, elaborating their trenches with deep protective dug-outs. However, to break the stalemate they experimented with poison gas attacks and the use of flamethrowers against emplacements at Ypres in 1915. The French had tried to use incendiaries and petrol vapours together in October 1914, but the Germans perfected a device that sprayed flaming oil from cylinders up to 40 yards (37 m). The British faced the *Flammenwerfer* at Hooge on 29 July 1915, but they were

outraged at this breach of the Hague Conventions of 1899 and 1907. Poison gas was first used (as opposed to irritant tear gas at Neuve Chappelle in October 1914) on 22nd April 1915 at Ypres. Cylinders were opened when the wind was favourable and an artillery bombardment was needed to suppress the Canadian and French colonial troops which held the sector. Many of these men died and the rest pulled back, leaving a gap five miles wide. However, the Germans had not expected such a complete success and they were slow to follow up. When they made a second gas attack on the 24th, the Canadians fell at their posts. Their only protection was wet cloths across their faces. However, 75 per cent were able to hold the Germans who found it difficult to sustain lethal densities of the gas for long periods.

Organisation of the state for war

There was an urgent need for men and munitions in the British Army
Opinions were divided on the solution to the stalemate which had developed on the Western Front. Churchill and Lloyd George favoured holding on the west, but attacking elsewhere, perhaps Germany's allies. Sir John French felt that the primary aim had been the support of the French, and that the war would be decided by the defeat of Germany in the west. However, in the short term the British army needed more men and it needed munitions. Field Marshal Lord Kitchener, the Secretary of State for War, disapproved of the Territorials ('town clerks' army') and was unfamiliar with the ponderous bureaucratic machinery of Whitehall so he launched his own appeal for men to enlist in the New Armies. The response was overwhelming. In just eight weeks 761,000 men joined up. Some of these new units were drawn almost exclusively from one area or profession, and the close camaraderie gave rise to the title 'Pals' Battalions'. The shortage of personnel to give training led to the re-employment of retired officers (called 'dugouts' because they had been dug out of retirement). There was also a shortage of uniforms and weapons. In France regulars and Indian Army troops were brought from the Empire to fill the trenches, but they too suffered shortages. There was an urgent need for sandbags, barbed wire, machine guns and, above all, ammunition.

The British offensives of 1915 were hamstrung by a lack of ammunition
Sir John French decided to attack at Neuve Chappelle and then to push on to Aubers Ridge whereupon the cavalry would fan out into the country beyond. The first assault on 10 March was successful but it was almost impossible to know what was happening at the front so the

attack on Aubers Ridge was delayed. Telephone wires were cut by shell fire. The shell-torn ground also made it difficult to get supplies and ammunition forward, and this greatly assisted the defenders. The Germans capitalised on the delay, which was extended by their own experimental attacks using poison gas at Ypres in April. Gas had proved effective against unprotected troops, but it failed to provide the Germans with any breakthrough. At Aubers Ridge the Germans built supporting trench lines and concrete pill boxes, increased the depth of their barbed wire and brought up more reserves. When the British attack went in on 8 May it had only one fifth of the artillery fire of before. There were 11,500 casualties. Sir John French was furious, particularly when he discovered that 22,000 shells had been sent to Gallipoli. In some cases guns were issued with three rounds per day. Charles Repington reported the news in *The Times* and French challenged his superiors. The government of the day was forced to form a coalition with other parties, but there was still no effective management of the country's resources.

The Battle of Loos illustrated the problems of the Western Front
Against Sir John French's advice the French commander, Joffre, and Lord Kitchener demanded an attack to suport a French assault at Artois and to support the Russians who had been driven out of Warsaw. The position was a strong one. Amongst the slag heaps of an industrial area the German army had constructed two belts of defences. They were supported by considerable numbers of reserves and artillery. The numerous towers of the mining operations offered excellent observation posts to direct their guns. The width of the attack on 25 September, reduced the intensity of the artillery fire and infantrymen were unable to cross uncut barbed wire. The first use of gas by the British army produced little result, and 2,000 were incapacitated when wind blew the gas back into British trenches. Once again, communication with the leading waves was difficult once the battle had begun. As a result of the battle Sir John French was sacked and Sir Douglas Haig, who had been critical of the Commander in Chief, was appointed to replace him.

Alternatives to the Western Front

The Gallipoli campaign was designed to 'knock away the props'
Turkish ships bombarded the Russian ports in the Black Sea prompting Russia, then France and Britain to declare war on 5 November 1914. However, the Turks closed the Dardenelles to all shipping and Russia

was soon dependent on the ice-bound ports of Archangel and Vladivostok for supplies. It was also hoped that Greece and Bulgaria might join the Entente powers against their old enemies, the Turks. Churchill, the First Lord of the Admiralty, aimed to send a flotilla of older vessels to force the Dardenelles straits and bombard Constantinople. The naval attack was checked by mines laid in the narrow channel on 15 March 1915, so it was clear that landings would be required to support the Royal Navy from the coast. On 25 April British troops went ashore at Cape Helles but were unable to penetrate the Turkish defences in the hills above them. Despite major attacks on 6–8 May, a stalemate developed. Fresh landings at Anzac Cove (named after the Australian and New Zealand Army Corps that landed there) and Suvla Bay failed to make any headway. In September, fresh German attacks on Serbia demanded that the British switch effort to Salonika where they could keep open communications. This decision was confirmed when Bulgaria joined the Central Powers in October. In January 1916 the Gallipoli beachheads were abandoned. In 1918 the Salonika force was able to break out of its position and contributed towards the defeat of Bulgaria. Nevertheless, Turkey was defeated by operations further south.

The Turks were attacked in the Near East and the Middle East
The Indian army was tasked with the protection of oil supplies at Abadan, at the head of the Persian Gulf. Basra was occupied in November 1914 and General Townshend led an expeditionary force up the Tigris, defeating Turkish forces at Kut el Amara and Ctesiphon in 1915. However, outnumbered, he was forced to retire to Kut which was besieged for five months. The garrison surrendered in April 1916, but most of the 12,000 prisoners of war died in Turkish camps. In 1917 General Maude recaptured Kut and drove on to Baghdad. British operations tied down Turkish troops and successfully protected vital oil supplies. A Turkish attack on the Suez Canal was repulsed in February 1915 and in early 1916, General Murray advanced as far as Gaza. Captain T.E. Lawrence worked alongside the Arabs, who had rebelled against Turkish rule in 1916 and captured the port of Aqaba on the Red Sea. In 1917 General Allenby outflanked Turkish defences at Gaza, and on 9 December he captured Jerusalem. Although delayed by the need to send troops to France, Allenby defeated the Turkish army at Megiddo in September 1918 and the following month Turkey sued for peace.

The war extended into Africa and Asia
South African troops launched attacks on German South West Africa

and captured it in July 1915, despite having to deal with a Boer uprising in December 1914. Togoland had fallen in August 1914, but Kamerun held out until the close of 1915, mainly because of disease among the Imperial troops. In German East Africa, Indian troops were repulsed in November 1914, and the war descended into a series of scattered cross border attacks. In early 1916 General Smuts (formerly a Boer commando leader) and South African forces drove the German garrison southwards. British-trained East African and West African forces then relieved Smuts' force and continued to drive the Germans south before pursuing them into Rhodesia. In the Pacific Japan seized German territories while Australian and New Zealand forces took Samoa and some of the German Pacific islands.

The effects of the naval blockade and Jutland were not apparent at first
Britain's naval supremacy proved vital in securing final victory in the First World War. Despite minor actions in 1914 and 1915, where German surface raiders were tracked down and sunk, the only major engagement of the war was the Battle of Jutland in January 1916. Although the Royal Navy lost more vessels, the German High Seas Fleet limped back to port and never reappeared. This enabled Britain to maintain a blockade of German North Sea Ports and protect the lifeline to Russia. The German response was to concentrate on U-boat warfare. There was a steady increase in the numbers of British merchant ships being sunk. In April 1917 the worst month of the war, Britain lost 869,000 tons of shipping (373 ships). It was estimated that Britain had barely six weeks' supply of food left in the summer of 1917. Defeating U-boats was difficult. In the 142 engagements between destroyers and German submarines, only seven U-boats had been sunk. The temptation to starve Britain through the total destruction of all merchant ships compelled Germany to announce unrestricted U-boat warfare in January 1917. With evidence of the sinking of the *Lusitania* in 1915, with the loss of 1,200 lives (including 128 Americans), the decision eventually brought the USA into the war.

Public opinion: the war effort was well supported by the public
The British people believed that the war was a righteous one. Germany had violated the borders of a neutral country and invaded France. Germany occupied French and Belgian soil and exploited the industry it found there for its own war effort. Germany was an autocracy and the Kaiser's plans were militaristic and acquisitive. News also filtered back to Britain through refugees that the German army treated Belgian

and French civilians with high-handedness. In 1915 the sinking of the passenger ship *Lusitania* seemed to indicate that Germany would not respect the protection of non-combatants in war, a fact reinforced by the first Zeppelin raids. Edith Cavell, a British nurse, had been captured in 1915, was accused of spying and was shot, while the use of poison gas (another breach of the Hague Protocol of 1907) was regarded as yet more evidence of German 'frightfulness'. Patriotism was a strong motivation for enlisting, but it also sustained those at home. However, once in the trenches soldiers tended to fight for their immediate friends, units and leaders.

Organisation of the state for war

The British Defence of the Realm Act (DORA) represented new wartime measures
The first DORA of 8 August 1914 gave special powers to the Cabinet. It did not have to wait for the approval of Parliament and could impose measures via the Admiralty and the Army Council necessary for the defence of the United Kingdom. This enabled the government to impose censorship to protect public morale, and intern anyone suspected of hostile sympathies. After the initial flood of volunteers, a scheme was designed in October 1915 to enable men to attest to their willingness to serve when the time came. The huge demand for manpower outstripped the supply of volunteers, and conscription on all unmarried men between 18 and 41 was imposed. At first, in the urgency of the first weeks of the war, there had been little concern about who had volunteered, but it became apparent that some men were needed at home in factories, mines and transport systems.'Reserved Occupations' were identified. In May 1916 all men were conscripted or directed in labour. Conscription was a deathblow to liberalism. It ran contrary to the concept of individual liberty and starkly demonstrated state direction.

Britain geared itself for total war
From the outset Britain faced some shortages, but they were limited. The government made bulk purchases of wheat and sugar which were scarce after U-boat attacks, and aimed to safeguard the supply of Indian jute (for sandbags) and Russian flax (tent canvas). However, prices did increase by 59 per cent between July 1914 and June 1916. This wartime inflation was to be expected. In 1916 there were some local rationing initiatives but no national scheme until 1918. The shell shortage had caused the biggest concern. Lloyd George was appointed the Minister

of Munitions and he applied great energy to the problem. In January 1915 the army received its first batch of Stokes' trench mortars, thanks to his efforts. Despite Kitchener's scepticism, Lloyd George also ordered 40 of Major Swinton's 'landships' under the codename of 'tanks'. The Munitions of War Act brought munitions and armaments factories under government control and banned strikes, lockouts and drunkenness. The ministry Lloyd George created was unorthodox. Housed in a hotel outside Parliament, it was staffed with businessmen of 'push and go', rather than civil servants. Despite the claim that it produced startling results, its first consignment of shells did not reach the front until October 1915 and the War Office had already produced a 19-fold increase in ammunition in the first six months of the war.

Domestic morale: there was also growing unrest at war conditions
Under the terms of the Treasury Agreement in March 1915, unions in war work would forego the right to strike. However, some union members were angry that the strike weapon had been abandoned so readily. On 'red' Clydeside there were angry protests and a hostile reception for Lloyd George in Glasgow in December 1915 led to the arrest of the union ringleaders. Industrial disputes actually increased during the war, from 532 in 1915 to 1,165 in 1918. However, in Russia disturbances became far more serious and a full-scale revolution developed in February 1917. The Tsar abdicated when his commanders lost faith in his leadership, and the monarchy was replaced by a provisional government. In France heavy casualties in 1917 caused soldiers to refuse to fight. They marched away from the front or argued that they would only take part in the defence of positions but would not attack. In Germany, food shortages were beginning to take their toll and, by 1918, bread riots were affecting many major cities.

War of attrition: the battle of Verdun

General von Falkenhayn, Chief of the General Staff, conceived a plan to 'bleed France white' by forcing it to commit thousands of troops in defence of the fortress town of Verdun. Reasoning that the French would not let the town fall for national prestige, he hoped that the French would deploy men who could be destroyed by artillery fire. The forts commanded good fields of fire but most of their heavy 155 cm guns had been withdrawn following the lesson of the defeat of the Belgian fortresses at Liege in 1914. As soon as the German build-up began, the French sent reserves to the area, but the main German bombardment was delayed by blizzards (which grounded artillery-spotting aircraft). Nevertheless, the Germans' 1,200 guns outnumbered the 270 French ones and they could muster only 34 divisions against the Germans' 74. Re-supply was along a secondary road, the *Voie Sacrée*, and 1,700 trucks a day sustained the garrisons. The Germans had fired thousands of shells by the time Fort Douaumont was captured (25 February), but they gradually seized their objectives: Hill 295 (29 May) and Fort Vaux (6 June). On 24 October General Nivelle counter-attacked (although operations were directed largely by General Mangin) and recaptured much of the lost ground. On 18 December the French had regained their original line. Forty million shells had fallen around Verdun. The French lost 543,000 and the Germans 434,000 men. This made it a battle of attrition, but Falkenhayn had not realised that the Germans would suffer as heavily as the French.

Strategy and tactics: the Battle of the Somme

There are criticisms of Haig's plans
The Somme is perhaps the best known and most remembered of all the battles of the First World War. This is largely because of the high casualties that were sustained on the first day of the battle; 57,000 were killed and wounded, which was the most costly day in the history of the British army. The Somme is also synonymous with the blunders of the war. However, the battle looks quite different when it is viewed in context. Haig chose the Somme for a grand set-piece offensive. The argument runs that the site was poorly chosen because the Germans had excellent views of the British as they attacked uphill from the Ancre valley. The second accusation is that his troops were too inexperienced compared with the German soldiers; Haig perhaps thought he could pit the enthusiasm of the British volunteer civilians against the machine guns of the German army. The third criticism was his use of artillery. A massive bombardment was supposed to smash the German trenches and barbed wire. Then, at the appointed hour, waves of British soldiers would get up out of their trenches and walk forward, carrying 60 lb of equipment, to occupy the German trenches.

Historians are divided about Haig's performance
In the event, when the British attacked, in many places they were cut down by German machine guns and artillery. Ever since, the enormous casualty figures have been put down to the incompetence of the generals. Thanks to *The Donkeys* (1963) by Alan Clark (a reference to the comment

alleged to have been made by the German commander Ludendorff, that British soldiers were 'lions led by donkeys'), Gerard de Groot's highly critical biography of Haig, and John Laffin's often inaccurate *British Butchers and Bunglers of World War One* (1998), the impression given is that the generals were incapable of any tactical imagination. Nevertheless, some military historians have taken a different view. John Terraine demonstrated that Haig's stoicism reflected the Field Marshal's view that the Western Front was one, long continuous engagement requiring the full mobilisation of national resources and some tough decisions. Keith Simpson listed the mitigating factors as: pre-war inexperience of total war, lack of preparation, the problem of adapting to new technology, the strength of the German army, restraints imposed by the coalition partners (France and Russia) and political interference. Paddy Griffith believed that the army's experiences were cumulative and contrasted the inexperience of the early years with the successes and scientific application of artillery in 1917–18.

Britain had to support France and Russia in 1916
The painful truth was that Britain was obliged to launch an offensive, and Haig insisted that it be planned carefully. The Germans occupied a large slice of Belgium and France, and would not negotiate while it was still strong. Russia was under pressure in the east and France was enduring a massive and costly offensive at Verdun to the south. General Joffre practically begged Haig to launch an attack to divert the Germans from Verdun. Haig was reluctant. The professional soldiers in the British army were few in number, and the volunteers of 'Kitchener's Army' were as yet untried in battle. Haig's first choice for a British offensive was Ypres because it was near the ports (making re-supply easier) and an attack here would try to capture the cluster of German railheads, and that would make the continued occupation of the north untenable for them. However, there was an alternative to the muddy and low-lying fields of Flanders. The Somme uplands were chalk where well-drained and drier conditions prevailed, especially in summer. The Somme was also the junction of the French and British armies so that a joint attack here, along a 30-mile front, would double its effect on the Germans.

Haig had learnt valuable lessons from 1914 and 1915
Valuable lessons had also been learnt from the fighting of 1914 and 1915 which could be applied here. Artillery fire was going to be delivered in a scientific way. Instead of a random bombardment there would be two

phases. A preparatory bombardment would pulverise trenches, wire, strongpoints and demoralise the enemy. On the day of the attack, a creeping barrage would be applied; shells falling just in front of the advancing troops and lifted and advanced every few minutes. To add to the effect, mine shafts would be dug so that explosives could be detonated underneath the German positions just before the infantry went in. As soldiers trained for the attack, there was a growing sense of optimism. It was felt that it might even be possible to break through the German lines after a day or two. This would enable the cavalry to pour through and pursue the Germans, disrupting their rear areas, perhaps even initiating a general collapse of the Kaiser's army.

Planning and preparation: the offensive required huge preparations
The British army had never before attempted an attack on this scale. Half a million men were involved. The logistics to support it were staggering. Thousands of shells, cartridges, explosives and guns were required. The army had to be fed, clothed, shod and equipped. Horses, fodder, water, barbed wire, stretchers, nurses, saddlery, workshops, communications wire, nails and a million other things were needed, and with the French under pressure at Verdun, time was short. The artillery firestorm began on 24 June and lasted a week. It was the largest artillery bombardment of the war to that date. The soldiers each carried a rifle, bayonet, 220 rounds of ammunition, gas helmet, wound dressing, two hand grenades, flares, a spade, greatcoat, haversack and two empty sandbags. Some also carried reels of barbed wire, pickets, mortar bombs, signalling equipment or a Lewis gun and ammunition belts. With these loads, it was hard to make progress over broken ground.

Heavy casualties: the battle was one of the costliest of the war for Britain
Prior to the attack, captured German soldiers produced mixed reports; some were demoralised by the shelling, others were unaffected. Behind the front line trenches was a warren of dugouts and galleries extending back into the hills. Sheltering from the bombardment, the German troops emerged as soon as the shelling lifted and poured fire into the advance. Casualties were high in many units. The 16th Middlesex Regiment (the Public Schools Battalion made up of students and staff) was in the first wave at 07.30, 800 strong. At 07.45 they fell back to their start line; 22 officers and 500 men were casualties. However, the 36th Ulster Division captured its first-day objectives, only to be forced back again by German counter-attacks. Some key villages were captured,

such as Mametz, and others fell a few days later. Thiepval, the centre of a series of German strongpoints, was not captured until September. Certain woods, such as Delville or High Wood, became the scene of intense struggles.

Technology

There was a continuing search for solutions amidst a grim struggle

On 15 September the first tanks were used and, despite their numbers, they were a remarkable success. Mechanical unreliability and vulnerability to artillery fire were their greatest weaknesses, but they were the greatest technical innovation of the war. They also allowed commanders to retain mobility on the battlefield of the Western Front. New types of poison gas were tried out too. However, the refinement in the use of artillery was becoming apparent and it was clear that gunfire dominated. Nevertheless bad weather, combined with the cratered soil, rendered the battlefield impassable and the offensive was halted in November. The Somme had not produced a breakthrough as expected and had developed into a battle of attrition. Although the British army suffered 400,000 killed, wounded and missing, the Germans losses are estimated to have been 600,000 (the French lost 200,000). A German officer described the Somme as 'the muddy grave of the German army'. Therefore, whilst British soldiers endured terrible conditions and suffered heavy losses, there was still a grim determination to win.

Tactics: the development of indirect fire

Between 1914 and 1916 techniques of indirect fire had made it possible to defend points without having to expose men to enemy fire. Gaps in barbed wire, for example, could be fired on from behind slopes, the bullets falling as a 'beaten zone'. Artillery was used less in the direct fire role, firing over 'open sights', in preference to the saturation of wide areas with high explosive. The density of artillery per yard gradually increased during the war, but the rate of fire was often so demanding that barrels quickly wore out. On 9 May 1915 the French had adopted a creeping barrage that shelled Vimy Ridge, but wire was left uncut and insufficient attention was paid to known machine-gun posts. When the infantry attacked, their reserves were too far back to help when the German machine guns cut down the French troops channelled by the wire. They sustained losses of 100,000 men (the Germans 60,000) for a gain of 1.5 miles on a front of 3.5 miles.

The Italian Front and the Balkans theatre

Italy joined the war on 23 May 1915 but much of the Italian army's effort concentrated on the mountainous border with Austria. Supplies, arms and ammunition had to be hauled up the slopes. The possession of the highest points became vital to success. Avalanche, frostbite and exposure accounted for many of the campaign's casualties. The difficulty of making any engagement decisive was revealed by the fact that 12 battles took place on the Isonzo River. In the Balkans the mountain regions were cut by valleys and plains, so the fighting was not as confined and Serbia was almost overrun in 1914. To relieve pressure on the Serbians, the Allies managed to persuade the Greeks to join the war, but an offensive was reduced to a trench stalemate in the Salonika area. Bulgaria joined the Central Powers in 1915, as did Turkey. Thus, by 1916, the war had extended in scale but there were no decisive victories.

Tutorial

Progress questions
1. What was the achievement of the small BEF in 1914?
2. What methods did Britain try to use to break the deadlock of the Western Front?
3. What was new about warfare between 1914 and 1916?

Seminar discussion
Were the Great War British generals incompetent?

Practical assignment
1. Make a list of all the measures nations were forced to consider to wage a total war.
2. What obstacles did an army face in trying to win the war? Consider how governments and generals dealt with these problems.

Study tips
1. It is easy to jump to conclusions about the leadership of the British war effort. Instead of condemnation, try to account for their limitations and the obstacles they faced. Try to be objective about the military leaders of other nations in the war.
2. Try to find out more about your local community and the Great War. How were local people affected?

12

Total War, 1916–1918

One Minute overview – The years 1917 and 1918 were marked by the maturation of fully operational war economies, and the perfection of tactics based on the battles of 1914–1916. British soldiers and their commanders had more experience and there was a better appreciation of how artillery should be used. However, the German army had also developed new tactics of defence which, along with atrocious and unseasonable weather, brought the 1917 Ypres offensive to a standstill. The French army began to crack up after the battle of Verdun, putting more emphasis on the British war effort. When Russia collapsed in 1918, German troops arrived on the Western Front to resume the attack on this front. Critically short of manpower, Haig and the British troops stemmed the tide as best they could. In the summer of 1918, American reinforcements arrived to assist in a gigantic counter-offensive. By the autumn, the British army had returned to mobile warfare. These attacks in France, and the Royal Navy's blockade caused Germany to sue for peace in November 1918. On the home front in each country, massive efforts were made to supply the food, equipment and munitions needed to sustain intense operations.

In this chapter you will learn:

▶ the development of total war
▶ how the allies tried to find solutions to the stalemate in 1917
▶ the collapse of Russia
▶ the methods by which the allies achieved victory in 1918

The organisation of the state for total war

The British Prime Minister, Lloyd George, made far-reaching changes
Lloyd George established a smaller, five-man War Cabinet and a Cabinet Secretariat to co-ordinate all government departments. He filled ministries with non-government experts, such as Joseph Maclay (ship-owner) in charge of shipping and newspaper magnate Lord Beaver-

brook in charge of propaganda. Lloyd George also set up a private secretariat (nicknamed 'the Garden Suburb') of advisors. He directed that food production be increased, and an additional 3 million acres was cultivated. Wheat production increased by 1 million tons, and potatoes by 1.5 million tons. Rationing was introduced, first for sugar and later other products. Bread was not rationed and prices of this staple crop were kept down by a subsidy. At sea, Maclay requisitioned almost all private merchant ships for war use. The Admiralty was slow to adopt convoys to protect merchant shipping, because it was thought the number of ships to protect was too vast and the number of protection vessels too few, but experiments in April 1917 proved a success.

The German war economy

The economic aspects of the war were apparent from the outset, and Germany's U-boat campaign was designed to wage an economic war on Britain and France. By the end of the war, Britain had inflicted 24 million Reichsmarks' worth of damage on German industry in bombing raids. In Germany the drain of manpower in the armed forces affected agriculture: production fell, despite the increased demand, by 50–70 per cent. Germany was the first country to introduce rationing, limiting the consumption of bread, meat, potatoes and fats. Horses were also in demand. In 1914 Germany took control of civilian resources and production with the War Materials Department. Women were enlisted in factory work for munitions and there were increasing controls over information. Censorship and propaganda became essential tools of the war effort. Food shortages eventually eroded German morale, and Austria's army suffered mass desertions when rations gave out in 1918.

Technology: the evolution of artillery and machine guns

Artillery was becoming more accurate. This was due to improvement in the reliability of fuses, and the matching of each gun to individual targets. Guns were carefully calibrated and surveyed into position so that it was no longer necessary to observe the fall of shot for every round. Accurate meteorological data could be used to calculate the effect of crosswinds and rain on the fall of shot too. Creeping barrages threw shells along a line, that could be 'lifted' a bound of 100 yards at the pace of walking troops, so that infantry could arrive on an objective behind a curtain of fire. The shelling of communication routes kept enemy reserves at bay. Counter-battery fire also developed. Almost every attack was preceded by a storm of high explosive and gas shells against gunners. Guns were being controlled centrally by specialised staff at headquarters. 'Artillery time' became the dominant feature of all battle planning. As artillery got heavier, so lighter machine guns were developed. The Lewis gun became a tactical support weapon that could be carried by one man in the attack. It weighed 25 lb (11 kg) compared with the Maxim's 125 lb (56 kg). The British had 40,000 Lewis guns by 1916. The Germans developed a lightweight Maxim, but their best weapon was the Gast which could fire 1,000 rounds a minute, twice the rate of other Maxim types. The machine gun represented the importance of area weapons. At close quarters, the hand grenade became the most valuable weapon for the infantry.

The campaigns of 1917

Trench warfare: Operation Albericht and the Hindenburg Line
In early 1917 the German High Command decided to remain on the defensive in both the eastern and western theatres, in order to break the Italians in the south. To this end the German army retired 20 miles within the Somme sector in Operation Albericht. The extraction was carried out in total secrecy, and the bewildered allies followed up cautiously. The Germans had booby-trapped and destroyed everything that could be of use in the abandoned areas, and they took up new, prepared positions on the so-called Hindenburg Line. Acres of barbed wire protected concrete bunkers and a five-mile deep defence line. Fifteen hundred yards in front of the 'battle zone' was an outpost line, an area that could absorb artillery fire without exposing men to destruction. Within the battle zone, troops were encouraged to surrender ground if necessary but to counter-attack aggressively any key positions. Isolated field guns were dug in as anti-tank weapons.

Nivelle's offensive failed
On 16 April General Nivelle launched an offensive in the Champagne region on the River Aisne. Over one million French troops in the Fifth and Sixth Armies, supported by the First and Tenth Armies, advanced behind a creeping barrage. Nevertheless, the Germans had prior warning of the attack. They shelled the assault trenches and cut down the human waves in front of concrete strongpoints. The repetition of these attacks, coupled with poor conditions out of the line, eroded the morale of the French *poilus* (soldiers).

The Italian were defeated at Caporetto
The Italians were routed at Caporetto on 24 October 1917, just at the

point where they had succeeded in throwing back the Austro-Hungarian army. The exhausted Italians were shocked when German and Austrian units infiltrated their lines using new tactics. The appearance of enemy troops in the rear, coupled with their exhaustion, broke the army. Attempts to stem the tide failed at Tagliamento on 31 October. British and French reinforcements were hurried to the River Piave and General Cadorna, the Italian commander, stabilised a line by 4 November. Much-needed British and French troops were diverted from the Western Front.

Domestic morale: the collapse of Russia

The failure of the Russian Brusilov offensive and its consequences
In 1916 General Alexei Brusilov launched a well-organised and gigantic offensive against two Austrian armies near Czernowitz. It was so successful that the Germans were forced to divert troops to assist the Austrians. When the Russians reached the Carpathians, exhaustion, lack of supplies and one million casualties halted the attack. Conditions in the Russian army were generally so poor, and food so scarce at home, that the people and the army revolted in February 1917. The army formed Soviets (councils) and, encouraged by Bolshevik agitators, discipline collapsed. The provisional government appointed Brusilov Chief of Staff, but the failure of his second offensive in 1917 (1–19 July) marked the total collapse of the Russian army. Russia had lost because it lacked the industrial capacity to wage a total war and suffered acute shortages.

The burden of the Western Front shifted towards the British army
Nivelle's offensive on the Aisne in April 1917 resulted in such heavy casualties that it led to mutinies in the French army. Coming on the back of revolutionary unrest in Russia, it was imperative that the British relieve pressure on the other Entente powers. Already at Arras the British and imperial forces had secured the vital Vimy Ridge (9–14 April). However, subsequent attacks were exhausted by the depth of the German positions, for belts of wire, trenches and emplacements succeeded each other behind the front line.

Tactics: the Battle of Messines Ridge was a success
General Sir Herbert ('Daddy') Plumer was the commander of 2nd Army tasked with capturing the Messines Ridge. Securing this high ground would be the prelude to an attack on the Menin-Broodseinde

Ridge which, once taken, would place the British army within striking distance of the main rail junction of Menin from which the Germans were supplying and reinforcing the entire northern front. Plumer's preparations were meticulous. Tunnels were dug under the German front line for explosives to be laid, light railways brought up ammunition in vast quantities, and 2,266 guns fired 3.5 million shells into the German positions. On 7 June 19 mines were detonated and the British attack captured three lines of German trenches and, with them, the entire ridge. The success illustrated what had been learned from the Somme. New fuses enabled artillery to destroy wire, the British infantry were better trained, the Royal Artillery dominated the battlefield and infantry–artillery co-ordination had been perfected. However, there were still heavy casualties: 25,000 had fallen in the battle.

Heavy casualties: the Third Battle of Ypres was a pyrrhic victory
The chief difficulty with the second phase of the operations around Ypres was that the low-lying and marshy ground had been smashed by years of shelling. Added to this was the appalling weather that dogged the attack almost from the start. Some sectors became impassable swamps and trenches filled with water. The infantry continued to attack, but often found it impossible to hold on to ground against German counter-attacks. Tanks foundered in the mud. Wounded men were drowned in shell holes. Even some of the concrete emplacements slid into the slough, trapping those inside. This battle, more than any other, inspired comments on war's futility from those who endured it. The conditions were not unfamiliar to the soldiers, but the heavy casualties, gas attacks, shelling and exhausting trial of moving in the quagmire of the Ypres Salient marked the battle out as particularly distinct. Estimates of the casualties by the end of the offensive in November vary, but are thought to be in the region of 260,000. The ridges were captured, but the casualty figures suggest that the price was too high to call it a success. The consolation was that the German army had suffered just as heavily and Ludendorff, the German Commander in Chief, doubted whether the Kaiser's forces could take another blow like Third Ypres, or Passchendaele as it became known.

Tactics: Cambrai proved more tanks would be used in future attacks
The sign of things to come was the remarkable success at Cambrai. Initially conceived of as a raid, massed tank formations of 476 vehicles captured 8 miles of German lines. A shortage of reserves meant that the ground could not be held for long, but it had proved the worth of

the tank. The Germans had lost 10,000 men, 123 guns, 79 trench mortars and 281 machine guns. British losses were 4,000 and 179 tanks. By 1918 British tanks had become far more reliable, and a new light version was being developed. The only problem with the tactics used at Cambrai was the continuing focus on reducing German strongpoints instead of driving in depth into the enemy rear.

Technology: air power had become more important
The Germans deployed airships, or Zeppelins, to carry out bombing raids behind the front and even across Britain. Bombers were developed by both sides too. Ground strafing raids by fighters were becoming more common, and hybrid fighter-bombers were being used by 1918. On 21 September 1918 the Turkish Seventh Army was caught in a defile called Wadi Fara when it came under RAF bomber and fighter attack (the Royal Air Force was formed in 1918 to supersede the RFC, or Royal Flying Corps). The road out was blocked and the men gradually began to disperse into the desert. After four hours of air attacks, the Turks lost 90 guns, 50 lorries and 1,000 other vehicles. Curiously, cavalry had also survived in this theatre and a number of charges were made (although dismounted action was more common). Cavalry still retained the mobility and cross-country capability that road vehicles did not have. Cavalry could also dismount to hold ground, unlike aircraft. This arm was therefore retained in some armies into the 1930s.

The victory of 1918

The German spring offensive was overwhelming
Having finally defeated Russia in March 1918, the German army swung its main effort at the British on the Somme. A series of sledgehammer blows drove the Third and Fifth Armies back, but Haig managed to hold the line. Despite criticism from Lloyd George, Haig also held back his reserves until it was clear where the attacks would fall. Unable to break though on the Somme, the Germans tried to break the Second Army at Ypres. Subsequent attacks were made against the French. Marshal Foch became the Supreme Allied Commander to co-ordinate the defence of the Western Front.

German tactics in the spring offensive were effective
General Oscar von Hutier had developed new 'breakthrough' tactics at Riga on the eastern front. Hutier abandoned the long preliminary bombardment (realising that most shells destroyed the ground and fell

into the empty outpost line) in favour of a short storm of shells, followed up by 'battle units'. These were teams of grenade throwers, infantry, machine-gunners, assault artillery and engineers, thus achieving close co-operation and faster decision-making. Small groups, 'storm troops', would be ordered to precede the battle units, skirting stiff opposition, but using grenades to blast a way through to the enemy rear. Strong-points could thus be isolated and neutralised later. At Riga the Russians were demoralised, but the tactics also began to work in the west. Mobility had been achieved by these tactics and the continual movement protected the troops from heavy artillery fire.

Problems in the logistics of the German offensive soon stalled the attack
Ludendorff, despite the success of the new tactics, was surprised at the resistance of the British after their initial shock. Although the British and the French had been thrown back, Ludendorff tried to secure strategic points, such as Vimy Ridge and Arras, instead of enveloping them. The distances of ground taken got progressively shorter as German troops became exhausted or met stiffer opposition. Local superiority of numbers was lost when Ludendorff tried to widen the front, attacking south of Ypres on the Lys or on the Aisne. The German's supply system began to give out, and the storm troops could no longer rely on captured British depots. The Germans lacked tanks (their version, the A7V, could not cross trenches) and all their cavalry was committed in the east.

The shortage of manpower for the allies was critical in early 1918
The number of battalions in British brigades was reduced from four to three, but there was no disguising the shortage of troops. With years of emphasis on attack, rear areas were ill-prepared to withstand the German attacks. However, the trickle of American troops was becoming a steady stream by early 1918. At first there were too few of these enthusiastic, but inexperienced troops to be used effectively as an independent command, but their presence released British and French troops from reserves. With these additional men, the German March offensive was checked and then thrown back.

Mobile war returned in the '100 Days' campaign from Amiens
Rawlinson, the commander of the 4th Army (combining British, Canadian and Anzac troops), maximised the use of tanks, machine guns and artillery co-ordination to achieve considerable success near Amiens. Aircraft dominated the skies, and a rolling barrage in front of the

advancing troops repeated the success of the 4th Army over several days. On 8 August, 8 miles were captured, and Ludendorff knew that the end was coming. He called it 'the black day of the German Army'. Six hundred and four Allied tanks had surprised the Germans after a short bombardment; light tanks and armoured cars then penetrated 20 miles into the rear, overrunning headquarters and supplies. J. F. C. Fuller helped devise a plan for massed tank action if the war continued for another year. He proposed a wave of 10,000 vehicles that would penetrate the German lines to attack control centres and communications nodes.

Breaking the Hindenburg Line marked the beginning of the end for Germany
The advance continued and the German Hindenburg Line, a strongly fortified system, was broken in September. The Germans continued to fight, but they were pressed back towards their own borders. Armour, artillery, aircraft and infantry all worked in close co-operation.

The effects of blockade ensured the final collapse of the German war effort
Shortages in Germany caused by the Royal Navy's blockade had reached crisis levels in many cities and food riots were an indication that the war effort could no longer be sustained. There was growing war weariness amongst the troops too. Germany's allies gave up. The news from the Western Front led to the collapse of the military government and the Kaiser abdicated. As Plumer cleared the Belgian coast and the British army advanced towards Germany, an armistice was declared on 11 November 1918.

Interpretations of the First World War

Casualties were an important legacy but not the determinant of victory
The Hundred Days and the German capitulation in November 1918 indicate that the Allies had won the Great War, but the scale of the losses gave rise to a determination never to go to war again. Seven hundred and fifty thousand British and Empire soldiers, sailors and airmen died on the Western Front. Britain alone lost a total of 650,000 with 1.6 million permanently disabled. Germany lost 1.8 million, France 1.3 million, Russia 1.7 million, Austria–Hungary 1.2 million and Italy 460,000. For a long time, it was thought that the 'flower' of European youth had perished: the best, brightest and fittest. This was probably because the junior officer corps, drawn from the educated middle classes and aristocracy, had suffered proportionally higher

casualties. However, the terrible losses amongst the British Pals' battalions on the Somme, or the territorial units of continental armies, devastated small communities. Thousands of families lost at least one family member. Death did not respect rank or status, the great and the humble lost sons, brothers, and friends. Yet Britain and France would have suffered far worse consequences if, as almost occurred in March–April 1918, the Germans had won. There was little sympathy for the Germans in 1918. An army of occupation stood on the Rhine and the allies demanded that Germany pay for the damage and sorrow it had inflicted on the rest of the world. Sadly, this nurtured a desire for revenge in the hearts of German nationalists that would lead to another, even more costly world war.

Tutorial

Progress questions
1. What measures did Lloyd George implement in the economy during the war?
2. Why was Plumer's attack at Messines Ridge in 1917 a success?
3. What went wrong in the attack at Third Ypres?
4. By what methods did the Allies achieve final victory in 1918?

Seminar discussion
1. How did the use of artillery evolve during the First World War, and why was the limited use of artillery at Neuve Chappelle as successful as the tremendous volume of artillery at Messines Ridge two years later?

Practical assignment
1. Assess the relative importance of the war at sea, wartime controls at home and battlefield tactics in producing the Allied victory of 1918.

Study tips
1. Note how, until 1916, the British failed to appreciate the full implications of total war, whereas Lloyd George dispensed with normal procedures for the sake of urgency.
2. Note that most military historians do not condemn the British generals; historians should try to appreciate the problems that contemporaries faced.

13

Conclusions: warfare and the experience of war

One minute overview – Warfare, as the preceding chapters have shown, did not develop in a smooth, linear fashion. Technological superiority was not the only determinant of victory. So many factors have influenced the outcomes of battles and campaigns, and, whilst conveniently labelled 'the friction of war', they have often been more important than a single advantage in firearms technology. Even superior weapons will not win a battle if the men are too tired, hungry or terrified to operate them, or if the ammunition isn't available to supply them. Wars are very human experiences that have influenced much of world history. Decisive battles have changed the course of history. Yet those battles depended on the performance of soldiers who were often concerned with much more mundane matters, or with their own personal survival. To fully understand a period of history, historians have to acknowledge the important role of armies, guerrillas and leaders. Equally, to understand change in warfare, a full appreciation of the historical forces are required; the political systems, the cause for which the soldiers felt they were fighting, the level of education of the troops, the experience of the leaders and the economic power of the states involved.

In this chapter you will learn:

▶ how the experience of soldiers played a part in determining the outcome of war
▶ the importance of tactics and technology relative to other historical factors
▶ the strengths and weaknesses of linear and non-linear explanations of warfare
▶ changes in warfare: an overview

The experience of war

Military life: enlistment and comradeship built unit cohesion
Military discipline came as a shock to civilian recruits, regardless of
whether they were volunteers or conscripts. Shared hardship and the
collective identity of regiment or corps was enough to bond strangers as
close friends who would support each other when the fighting began.
The pride, or *esprit de corps*, was fostered by the officers and NCOs in
their men so that, even after leaving their parent organisations, the
loyalties to them continued for many years, if not for life. The regimental tradition was vital when a unit faced heavy casualties. If most of the
unit was killed, an identity could be maintained. Soldiers were
prepared to sacrifice themselves in the knowledge that the regiment
would survive. Selfless acts of courage were also performed for the regimental honour and recorded in regimental history, helping to build the
esteem of those who enlisted later. Professional soldiers became disdain-
ful of 'causes', valuing the regiment and duty above any other reason
for fighting. In combat, a soldier would fight for his immediate friends:
this was often more important than the higher cause of the regiment or
patriotism.

On campaign, conditions were tough
Life on campaign was hard. Weather conditions were the most important concern for soldiers not actually in combat. In hot weather, dehy-
dration and heat could exhaust heavily laden men. In freezing
conditions, frostbite or exposure could create casualties. Throughout
the period 1792–1918 soldiers usually marched to war, often vast
distances. In temperate climates, assembly before dawn to cook break-
fast would be necessary. Parades would precede the march. Pauses
would be made along the line of march and troops would bivouac for
the night, unless they were fortunate enough to occupy barracks or
billets (civilian homes requisitioned for military use). Many troops had
no tents, having to make do with a greatcoat or blanket. These, and
simple kitchen tools, would be carried in a knapsack. A canteen of
water, ammunition, rifle and bayonet, and perhaps an entrenching
tool, would complete the marching load, averaging 60 pounds. Troops
sometimes would have to dig in at the end of a march, especially if the
enemy was near, creating some earthwork or shallow trench to shelter
from enemy fire. Cavalrymen had other duties. Horses always took
priority, so that watering and providing fodder came before the troo-
per's personal welfare. For the artillery, the guns and horses were simi-

larly placed before the individual's own interests. Officers were expected to command their men, but those who neglected welfare would rarely get any good performance from them. The Duke of Wellington knew that there was a direct relationship between soldiers who were fed and paid regularly and battlefield success.

Disease was a hidden enemy

Until 1944 more men died on campaign from disease than from enemy action. In poor weather conditions soldiers who were ill-fed and run down were more susceptible to infections and diseases. In tropical climates soldiers often fell victim to diseases typical in the region. In swamps and coastal areas, malaria accounted for many casualties. Yellow fever was common in the Caribbean stations. Beri-beri affected south-east Asian campaigns. Cholera and typhoid were prevalent whenever water supplies were unclean. Many soldiers suffered from diarrhoea and dysentery. Soldiers died of heat stroke in India during the Mutiny campaigns, as the battles were fought at the height of the hot season. Wounded soldiers were also vulnerable to infections like gangrene and septicaemia. There were other 'inconveniences'. Keeping clean in the field, finding adequate sanitation, or being covered in lice were irritations that soldiers had to live with from Valmy to Verdun.

'An army marches on its stomach': food was vital in any period

All soldiers complained, and top of the list was food. Napoleon's men, who foraged for their supplies if they were beyond depots, descended like locusts on central and eastern Europe. In 1813, after years of war, there was a general shortage of food. The Confederacy, in the latter stages of the American Civil War, began to run out of food, and even Union troops, such as those of Major General William Rosecrans in the Chattanooga campaign, fought on half rations.

Fatigue was a typical experience of war

Living rough on campaign and marching for hours or days or weeks was exhausting. Stephen Westman, a soldier of the German 113th Infantry, recalled marching 'in a coma'. A. W. Hancox of the Royal Field Artillery on the Western Front in 1917 described having to live in eight-man bell tents that were surrounded by a lake of ankle deep, liquid mud. On the Western Front rats, which fed on corpses, grew to enormous sizes and soldiers grew tired of their presence amongst them, especially at night. In darkness First World War soldiers had to perform sentry duties to prevent raids, dig trenches, fill sandbags, erect barbed wire entanglements, man listening posts in No-Man's Land, bring up 'trench stores' (rations and equipment) or go on patrol. Fatigue affected performance, but also morale. Sergeant Wheeler of the 51st explained that on the night before Waterloo the rain 'ran in streams from the cuffs of our jackets … we were as wet as if we had been plunged over head in a river'. However, men from working-class or rural backgrounds were used to the toil of hard labour and fared better than the middle-class intellectuals in the turmoil of the First World War.

Pre-battle enthusiasm and anxiety was a unique experience for soldiers
Soldiers often share mixed emotions about going into battle: a desire to do well contrasting with a sense of danger. Anxieties often concern a fear of failure, of letting down comrades or of letting terror gain the upper hand. Combat itself actually released many soldiers from fear. Richard Holmes, in *Firing Line*, has analysed the range of feeling of soldiers both in and out of combat, and reached this conclusion. In January 1917 Captain J. E. H. Nevill wrote that he was only 'afraid of getting the wind up … I'm afraid of being afraid'. NCOs and officers were frequently busy enough before a battle not to suffer the effects of pre-battle stress so acutely, and concern for the performance or welfare of their men helped them forget their own vulnerability. Officers were expected to lead though, and this accounts for the frequently higher proportion of casualties amongst leaders. The officers of the 23rd Regiment continued to stroll about in full view of the enemy after capturing the Great Redoubt at the battle of the Alma in 1854, because courage was expected of them, but many were hit as a result. In 1915 officers of the Royal Welch Fusiliers complained about new uniforms that concealed badges of rank for officers, even though the old ones drew the attention of enemy snipers. Lieutenant H. Allen described the moment of being in action and under fire as 'wonderfully inspiring'. Equally, without irony, Sergeant R. H. Tawney (Manchester Regiment, Somme, 1916) felt 'a load fall' from him when he went over the top because he realised he wasn't scared.

Effects of shelling could be mental as well as physical
Most soldiers found battle a disorientating experience, particularly when friends became casualties. Explosions and changes to the landscape also added to the sense of the unreal. Bunching together offered solace and cohesion, but made groups more vulnerable to enemy fire. Advancing troops, often bent double as if walking into a rainstorm, were discouraged from taking cover because they were less likely to get

going again. Advancing, or at least moving, was far easier to bear than remaining stationary under artillery fire. Gas shells were a particular terror, because they could arrive at any time, during any bombardment. H. S. Clapham described being under bombardment at Hooge in June 1915 and, longing for one shell to put an end to the torture, found himself quite stupefied. At the battle of the Alma British soldiers were constantly reminded of their dressing and their appearance so as to take their mind off the fearful cannonade that was tearing through the ranks. Major Charles Napier made his men of the 50th Foot do rifle drill whilst under fire at Corunna in 1809. At Verdun, under heavy shelling, inactive French soldiers sometimes went mad or committed suicide. Fatalism could settle in when soldiers who dived for cover were killed. An Australian artillery officer in the First World War described soldiers who gave up ducking, believing that fate would take them anyway. For others, religion became important. Rum rations were issued to British soldiers from the Peninsular War to the Great War, as alcohol had long been used to keep up the spirits or keep out the cold.

Attitudes towards the enemy varied from indifference to hatred
Despite contemporary Western attitudes to war, that it is a futile exercise that can only result in a pointless loss of human life, historical figures sometimes took a different view. Captain Julian Grenfell, writing of the First World War, said that he adored the experience. Danger and the sense of participating in an historic or worthwhile enterprise, or life with a special object or mission, were thought preferable to a mundane, peacetime and purposeless existence. Robert E. Lee, proud of the victory his men had achieved at Fredericksburg, pointed out that it was as well that war was terrible, 'lest we become too fond of it'. British soldiers who shot down German infantry attacks in 1914 found pleasure in the sense of power it gave them. However, professional soldiers were often indifferent towards their enemies. Major Tom Bridges of the 4th Dragoon Guards wrote that he would have fought the French or Belgians as readily as the Germans in 1914. After the battle of Spion Kop in 1900, a Boer asked a British officer how they could endure such heavy casualties. The officer replied dismissively that this 'is the life we always lead'. The misuse of white flags by Boers and German troops, however accidental, tended to change attitudes. The breach of rules was important in combat too. German machine gunners who kept firing up to the point when British and Imperial troops were upon them in the trenches of Flanders and then tried to surrender were bayoneted with the comment: 'Too late, chum'. There are accounts of soldiers who had

lost close friends and found themselves in charge of small groups of prisoners, shooting them. Poor discipline might lead to atrocities, but also
sheer frustration stemming from the inability to combat guerrillas.
Those who fought in civilian clothing risked reprisals being inflicted on
their own population, as in Spain between 1808 and 1813.

Casualties: the sight of the dead was shocking
The dead were the most shocking features of the battlefield, and the
sight of wounds often profoundly affected the living for the rest of their
lives. Blasts ruptured bodies and severed heads or limbs. William Frassi-
nato remarked that the battlefield of Antietam could be smelt a mile
away, and Charles Carrington remembered the Western Front had an
odour of 'burnt and poisoned mud ... and the stink of corrupting flesh'.
In the trenches of France and Flanders hastily buried corpses could be
churned up by artillery fire or by men digging new trenches. However,
familiarity with the dead bred indifference: soldiers used protruding
limbs as hooks for everyday bits of equipment and bodies hanging on
the wire became just another landmark. The destruction of bodies
made soldiers all the more determined that their comrades should
enjoy the dignity of burial and remembrance when the war was over.

The suffering of the wounded was a common feature of war
Although severe wounds might cripple a soldier for life, and was a
universal fear, a slight wound in the First World War was called a
'Blighty' by British troops because it would mean a short spell out of
the firing line and a visit home. While some soldiers gave themselves
SIWs (self-inflicted wounds), the punishments were severe and for each
of these men there were others who continued fighting in spite of quite
serious injuries. Lieutenant John Glubb, wounded in the foot, hobbled
on because he did not want to leave his men in danger without his
leadership. Some bore their wounds with remarkable courage. General
Strangeways, the commander of the Royal Artillery in the Crimea,
had his leg blown off by a cannon ball at the battle of Inkerman, but
nonchalantly asked if someone 'might have the kindness to help me off
my horse'. When the surgeon told him his survival was hopeless, he
asked if he would be taken to the battle so that he 'might die amongst
my gunners'. Those in pain often sobbed. Lieutenant Vaughan of the
Royal Warwicks remembered hearing the wounded in No-Man's Land
crying, until the water in the shell holes that sheltered them rose up
and drowned them. Nevertheless, stretcher-bearers accompanied every
British unit at the front. Casualties were brought back to an advanced

dressing station, where the most critical patients were stabilised. Wounded men were then taken to a casualty clearing station and then, if necessary, to a field hospital. Advances in medical science greatly improved chances of survival.

Prisoners would be taken when the will to fight was lost

Soldiers often gave up when their position seemed hopeless and death was the only alternative. Indeed, victorious armies have often offered terms of surrender to avoid unnecessary bloodshed. These are not always accepted. The Imperial Guard at Waterloo, holding a line when the battle was clearly lost, aimed to retain its military honour by fighting to the death. When called upon to surrender, their only reply was '*merde!*' They were killed. At the end of the Boer War, and of the First World War, troops on either side were more likely to surrender. The Boers could not hold on to British prisoners and released them. The Boers could see no reason for losing their lives at the end of the war. In 1918 the Germans took thousands of British prisoners who found themselves isolated from any support in strongpoints. When the Hindenburg line was breached, German troops gave up in large numbers. Refusal to fight, or mutiny, was also a feature of the First World War in several armies. Whilst this indiscipline was rarely tolerated, there was tacit acknowledgement that both sides needed 'quiet sectors' to rest their men. In these sections of the line, neither side initiated hostilities.

Courage was an 'account'

Lord Moran, who served as an officer in the trenches of the First World War, analysed courage in battle and likened it to a bank account. Progressively, courage could be drawn upon, but unless courage was replenished by a respite, the account could be overdrawn. Soldiers who suffered from battle shock could return to the fighting if they were given light duties out of the firing line. Withdrawing them from the war altogether tended to produce worse symptoms and feelings of guilt. Surveys of soldiers in the Second World War revealed that, on average, men could endure 35 days of continuous fighting before 'combat exhaustion' set in. The intensity of artillery fire at Waterloo caused some men to lose their courage after several hours. Yet other factors could militate against combat fatigue. Gallows humour, a peculiarity of British soldiers, alleviated stress. Music or drumming had often been an encouragement to soldiers before the modern age, but it survived through to the First World War. Drummer Ritchie of the 2nd Seaforth Highlanders won the Victoria Cross on 1 July 1916 for encouraging his battalion into the attack on the Somme by drumming the 'charge'. Even voices could encourage troops: Confederates had their own 'rebel yell' and the Zulus cried '*Usuthu*' before a charge. Conversely, all cohesion could be lost in a collective panic. General Louis Tronchu remembered French troops before Austerlitz taking on this crowd mentality. Yet troops who found the strain of having to endure gunfire too much could just as easily demand to attack, as the Imperial Guard did of their officers at Rezonville (16 August 1870). Yet in the face of adversity the presence of brave men fostered courageous acts (known as Adlerian psychology). British soldiers volunteered, and competed with each other, to serve in the forlorn hope of a siege. This little band, their objective to place ladders against a wall or precede an assault, faced almost certain death, but earned little reward for doing so.

Leadership was a key factor that determined success in warfare
It has often been said there are no good or bad regiments, just good or bad officers. This illustration of the importance of leadership to military performance cannot be gainsaid. Euripides once wrote: 'Ten good soldiers wisely led will beat a hundred without a head'. Corporal Morley (17th Lancers) epitomised this in the charge of the Light Brigade (1854) when, by command of his voice alone, he rallied his comrades. His broad Nottingham accent could be heard above the sound of battle: 'Coom 'ere, fall in, lads, fall in.' His cool head saved the lives of his men, as he was able to lead them in an organised withdrawal. Professor John Adair has analysed military leadership in an action-centred model where the overlapping needs of the individual, the team and the task are fulfilled in good leadership. Poor leaders neglect one or more of these areas. Leadership is also thought to be embodied in certain personal qualities or traits: decisiveness, confidence, integrity, moral and physical courage, knowledge, the ability to communicate, selflessness and discipline. Knowledge of and rapport with the soldiers they led made some commanders not only popular but also skilled at knowing which regiment to use. All armies' guard or élite units were used for the key task, perhaps the crucial attack at the critical moment of a battle, or the spearhead of a difficult operation. These units often performed well because they believed themselves to be the leaders of an army. In democratic societies leadership is often misunderstood, but in the crisis of battle men look to leaders to provide success.

Tactics

Mobility and shock arms remained important
Throughout the period 1792–1918, the ability to manoeuvre was regarded as an essential feature of conducting operations. Armies that pinned themselves exclusively to defensive positions found that they could be enveloped or besieged. Defensive localities worked well when mobile units could operate around them. Thus if an enemy made an attack on a defended position, a counter-attack could be launched at the critical moment, just as the attackers were becoming exhausted or depleted, with resounding success. This was achieved by the British cavalry at Waterloo and by German troops in the battles on the Western Front. Shock action was also universally favoured throughout the period. The 'weight' and speed of a cavalry charge was diminished after the Napoleonic Wars, but the development of armour in 1916 saw a return of shock action. The tank also combined mobility and firepower. Aircraft too would go on to provide the speed and shock effect of the charge in the twentieth century. In the period between 1870 and 1916 commanders faced considerable difficulties in getting troops across the open to secure vital ground. Firepower had itself become the 'shock' effect instead of mobility. It took decades for this to be truly appreciated.

The importance of committing reserves at the critical moment remained constant
Battles could be won or lost because of the reserve. The timing of the committing of reserves could be critical. At Bull Run in 1861 the arrival of Confederate reserves stabilised a line that was breaking. At Waterloo Napoleon probably delayed one hour too long before committing the Old Guard, and then in too small numbers to really effect a change to the tide of battle. At Antietam in 1862 McClellan refused to send in his reserves, even though Lee's force was exhausted, because defeat would destroy the 'last army of the republic'. The ability of the commander to read a battle, and know just when to order a counter-attack, could therefore be crucial in battle.

Linear formations and firepower developed through the period
Linear formations pre-date the 1790s, as it was already appreciated that there was considerable importance in bringing as many muskets to bear as possible. In the British army, three-deep lines gave way to two-deep lines. To maximise the shock effect of the fire, British units often waited until the enemy were within yards and then fired volleys in succession. Bayonet charges followed swiftly, adding to the morale

effect, encouraging the attackers who moved forward, whilst discouraging those just subjected to the blast of musket balls. The French Napoleonic army combined units in line and columns, but the columns themselves were made up of a series of lines. Only the leading units could fire, but any casualties could be replaced from the large numbers coming on behind. The cohesion of such a large crowd tended to keep morale up too. The vulnerability of dense formations to artillery and then small arms fire caused gradual dispersion. Skirmish lines, then open order, with several yards between each man, tended to reduce casualties, but increased the sense of isolation of the individual under fire. Attacking in lines meant that troops were less likely to fire on their own side by accident. Yet it was hard to control troops in broken country, trenches or built-up areas. This meant that smaller formations, led by junior commanders with initiative, could succeed in the later battles of 1918. The improvement in firepower meant that smaller, non-linear formations (such as machine-gun teams) could pack a considerable punch.

Light formations were also important
Light troops (light infantry, cavalry and horse artillery) were essential components in many European armies from the 1790s. In the British army, light infantrymen were picked men who displayed initiative. The British riflemen were a *corps d'élite* of marksmen dressed in 'rifle green' so that they were less conspicuous on the battlefield. The emphasis in light units was on mobility. Light cavalry were fast-moving, ideal for reconnaissance or even raiding. Lightweight guns were also invaluable for moving across broken terrain, where they could accompany advancing infantry and cavalry formations. In the colonial wars, light cavalry were sometimes 'irregulars' following the tradition of the Hussars in Europe (the freebooters of fifteenth-century Hungary). The most successful ones of the North-West Frontier of India were the Punjab Frontier Force ('Piffers'), the Guides, and Hodson's Horse. Dragoons, traditionally mounted men who fought on foot, also appeared in frontier wars, and mounted infantry became an integral arm of the British army in the South African War (1899–1902). In the First World War the importance of fast, 'light' units was still recognised. In the Middle East cavalry continued to operate, but aircraft and light tanks were replacing them in Europe.

Field fortifications became more important
Armies had used ditches and earthworks to protect themselves since

Roman times, and fortresses had evolved with the use of gunpowder weapons. Walls became lower but deeper. Outworks, armed with artillery, began to cover the approaches to forts and cities, rather than being on the walls themselves. Whereas curtain walls had been designed to keep an enemy out, new fortifications allowed enemies to proceed into designated killing zones. Barbed wire was used to channel as well as delay attackers. In the First World War traditional siege tactics were still in use: mining, trenches, bombardment. The Germans developed the defence in depth, using an outpost line to absorb artillery fire but placing the emphasis on retaining positions further back and counterattacking at vital positions. In the churned-up battlefields around Ypres, trenches almost disappeared as troops took up scattered positions in shell holes or clustered near concrete pillboxes.

Weapons

Small arms developed but ammunition expenditure remained high

In battle many rounds had to be fired to hit an opponent, even in relatively modern wars. The British infantry of the Napoleonic Wars were often excellent shots. At the battle of Maida (4 July 1806), 630 men from light companies fired three volleys at a range of between 115 and 30 yards, firing a total of 1,890 rounds. They inflicted 430 casualties, at a ratio of 4.4 rounds per hit. This was a high hit rate for the period, reflecting the skill and discipline of the British troops. Most battalions armed with muzzle-loading muskets were inaccurate and inefficient. But rifled breechloaders increased the rate of fire without necessarily improving the hit rate per man. At the battle of Weissembourg (4 August 1870), General Abel Douay's division fired 48,000 Chassepot rounds to hit 404 Germans. The Germans fired 80,000 needle-gun bullets to hit 400 French troops. In 1914 the expert riflemen of one company of the 2nd Grenadier Guards repeatedly stopped German infantry attacks with accurate small arms fire. In one day's fighting they killed 300 with perhaps a further 600 others wounded. The expenditure of ammunition was nevertheless high. On 23 October 1914 Private J. S. Barton of the Gloucesters recorded firing 600 rounds that day. Ranges also grew and trajectories flattened so that, in theory, firing became more accurate. High-velocity bullets were less affected by the wind and rain than musket balls. Sealed breaches meant that soldiers no longer had to worry about keeping their powder dry.

Close-quarter battle became less common, except in built-up areas or trenches
With improvements in ballistics and ranges, close-order formations
became less common. Loose, open-order skirmish lines made troops
less vulnerable to artillery and rifle fire. The Napoleonic tactic of volley
firing, followed by a charge with the bayonet, was gradually superseded
by firing from prepared positions, or attacking with hand grenades and
lightweight machine guns, both area weapons, the latter with high
rates of fire. There were exceptions. To clear trenches, bunkers, villages,
towns and forests, close-quarter action was necessary. Even in recent
wars armies have 'crossed bayonets', but the lines of soldiers, two-deep
and shoulder-to-shoulder, had gone. Moreover, artillery underwent
the greatest change. Guns used to demolish positions as well as inflict
casualties could consume vast quantities of ammunition. On the
Somme, on 1 July, British artillery fired 224,221 rounds, inflicting
6,000 casualties. Between 15 July and 2 August 1917 4,283,550 shells
were fired onto Messines ridge to destroy German positions. The calibre
of the guns had increased as engineering and foundry techniques
improved. The fuses became more reliable, and there were mechanical
ones as well as chemical.

Conclusion: technology and linear development

It is very easy to relegate the changes in warfare to the argument that it
was all determined by technological development. It is also easy to
assume that European techniques in warfare followed some linear
pattern of development, leaping from improvement to improvement.
Such arguments provide convenient explanations for the emergence of
colonial empires, and are often used to reinforce the outcomes of battles
where the emphasis is on casualty figures. Contemporary media's
reporting of wars involving Europeans tends to highlight even the lightest casualties. Wars are fought by the West with the expectation that
casualties will be minimised. When this view is projected onto the past,
the success or failure of modes of war is assessed in terms of casualties.
Whilst the loss of life of any war is to be deplored, casualties alone do
not determine the outcomes of battles or wars. Wellington won the
battle of Salamanca in 1812, and has often been praised for defeating
'40,000 men in 40 minutes'. Nevertheless, the 11th Foot had to advance
into a fusillade of muskets and grapeshot and fight with the bayonet to
win the day, and lost 16 officers and 325 men out of a total of 412. In
1918 the 2nd Battalion of the same regiment was almost wiped out as it
held up a German attack at Bois de Buttes. The sacrifice of 28 officers

and 552 men enabled a defence line to be established on the River Aisne. Weapons superiority appears to offer a convenient explanation for warfare, until one remembers that the French army of 1870 possessed superior Chassepot rifles and the *mitrailleuse* machine gun. The German troops frequently suffered heavier casualties than the French in the opening battles of the Franco-Prussian War, but they undoubtedly won the war. When analysing warfare, it is thus not just a story of weapons, but how they are used and how armies respond to them that is also important.

Change and continuity: non-linear explanations of warfare

Change and continuity featured in warfare between 1792 and 1918

The history of warfare is a complex interaction of change and continuities. European armies adapted constantly to new developments and experiences. The British army began to adopt khaki uniforms for campaigning after its experience in India. The French picked up the *Razzia* tactic after suffering repeated raids by Algerian horsemen. Regression or stagnation was also apparent, but served a local purpose. Thus the British retained the 'square' to repel charges by tribesmen, protect vulnerable baggage and maintain all-round defence. Cavalry and mounted infantry were vital to victory in the South African War of 1899–1902, even though cavalry had been defeated by the effectiveness of rifle fire in the European theatre. There were also continuities in warfare unrelated to technology. Leadership principles remained important. The terrain, the weather, the logistical supply of food and ammunition, the exhaustion of soldiers, and morale continued to exert influences over the outcomes of war. Indian troops were starved into surrender at Kut el Amara in Mesopotamia in 1916 and Russian morale was lowered to breaking point on the Eastern Front when supplies of food became intermittent and munitions failed to arrive in 1917.

Technological change was significant

New technologies and developments did have a considerable impact on warfare. The Confederacy lost the American Civil War because of economic factors as well as military ones: it could not reproduce war *materiel* as fast as the industrialised northern states. Rifled barrels gave greater accuracy, breech-loading mechanisms and magazines gave higher rates of fire and artillery ammunition became more reliable when engineering improvements were made. The industrial revolution meant that these weapons could be manufactured rapidly and to the same standard. Weapon ranges generally increased. In the 1790s, infantry engagements had to take place over a distance of a few yards, but in 1918 infantrymen could hit targets out to 1,500 yards. Area weapons also became more important: machine guns could be used in an indirect role, artillery fired to saturate a zone to suppress as well as to kill, hand grenades were indispensable to clearing small defended areas. The battlefield itself had also extended. Waterloo was fought across a front of 4,500 yards. The Western Front was 460 miles long and 20 miles broad, but it could be argued that, as a total war, the civilian population of Europe was also part of a vast battlefield. Bombing raids by Zeppelins and aircraft reinforced this fact. However, civilians had long been caught up in war. The crowds of refugees that fled the battlefields of the Revolutionary Wars were a recognisable and distressing feature of the battles of 1914. When guerrillas ambushed and sniped at the conventional forces, all too often it was the civilian population who paid the price with their property or even their lives. Warfare changed dramatically between 1792 and 1918, but its agonies remained the same. Whether one regards war as futile or necessary, the readiness of some powers to seek violence as a policy requires a fundamental response: *si vis pacem, para bellum* (he who would see peace, should prepare for war).

Tutorial

Progress questions
1. How might fatigue and morale affect the outcome of a battle or campaign? Give examples to support your answer.
2. Why do atrocities occur in war between 'civilised' states?
3. How did soldiers cope with fear in war?
4. What were the chief developments in weapons technology between 1792 and 1918?

Seminar discussion
1. Had war become more 'destructive' by 1918, or not?
2. Are heavy casualties an unavoidable feature of modern wars?

Practical assignment
Review all your notes so far. Try to construct summary diagrams of each of the periods and highlight, or underline, the main developments.

Alternatively, list changes in warfare under the headings of technology, leadership, tactics, or strategy.

Study tips

1. The theme of this book has been that wars are not determined by technology alone. Try to identify a few good examples of this from across the period of this book.
2. Learn a collection of good examples to illustrate change and continuity. Make sure you do not omit the typical examples for the sake of exceptional single battles.
3. Review and practise recalling information from this book at regular intervals. Reading the headings that are in italics will help you summarise the key points.
4. Remember that soldiers often bore their hardships with good humour. Don't forget to enjoy your studies too!

Glossary

abattis Sharpened stakes to impede an attacker.

arquebus An early form of musket.

artillery The branch of an army concerned with cannons and large guns.

attrition Fighting that results in heavy casualties.

battalion A formation circa 1,000 strong.

bayonet Knife attached to the end of a rifle or musket.

breastworks Earthworks, at the front of a position.

breech-loader A firearm which takes cartridges in the breech as opposed to the muzzle.

brigade A formation circa 5,000 strong.

canister A case of small balls fired from cannons that explodes on leaving the muzzle like a shotgun.

cavalry Soldiers who fight on horseback.

cheveaux de frise Sharpened stakes or iron poles to obstruct an attacker.

colours Regimental flags (British army).

commissariat The supply of food and munitions (nineteenth-century term).

company A formation circa 100 strong.

corps A formation circa 30,000 strong.

creeping barrage A belt of fire from artillery that is dropped in front of advancing troops as they move.

cuirassier A cavalryman who wears a breast and back plate.

division A formation circa 15,000 strong.

dragoon A mounted soldier who dismounts to fight with firearms.

dressing The alignment of formations, or a pad placed over a wound.

drill The repeated practice of movement in unison by soldiers.

enfilade fire Fire that is delivered from a flank.

flintlock musket Firearm which ignites propellant with a flint on a mechanical arm.

guerrilla Irregular fighter who uses hit-and-run tactics.

horse artillery Cannons pulled by teams of horses that accompany the cavalry.

howitzer A cannon that fires on a high trajectory, plunging explosive shells over defences.

Impis Zulu armies.

infantry Soldiers who fight on foot.

interior lines Communication and transport routes that radiate in favour of the defenders.

irregulars Soldiers who are affiliated to an army but who fight according to their own practices.

light infantry Foot soldiers who move quickly and can fight without formation.

line of communication A supply and information route.

linear tactics Fighting using formations in thin lines.

logistics The business of supplying armies.

magazine A case, attached to a weapon, that feeds cartridges, or a store.

matchlock musket Firearm where a slow burning match ignites the powder.

meeting engagement A battle where two sides fight from the line of march.

morale Psychological condition of troops.

mounted infantry Foot soldiers temporarily mounted on horseback.

munitions Ammunition and weapons.

NCO Non-commissioned officer, a junior leader.

oblique order An advance that is hidden by natural or mass man obstacles.

ordnance Artillery and siege weapons, all matters to do with weaponry.

percussion cap Device fitted to the end of a cartridge to ignite propellant.

pyrrhic victory A battle won at too great a cost to call it victory.

redan An earthwork with open sides.

redoubt An earthwork with enclosed flanks.

repeating rifle Firearm that does not require each shot to be loaded.

reserved occupation Essential tasks to maintain a country during wartime.

reverse slope The rear slope of a ridge line.

rifling A spiral groove in the barrel of a firearm.

sabre A light, curved sword used by cavalrymen.

skirmish line A ragged line from which soldiers fire and move as individuals.

soldier's battle A battle where commanders are unable to influence events and where soldiers struggle without direction.

square A formation used by infantry to give all-round defence.

U-boat A German submarine.

wheel lock musket Firearm with a mechanism that rotates a fuse to fire it.

Further Reading

Jeremy Black, *War and the World*. London, 1998; *Western Warfare, 1775–1882*. London, 2001.

Brian Bond, *War and Society in Europe, 1870–1970*. London, 1984.

David Chandler and Ian Beckett, *The Oxford History of the British Army*. Oxford, 1994.

D. G. Chandler, *The Campaigns of Napoleon*. New York, 1966.

O. Connelly, *Blundering to Glory: Napoleon's Military Campaigns*. USA: 1988.

Gary Gallagher, *The American Civil War: The War in the East 1861–3*. London, 2001.

D. Gates, *The Spanish Ulcer: A History of the Peninsular War*. London, 1986.

Michael Glover, *Wellington's Peninsular Victories*. London, 1963.

Richard Holmes, *Firing Line*. London, 1985; *The Western Front*. London, 1999.

Michael Howard, *The Franco-Prussian War*. London, 1961.

Lynn MacDonald, *1914*. London, 1987; *1915: Death of Innocence*. London, 1993; *Somme*. London, 1983; *They Called it Passchendaele*. London, 1978.

W. McElwee, *The Art of War: Waterloo to Mons*. London, 1974.

Robin Neillands, *The Great War Generals on the Western Front*. London, 1999.

Thomas Pakenham, *The Boer War*. London and New York, 1979.

Geoffrey Parker, *The Cambridge Illustrated History of Warfare*. Cambridge, 1995.

G. Rothenburg, *The Art of Warfare in the Age of Napoleon*. London, 1978.

Trevor Royle, *Crimea*. London, 1999.

Lawrence Sondhaus, *Naval Warfare, 1815–1914*. London, 2000.

David Walder, *The Short Victorious War: The Russo-Japanese Conflict, 1904–05*. London, 1973.

Geoffrey Wawro, *The Austro-Prussian War*. Cambridge, 1996; *Warfare and Society in Europe, 1792–1914*. London, 2000.

For website links visit www.studymates.co.uk

Index

Liverpool
Community
College